THE ROUGH GUIDE

RUSSIAN

PHRASEBOOK

Compiled by

LEXUS

ROUGH
GUIDES

www.roughguides.com

Credits

Compiled by Lexus with Irina and Alistair MacLean
Lexus Series Editor: Sally Davies
Rough Guides Reference Director: Andrew Lockett
Rough Guides Series Editor: Mark Ellingham

First edition published in 1997.
Revised in 2001.
This updated edition published in 2006 by
Rough Guides Ltd,
80 Strand, London WC2R 0RL
345 Hudson St, 4th Floor, New York 10014, USA
Email: mail@roughguides.co.uk.

Distributed by the Penguin Group.

Penguin Books Ltd, 80 Strand, London WC2R 0RL
Penguin Putnam, Inc., 375 Hudson Street, NY 10014, USA
Penguin Group (Australia), 250 Camberwell Road, Camberwell,
Victoria 3124, Australia
Penguin Books Canada Ltd, 10 Alcorn Avenue, Toronto,
Ontario, Canada M4V 1E4
Penguin Group (New Zealand), Cnr Rosedale and Airborne Roads,
Albany, Auckland, New Zealand

Typeset in Bembo and Helvetica to an original design by Henry Iles.
Printed in Italy by LegoPrint S.p.A

British Library Cataloguing in Publication Data
A catalogue for this book is available from the British Library.

ISBN 13: 978-1-84353-643-7
ISBN 10: 1-84353-643-9

1 3 5 7 9 8 6 4 2

The publishers and authors have done their best to ensure the
accuracy and currency of all information in The Rough Guide
Russian Phrasebook however, they can accept no responsibility for
any loss or inconvenience sustained by any reader using the book.

Online information about Rough Guides can be
found at our website www.roughguides.com

CONTENTS

Introduction

The Rough Guide Russian phrasebook is a highly practical introduction to the contemporary language. Laid out in clear A-Z style, it uses key-word referencing to lead you straight to the words and phrases you want – so if you need to book a room, just look up 'room'. The Rough Guide gets straight to the point in every situation, in bars and shops, on trains and buses, and in hotels and banks.

The main part of the Rough Guide is a double dictionary: English-Russian then Russian-English. Before that, there's a section called **Basic Phrases** and to get you involved in two-way communication, the Rough Guide includes, in this new edition, a set of **Scenario** dialogues illustrating questions and responses in key situations such as renting a car and asking directions. You can hear these and then download them free from **www.roughguides.com/phrasebooks** for use on your computer or MP3 player.

Forming the heart of the guide, the **English-Russian** section gives easy-to-use transliterations of the Russian words wherever pronunciation might be a problem. Throughout this section, cross-references enable you to pinpoint key facts and phrases, while asterisked words indicate where further information can be found in a section at the end of the book called **How the Language Works**. This section sets out the fundamental rules of the language, with plenty of practical examples. You'll also find here other essentials like numbers, dates, telling the time and basic phrases. In the **Russian-English** dictionary, we've given you not just the phrases you'll be likely to hear (starting with a selection of slang and colloquialisms) but also many of the signs, labels, instructions and other basic words you may come across in print or in public places.

Near the back of the book too the Rough Guide offers an extensive **Menu Reader**. Consisting of food and drink sections (each starting with a list of essential terms), it's indispensable whether you're eating out, stopping for a quick drink, or browsing through a local food market.

счастливого пути!
sh-chas**lee**vava poo**tee**!
have a good trip!

Basic
Phrases

yes
да
da

no
нет
nyet

OK
хорошо
Harasho

hello
здравствуйте
zdrasvooytyeh

good morning
доброе утро
dobra-yeh ootra

good evening
добрый вечер
dobri vyechyer

good night (when leaving)
до свидания
da sveedanya

good night (when going to bed)
спокойной ночи
spakoyni nochee

goodbye
до свидания
da sveedanya

hi!
привет!
preevyet!

cheerio!
пока!
paka!

see you!
пока!
paka!

please
пожалуйста
paJalsta

yes please
да, спасибо
da, spaseeba

thank you, thanks
спасибо
spaseeba

no, thank you
нет, спасибо
nyet, spaseeba

thank you very much
большое спасибо
balsho-yeh spaseeba

don't mention it
не за что
nyeh-za-shta

how do you do?
здравствуйте
zdra**s**vooytyeh

how are you?
как дела?
kak dyela?

fine, thanks
хорошо, спасибо
Harash**o**, spas**ee**ba

nice to meet you
приятно познакомиться
pree-**ya**tna paznak**o**meetsa

excuse me (to get past, to say sorry)
извините
eezveen**ee**tyeh

excuse me! (to get attention)
простите!
prast**ee**tyeh!

excuse me (addressing someone with question)
извините, пожалуйста ...
eezveen**ee**tyeh, paJ**a**lsta ...

(I'm) sorry
прошу прощения
prash**oo** prash-ch**ye**nee-ya

sorry?/pardon me? (didn't understand)
простите?
prast**ee**tyeh?

what?
что?
shto?

what did you say?
что вы сказали?
shto viy skaz**a**lee?

I see (I understand)
понятно
pan**ya**tna

I don't understand
я не понимаю
ya nyeh paneem**a**-yoo

do you speak English?
вы говорите по-английски?
viy gavar**ee**tyeh pa-angl**ee**skee?

I don't speak Russian
я не говорю по-русски
ya nyeh gavar**yoo** pa-r**oo**skee

could you speak more slowly?
вы не могли бы говорить помедленнее?
viy nyeh magl**ee**bi gavar**ee**t pam**ye**dlyenyeh-yeh?

could you repeat that?
повторите, пожалуйста
paftar**ee**tyeh, paJ**a**lsta

could you write it down?
запишите, пожалуйста
zapeesh**iy**tyeh, paJ**a**lsta

9

I'd like ... (said by man/woman)
я бы хотел/хотела ...
ya biy наtyel/наtyela ...

can I have ...?
можно, пожалуйста ...?
moжna, paжalsta ...?

do you have ...?
у вас есть ...?
oo vas yest ...?

how much is it?
сколько это стоит?
skolka eta sto-eet?

cheers! (toast)
ваше здоровье!
vasheh zdarovyeh!

it is ...
это ...
eta ...

where is the ...?
где ...?
gdyeh ...?

is it far from here?
это далеко отсюда?
eta dalyeko atsyooda?

what's the time?
который час?
katori chas?

Scenarios

1. Accommodation

what's an inexpensive hotel you can recommend?
▶ вы можете порекомендовать недорогую гостиницу?
[viy moJetyeh paryekamyendavat nyedaragoo-yoo gasteeneetsoo?]

к сожалению, похоже, ни в одной нет мест ◀
[k saJalyenee-yoo, paнoJeh, neevadnoy nyet myest]
I'm sorry, they all seem to be fully booked

---

can you give me the name of a good middle-range hotel?
▶ есть ли хорошая гостиница средней категории?
[yestlee нarosha-ya gasteeneetsa sryednyay katyegoree-ee?]

давайте посмотрим, вы хотите быть в центре? ◀
[davltyeh pasmotreem, viy нateetyeh biyt ftsentryeh?]
let me have a look; do you want to be in the centre?

---

if possible
▶ если возможно
[yeslee vazmoJna]

вас устроит, если это будет за городом? ◀
[vas oostro-eet, yeslee eta boodyet zagaradam?]
do you mind being a little way out of town?

---

not too far out
▶ если не слишком далеко
[yeslee nyeh sleeshkam dalyeko]

where is it on the map?
▶ где это на карте?
[gdyeh eta na kartyeh?]

can you write the name and address down?
▶ напишите, пожалуйста, название и адрес
[napeeshiytyeh, paJalsta, nazvanee-yeh ee adryes]

I'm looking for a room in a private house
▶ я хочу снять комнату в частном доме
[ya нachoo snyat komnatoo fchastnam domyeh]

2. Banks

bank account	банковский счет	[bankofskee sh-chot]
cheque	чек	[chyek]
to deposit	класть/положить на счет	[klast/palaJiyt na sh-chot]
rouble	рубль	[roobl]
pin number	пин-код	[peen kod]
pound	фунт	[foont]
to withdraw	снимать/снять со счета	[sneemat/snyat sa sh-chota]

can you change this into roubles?
▶ вы не могли бы обменять это на рубли?
[viy nyeh magleebi abmyenyat eta na rooblee?]

какие купюры вы хотите? ◀
[kakee-yeh koopyooriy viy Hateetyeh?]
how would you like the money?

small notes
▶ мелкие купюры
[myelkee-yeh koopyooriy]

big notes
▶ крупные купюры
[kroopniy-yeh koopyooriy]

do you have information in English about opening an account?
▶ есть ли у вас информация на английском языке об открытии счета?
[yestlee oo vas eenfarmatsi-ya na angleeskam yaziykyeh ab atkriytee-ee sh-chota?]

▶ да, какой счет вы хотите открыть?
[da, kakoy sh-chot viy Hateetyeh atkriyt?]
yes, what sort of account do you want?

I'd like a current account
текущий счет
[tyekoosh-chee sh-chot]

▶ ваш паспорт, пожалуйста
[vash paspart, paJalsta]
your passport, please

can I use this card to draw some cash?
я могу снять деньги по этой карточке? ◀
[ya magoo snyat dyengee pa-etl kartochkyeh?]

вам нужно подойти к кассе ◀
[vam nooJna padltee k-kas-syeh]
you have to go to the cashier's desk

I want to transfer this to my account at Citybank
▶ я хотела бы перевести это на мой счет в Ситибанке
[ya Hatyela biy pyeryevyestee eta na moy sh-chot v seeteebankyeh]

хорошо, но вам придется оплатить телефонный звонок ◀
[Harasho, no vam preedyotsa aplateet tyelyefon-ni zvanok]
OK, but we'll have to charge you for the phonecall

download these scenarios as MP3s from:

3. Booking a room

shower	душ	[doosh]
telephone in the room	телефон в номере	[tyelyefon vnomyeryeh]
payphone in the lobby	таксофон в фойе	[taksafon f-fa-yeh]

do you have any rooms?
▶ у вас есть свободные номера?
[oo vas yest svabodni-yeh namyera?]

на сколько человек? ◀
[na skolka chyelavyek?]
for how many people?

for one/for two
▶ на одного/на двоих
[na adnavo/na dva-eeн]

да, у нас есть свободные номера ◀
[da, oo nas yest svabodni-yeh namyera]
yes, we have rooms free

▶ на сколько ночей?
[na skolka nachyay?]
for how many nights?

just for one night
только на одну ночь ◀
[tolka na adnoo noch]

how much is it?
▶ сколько это стоит?
[skolka eta sto-eet?]

3060 рублей с ванной и 2380 без ванной ◀
[tree tiysyachee shesdyesyat rooblyay svan-nl ee dvyeh tiysyachee treesta vosyemdyesyat byez van-ni]
3060 roubles with bathroom and 2380 roubles without bathroom

does that include breakfast?
▶ это включает завтрак?
[eta fklyoocha-yet zaftrak?]

can I see a room with bathroom?
▶ можно посмотреть номер с ванной?
[moЈna pasmatryet nomyer svan-nl?]

ok, I'll take it
▶ хорошо, это подойдет
[Harasho, eta padldyot]

when do I have to check out?
▶ во сколько нужно освободить номер?
[va skolka nooЈna asvabadeet nomyer?]

is there anywhere I can leave luggage?
▶ где можно оставить багаж?
[gdyeh moЈna astaveet bagaЈ?]

4. Car hire

automatic	автоматическая передача	[aftamateechyeska-ya pyeryedacha]
full tank	полный бак	[polni bak]
manual	ручная передача	[roochna-ya pyeryedacha]
rented car	прокатная машина	[prakatna-ya mashiyna]

I'd like to rent a car
▶ я хотела бы взять на прокат машину
[ya Hatyela biy vzyat na prakat mashiynoo]

на какой срок ◀
[na kakoy srok?]
for how long?

two days
▶ на два дня
[na dva dnya]

I'll take the ...
▶ я возьму ...
[ya vazmoo ...]

is that with unlimited mileage?
▶ это с неограниченным километражем?
[eta snyeh-agraneechyen-niym keelamyetraJem?]

да ◀
[da]
it is

ваши водительские права, пожалуйста ◀
[vashiy vadeetyelskee-yeh prava, paJalsta]
can I see your driving licence, please?

и ваш паспорт ◀
[ee vash paspart]
and your passport

is insurance included?
▶ входит ли сюда страховка?
[fHodeetlee syooda straHofka?]

да, но вам придется заплатить первые 3400 рублей ◀
[da, no vam preedyotsa zaplateet pyervi-yeh tree tiysyachee chyetiyrryesta rooblyay]
yes, but you have to pay the first 3400 roubles

вы сможете оставить задаток в размере 3400 рублей? ◀
[viy smoJetyeh astaveet zadatak vrazmyeryeh tryoH tiysyach chyetiyrryoHsot rooblyay?]
can you leave a deposit of 3400 roubles?

and if this office is closed, where do I leave the keys?
▶ если офис закрыт, где нужно оставить ключи?
[yeslee ofees zakriyt, gdyeh nooJna astaveet klyoochee?]

бросьте их в тот ящик ◀
[brostyeh eeH ftot yash-cheek]
you drop them in that box

5. Communications

ADSL modem	ADSL-модем	[ADSL-modem]
at	"собачка"	[sabachka]
dial-up modem	модем	[modem]
dot	точка	[tochka]
Internet	интернет	[eenternet]
mobile (phone)	мобильный (телефон)	[mabeelni (tyelyefon)]
password	пароль	[parol]
telephone	адаптер для	[adaptyer dlya tyelyefon-
socket adaptor	телефонной розетки	nl razyetkee]
wireless hotspot	точка доступа WiFi	[tochka dostoopa WiFi]

is there an Internet café around here?
▸ есть ли поблизости Интернет-кафе?
[yestlee pableezastee eenternet-kafe?]

can I send email from here?
▸ можно ли отсюда отправить email?
[moJnalee atsyooda atpraveet eemayl]

where's the at on the keyboard?
▸ где на клавиатуре "собачка"?
[gdyeh na klavee-atooryeh sabachka?]

zero	ноль	[nol]
one	один	[adeen]
two	два	[dva]
three	три	[tree]
four	четыре	[chyetiyryeh]
five	пять	[pyat]
six	шесть	[shest]
seven	семь	[syem]
eight	восемь	[vosyem]
nine	девять	[dyevyat]

can you switch this to a UK keyboard?
▸ как переключиться на английскую клавиатуру?
[kak pyeryeklyoocheetsa na angleeskoo-yoo klavee-atooroo?]

can you help me log on?
▸ вы можете мне помочь войти в систему?
[viy moJetyeh mnyeh pamoch vltee fseestyemoo?]

I'm not getting a connection, can you help?
▸ не соединяется – вы не могли бы помочь?
[nyeh sa-yedeenya-yetsa – viy nyeh magleebiy pamoch?]

where can I get a top-up card?
▸ где я могу купить карту экспресс-оплаты?
[gdyeh ya magoo koopeet kartoo ekspres-aplatiy?]

can you put me through to ...?
▸ соедините меня, пожалуйста, с …
[sa-yedeeneetyeh myenya, paJalsta s …]

6. Directions

hi, I'm looking for Kozitsky Lane
▶ добрый день, я ищу Козицкий переулок
[dobri dyen, ya eesh-choo kazeetskee pyeryeh-oolak]

извините, никогда о таком не слышала ◀
[eezveeneetyeh, neekagda atakom nyeh sliyshala]
sorry, never heard of it

hi, can you tell me where Kozitsky Lane is?
▶ добрый день, не подскажете, где
Козицкий переулок?
[dobri dyen, nyeh patskaJetyeh, gdyeh kazeetskee
pyeryeh-oolak?]

я тоже приезжая ◀
[ya toJeh pree-yezJa-ya]
I'm a stranger here too

hi, Kozitsky
Lane, do you
know where
it is?
добрый день,
вы не знаете,
где находится
Козицкий
переулок?
[dobri dyen, viy
nyeh zna-yetyeh,
gdyeh kazeet-
skee pyeryeh-
oolak?]

where?	which direction?
где?	в каком направлении?
[gdyeh?]	[fkakom napravlyenee-ee?]

▶ за углом
[za ooglom]
around the corner

▶ налево после второго светофора
[nalyeva poslyeh ftarova svyetafora]
left at the second traffic lights

▶ затем первая улица справа
[zatyem pyerva-ya ooleetsa sprava]
then it's the first street on the right

вон там	напротив	прямо	справа
[von tam]	[naproteef]	[pryama]	[sprava]
over there	opposite	straight ahead	on the right
дальше	недалеко (от)	слева	сразу за
[dalsheh]	[nyedalyeko (ot)]	[slyeva]	[srazoo za]
further	near	on the left	just after
мимо …	перед	следующий	улица
[meema …]	[pyeryet]	[slyedoosh-chee]	[ooleetsa]
past the …	in front of	next	street
назад	поворот		
[nazat]	[pavarot]		
back	turn off		

7. Emergencies

accident	несчастный случай	[nyesh-chasni sloochee]
(in a car)	авария	[avaree-ya]
ambulance	скорая помощь	[skora-ya pomash-ch]
consul	консул	[konsool]
embassy	посольство	[pasolstva]
fire brigade	пожарная команда	[paJarna-ya kamanda]
police	милиция	[meeleetsi-ya]

help!
▶ помогите!
[pamageetyeh!]

can you help me?
▶ вы можете мне помочь?
[viy moJetyeh mnyeh pamoch?]

please come with me! it's really very urgent
▶ пожалуйста, пойдемте со мной – это очень срочно!
[paJalsta, pldyomtyeh samnoy – eta ochyen srochna!]

I've lost (my keys)
▶ я потеряла (ключи)
[ya patyeryala (klyoochee)]

(my car) is not working
▶ (моя машина) сломалась
[(ma-ya mashiyna) slamalas]

(my purse) has been stolen
▶ у меня украли (кошелек)
[oo myenya ookralee (kashelyok)]

I've been mugged
▶ меня обокрали
[myenya abakralee]

как ваше имя? ◀
[kak vasheh eemya?]
what's your name?

ваш паспорт, пожалуйста ◀
[vash paspart, paJalsta]
I need to see your passport

I'm sorry, all my papers have been stolen
▶ извините, у меня украли все документы
[eezveeneetyeh, oo myenya ookralee fsyeh dakoomyentiy]

8. Friends

hi, how're you doing?
▶ привет, как дела?
[preev**yet**, kak d**ye**la?]

хорошо, а у тебя? ◀
[Harash**o**, a-ootyeb**ya**?]
OK, and you?

---

yeah, fine
▶ хорошо
[Harash**o**]

not bad
▶ неплохо
[nyepl**o**Ha]

---

d'you know Andrei?
▶ ты знаком с Андреем?
[tiy znak**o**m sandr**yeh**-yem?]

---

and this is Olga
▶ а это – Ольга
[a-**e**ta – **o**lga]

да, мы знакомы ◀
[da, miy znak**o**miy]
yeah, we know each other

---

where do you know each other from?
▶ где вы познакомились?
[gd**yeh** viy paznak**o**meelees?]

мы познакомились у Саши ◀
[miy paznak**o**meelees oos**a**shiy]
we met at Sasha's place

---

that was some party, eh?
▶ неплохая была вечеринка, а?
[nyeplaH**a**-ya biy**la** vyechyer**ee**nka, ah?]

отличная ◀
[atl**ee**chna-ya]
the best

---

are you guys coming for a beer?
▶ вы пойдете с нами выпить пива?
[viy pdy**o**tyeh sn**a**mee v**iy**peet p**ee**va?]

отлично, пойдем ◀
[atl**ee**chna, pldy**o**m]
cool, let's go

нет, я встречаюсь с Юлей ◀
[nyet, ya fstryech**a**-yoos s **yoo**lyay]
no, I'm meeting Yulia

---

see you at Sasha's place tonight
▶ увидимся у Саши сегодня вечером
[oov**ee**deemsya oo s**a**shiy syev**o**dnya v**ye**chyeram]

пока! ◀
[pak**a**!]
see you

9. Health

I'm not feeling very well
▶ мне нехорошо
[mnyeh nyeh Harasho]

can you get a doctor?
▶ вы не могли бы вызвать врача?
[viy nyeh magleebiy viyzvat vracha?]

где у вас болит? ◀
[gdyeh oo vas baleet?]
where does it hurt?

it hurts here
▶ здесь
[zdyes]

▶ боль постоянная?
[bol pasta-yan-na-ya?]
is the pain constant?

it's not a constant pain
нет, не постоянная ◀
[nyet, nyeh pasta-yan-na-ya]

can I make an appointment?
▶ могу ли я записаться к врачу?
[magoolee ya zapeesatsa kvrachoo?]

can you give me something for ...?
▶ вы можете дать мне что-нибудь от ...?
[viy moJethyeh dat mnyeh shtoneeboot at ...?]

yes, I have insurance
▶ да, у меня есть страховка
[da, oo myenya yest straHofka]

antibiotics	антибиотики	[anteebee-oteekee]
antiseptic ointment	антисептическая мазь	[anteesyepteechyeska-ya mas]
cystitis	цистит	[tsisteet]
dentist	зубной врач	[zoobnoy vrach]
diarrhoea	диарея	[dee-aryeh-ya]
doctor	врач	[vrach]
hospital	больница	[balneetsa]
ill	болен	[bolyen]
medicine	лекарство	[lyekarstva]
painkillers	болеутоляющие средства	[bolyeh-ootalya-yooshchee-yeh sryetstva]
pharmacy	аптека	[aptyeka]
to prescribe	прописывать/ прописать	[prapeesiyvat/ prapeesat]
thrush	молочница	[malochneetsa]

10. Language difficulties

a few words	несколько слов	[**ny**eskalka slof]
interpreter	переводчик	[pyeryev**o**tcheek]
to translate	переводить/	[pyeryevad**ee**t/
	перевести	pyeryev**ee**st**ee**]

ваша кредитная карта не проходит ◀
[**va**sha kryed**ee**tna-ya k**a**rta nyeh prah**o**deet]
your credit card has been refused

what, I don't understand; do you speak English?
▶ Что? Я не понимаю; Вы говорите по-английски?
[shto? ya nyeh paneem**a**-yoo; viy gavar**ee**tyeh pa-angl**ee**skee?]

это не действительно ◀
[**e**ta nyeh dyaystv**ee**tyelna]
this isn't valid

could you say that again?
▶ повторите, пожалуйста
[paftar**ee**tyeh, pa**Ja**lsta]

slowly
▶ медленно
[m**ye**dlyen-na]

I understand very little Russian
▶ я понимаю чуть-чуть по-русски
[ya paneem**a**-yoo choot-choot par**oo**s-skee]

I speak Russian very badly
▶ я очень плохо говорю по-русски
[ya **o**chyen pl**o**Ha gavar**yoo** par**oo**s-skee]

вы не можете платить этой карточкой ◀
[viy nyeh m**o**Jetyeh plat**ee**t et**i** kart**a**chkl]
you can't use this card to pay

▶ вы понимаете?
[viy paneem**a**-yetyeh?]
do you understand?

sorry, no
извините, нет
[eezveen**ee**tyeh, nyet]

is there someone who speaks English?
▶ кто-нибудь здесь говорит по-английски?
[kt**o**neeboot zdyes gavar**ee**t pa-angl**ee**skee?]

oh, now I understand
▶ а, теперь я понимаю
[ah, tyep**ye**r ya paneem**a**-yoo]

is that ok now?
▶ теперь все в порядке?
[tyep**ye**r fsyo fpar**ya**tkyeh?]

download these scenarios as MP3s from:

11. Meeting people

hello
▶ добрый день
[**do**bri dyen]

добрый день, меня зовут Таня ◀
[**do**bri dyen, men**ya** zav**oo**t t**a**nya]
hello, my name's Tanya

Graham, from England, Thirsk
▶ меня зовут Грээм, из Англии, из города Тирск
[men**ya** zav**oo**t Graham, eez **a**nglee-ee, eez g**o**rada Thirsk]

не слышала о таком, где это? ◀
[nyeh sl**iy**shala atak**o**m, gd**ye**h**e**ta?]
don't know that, where is it?

not far from York, in the North; and you?
▶ не далеко от Йорка, на севере, а вы?
[nyeh dalyek**o** at **yo**rka, na s**ye**vyeryeh, av**iy**?]

я из Москвы; вы здесь один? ◀
[ya eez maskv**iy**; viy zdyes ad**ee**n?]
I'm from Moscow; here by yourself?

no, I'm with my wife and two kids
▶ нет, я с женой и двумя детьми
[nyet, ya sJen**oy** ee dvoom**ya** dyetm**ee**]

what do you do?
▶ кем вы работаете?
[kyem viy rab**o**ta-yetyeh?]

я занимаюсь компьютерами ◀
[ya zaneem**a**-yoos kamp**yoo**teramee]
I'm in computers

me too
▶ я тоже
[ya t**o**Jeh]

here's my wife now
▶ а вот и моя жена
[av**o**t ee ma-**ya** Jena]

приятно познакомиться ◀
[pree-**ya**tna paznak**o**meetsa]
nice to meet you

12. Post offices

airmail	авиапочта	[avee-a pochta]
post card	открытка	[atkriytka]
post office	почта	[pochta]
stamp	марка	[marka]

what time does the post office close?
▶ во сколько закрывается почта?
[vaskolka zakriyva-yetsa pochta?]

в восемь часов по будням ◀
[v-vosyem chasof pa boodnyam]
eight o'clock weekdays

is the post office open on Saturdays?
▶ открыта ли почта по субботам?
[atkriytalee pochta pa soobotam?]

до двух часов ◀
[da dvooH chasof]
until two o'clock

I'd like to send this registered to England
▶ я хотела бы послать это заказным в Англию
[ya Hatyela biy paslat eta zakazniym vanglee-yoo]

да, конечно, это будет стоить 340 рублей ◀
[da, kanyeshna, eta boodyet sto-eet treesta sorak rooblyay]
certainly, that will cost 340 roubles

and also two stamps for England, please
▶ а также две марки для Англии, пожалуйста
[ah takJeh dvyeh markee dlya anglee-ee, paJalsta]

do you have some airmail stickers?
▶ есть ли у вас наклейки авиапочты?
[yestlee oo vas naklyaykee avee-a pochtiy?]

do you have any mail for me?
▶ есть ли у вас почта для меня?
[yestlee oo vas pochta dlya myenya?]

международный	[myeJdoonarodni]	international
письма	[peesma]	letters
внутренний	[vnootryen-nee]	domestic
посылки	[pasiylkee]	parcels
до востребования	[da vastryebiyvanee-ya]	poste restante

13. Restaurants

bill	счет	[sh-chot]
menu	меню	[myenyoo]
table	стол	[stol]

can we have a non-smoking table?
▶ есть ли у вас столик для некурящих?
[**yes**tlee oo vas st**o**leek dlya nyekoor**ya**sh-cheeH?]

there are two of us
▶ нас двое
[nas dv**o**-yeh]

there are four of us
▶ нас четверо
[nas ch**ye**tvyera]

what's this?
▶ что это?
[sht**o**-eta?]

это такая рыба ◀
[**e**ta tak**a**-ya r**i**yba]
it's a type of fish

это местное фирменное блюдо ◀
[**e**ta my**e**stna-yeh f**ee**rmyen-na-yeh bly**oo**da]
it's a local speciality

входите, я вам покажу ◀
[fHad**ee**tyeh, ya vam pakaJ**oo**]
come inside and I'll show you

we would like two of these, one of these, and one of those
▶ нам, пожалуйста, две порции этого, одну - этого и одну – этого
[nam, paJ**a**lsta, dvyeh p**o**rtsiy-ee **e**tava, adn**oo** **e**tava ee adn**oo** **e**tava]

▶ а выпить?
[av**iy**peet?]
and to drink?

red wine
▶ красное вино
[kr**a**sna-yeh veen**o**]

white wine
▶ белое вино
[b**ye**la-yeh veen**o**]

a beer and two orange juices
▶ одно пиво и два апельсиновых сока
[adn**o** p**ee**va ee dva apyels**ee**naviyH s**o**ka]

some more bread please
▶ еще хлеба, пожалуйста
[yesh-ch**o** Hl**ye**ba, paJ**a**lsta]

▶ вам понравилось?
[vam panr**a**veelas?]
how was your meal?

excellent!, very nice!
да, замечательно, очень вкусно! ◀
[da, zamyech**a**tyelna, **o**chyen fk**oo**sna!]

▶ еще что-нибудь?
[yesh-ch**o** sht**o**neeboot?]
anything else?

just the bill thanks
нет, спасибо, только счет ◀
[nyet, spas**ee**ba, t**o**lka sh-chot]

14. Shopping

я могу вам помочь? ◄
[ya magoo vam pamoch?]
can I help you?

can I just have a look around?
▶ я могу просто посмотреть?
[ya magoo prosta pasmatryet?]

yes, I'm looking for ...
▶ да, я ищу …
[da, ya eesh-choo …]

how much is this?
► сколько это стоит?
[skolka eta sto-eet?]

семьсот шестьдесят восемь рублей ◄
[syemsot shesdyesyat vosyem rooblyay]
seven hundred and sixty-eight roubles

OK, I think I'll have to leave it; it's a little
too expensive for me
▶ пожалуй, это слишком дорого для меня
[paJalooy, eta sleeshkam doraga dlya myenya]

а вот это? ◄
[ah vot eta?]
how about this?

can I pay by credit card?
▶ я могу заплатить кредитной картой?
[ya magoo zaplateet kryedeetnl kartl?]

it's too big
▶ это велико
[eta vyeleeko]

it's too small
▶ это мало
[eta malo]

it's for my son – he's about this high
▶ это для моего сына – он примерно такого роста
[eta dlya ma-yevo siyna – on preemyerna takova rosta]

▶ что-нибудь еще?
[shto-neeboot yesh-cho?]
will there be anything else?

that's all thanks
нет, спасибо, это все ◄
[nyet, spaseeba, eta fsyo]

make it seven hundred roubles and I'll take it
▶ я возьму, если отдадите за семьсот рублей
[ya vazmoo, yeslee atdadeetyeh za syemsot rooblyay]

fine, I'll take it
▶ хорошо, я возьму это
[Harasho, ya vazmoo eta]

закрыто	[zakriyta]	closed
касса	[kas-sa]	cash desk
обменивать/ обменять	[abmyeneevat/abmyenyat]	to exchange
открыто	[atkriyta]	open
распродажа	[raspradaJa]	sale

download these scenarios as MP3s from:

15. Sightseeing

art gallery	картинная галерея	[kar**tee**n-na-ya galyer**yeh**-ya]
bus tour	автобусная экскурсия	[aft**o**boosna-ya eksk**oo**rsee-ya]
city centre	центр города	[tsentr g**o**rada]
closed	закрыто	[zak**ri**yta]
guide	гид	[geed]
museum	музей	[mooz**yay**]
open	открыто	[atk**ri**yta]

I'm interested in seeing the old town
▶ хотела бы посмотреть на старый город
[ya Hat**ye**la biy pasmatr**ye**t na st**a**ri g**o**rat]

are there guided tours?
▶ есть ли экскурсии с гидом?
[**ye**stlee eksk**oo**rsee-ee sg**ee**dam?]

к сожалению, мест нет ◀
[k saJal**ye**nee-yoo, myest nyet]
I'm sorry, it's fully booked

how much would you charge to drive us around for four hours?
▶ сколько вы возьмете за четырехчасовую поездку по городу?
[sk**o**lka viy vazm**yo**tyeh za chyetiyr**yo**H-chasav**oo**-yoo pa-**ye**stkoo pa g**o**radoo?]

can we book tickets for the concert here?
▶ здесь можно заказать билеты на концерт?
[zdyes m**o**Jna zakaz**a**t beel**ye**tiy na kants**e**rt?]

да, на чье имя? ◀
[da, na chyo **ee**mya?]
yes, in what name?

какой кредитной картой вы будете платить? ◀
[kak**oy** kryed**ee**tnl k**a**rtl viy b**oo**dyetyeh plat**ee**t?]
which credit card?

where do we get the tickets?
▶ где можно получить билеты?
[gdyeh m**o**Jna palooch**ee**t beel**ye**tiy?]

заберите их при входе ◀
[zabyer**ee**tyeh eeH pree fH**o**dyeh]
just pick them up at the entrance

is it open on Sundays?
▶ открыт ли он по воскресеньям?
[atr**iy**tlee on pa vaskryes**ye**nyam?]

how much is it to get in?
▶ сколько стоит входной билет?
[sk**o**lka st**o**-eet fH**a**dn**oy** beel**ye**t?]

are there reductions for groups of 6?
▶ есть ли скидки для групп из 6 человек?
[**ye**stlee sk**ee**tkee dlya groop eez shest**ee** chyelav**ye**k?]

that was really impressive!
▶ это было очень впечатляюще!
[**e**ta b**iy**la **o**chyen fpyechatl**ya**-yoosh-chyeh!]

16. Trains

to change trains	делать/сделать пересадку	[dyelat/zdyelat pyeryesatkoo]
platform	платформа	[platforma]
return	обратный билет	[abratni beelyet]
single	билет в один конец	[beelyet vadeen kanyets]
station	вокзал	[vakzal]
(underground, bus)	станция	[stantsiy-ya]
stop	остановка	[astanofka]
ticket	билет	[beelyet]

how much is ...?
▶ сколько стоит …?
[skolka sto-eet …?]

a single, second class to ...
▶ купейный билет в один конец до …
[koopayni beelyet vadeen kanyets da …]

two returns, second class to ...
▶ два обратных купейных билета до …
[dva abratniyH koopayniyH beelyeta da …]

for today	**for tomorrow**	**for next Tuesday**
▶ на сегодня	▶ на завтра	▶ на следующий вторник
[na syevodnya]	[na zaftra]	[na slyedoosh-chee ftorneek]

за поезд дальнего следования нужно доплатить ◀
[za po-yest dalnyeva slyedavanee-ya nooɹna daplateet]
there's a supplement for the Intercity

вы хотите забронировать место? ◀
[viy Hateetyeh zabraneeravat myesta?]
do you want to make a seat reservation?

вам нужно сделать пересадку в Москве ◀
[vam nooɹna zdyelat pyeryesatkoo vmaskvyeh]
you have to change at Moscow

is this seat free?
▶ это место свободно?
[eta myesta svabodna?]

excuse me, which station are we at?
▶ извините, пожалуйста, что это за станция?
[eezveeneetyeh, paɹalsta, shto eta zastantsiy-ya?]

is this where I change for Rostov?
▶ это здесь нужно сделать пересадку на Ростов?
[eta zdyes nooɹna zdyelat pyeryesatkoo na rastof?]

English

→

Russian

A

a, an* (see page 288)

about: about 20 около двадцати [okala dvatsatee]

it's about 5 o'clock около пяти часов [okala pyatee chasof]

a film about Russia фильм о России [feelm a rassee-ee]

above над [nad]

abroad за границей [za graneetsay]

absolutely! конечно! [kanyeshna!]

absorbent cotton вата [vata]

accelerator акселератор [aksyelyeratar]

accept принимать/принять [preeneemat/preenyat]

accident несчастный случай [nyesh-chasni sloochee]

there's been an accident произошёл несчастный случай [pra-eezashol nyesh-chasni sloochee]

accommodation жильё [Jilyo]

ache боль f [bol]

my back aches у меня болит спина [oo menya baleet speena]

across: across the road через дорогу [chyeryes darogoo]

adaptor адаптер [adapter]

address адрес [adryes]

what's your address? какой ваш адрес? [kakoy vash adryes?]

address book алфавитная записная книжка [alfaveetna-ya zapeesna-ya kneeshka]

admission charge: how much is the admission charge? сколько стоит билет? [skolka sto-eet beelyet?]

adult взрослый человек [vzrosli chyelavyek]

advance: in advance заранее [zaranyeh-yeh]

aeroplane самолёт [samalyot]

after после [poslyeh]

after you после вас [poslyeh vas]

after lunch после обеда [poslyeh abyeda]

afternoon: in the afternoon днём [dnyom]

this afternoon сегодня днём [syevodnya dnyom]

aftershave лосьон после бритья [lasyon poslyeh breetya]

aftersun cream крем после загара [kryem poslyeh zagara]

afterwards потом [patom]

again снова [snova]

against против [proteef]

age возраст [vozrast]

ago: a week ago неделю назад [nyedyelyoo nazat]

an hour ago час назад [chas nazat]

agree: I agree (said by man/woman) я согласен/согласна [ya saglasyen/saglasna]

Aids СПИД [speed]

air воздух [**vo**zdooн]

by air самолётом
[samal**yo**tam]

air-conditioning: with
air-conditioning с
кондиционером [skandeetsi-
an**ye**ram]

airline авиалиния [**a**vee-a-
l**ee**nee-ya]

airmail: by airmail
авиапочтой [**a**vee-a-p**o**chtɪ]

airmail envelope
международный конверт
[myeʒdoonar**o**dni kanv**ye**rt]

airport аэропорт [a-erap**o**rt]

to the airport, please в
аэропорт, пожалуйста
[va-erap**o**rt, paʒa**l**sta]

airport bus автобус-
экспресс в аэропорт
[aft**o**boos-ekspr**e**s va-erap**o**rt]

aisle seat место у прохода
[m**ye**sto oo pran**o**da]

alcohol спиртное [speertn**o**-
yeh]

alcoholic: is it alcoholic? это
спиртное? [**e**ta speertn**o**-yeh?]

all* (things) всё [fsyo]
(people) все [fsyeh]

all the children все дети
[fsyeh d**ye**tee]

all of it всё [fsyo]

all of them все [fsyeh]

all day весь день [vyes dyen]

that's all, thanks это всё,
спасибо [**e**ta fsyo, spas**ee**ba]

allergic: I'm allergic to ... у
меня аллергия на ... [oo

menya alyergee-ya na ...]

allowed: is smoking allowed
here? можно ли здесь
курить? [m**o**ʌnalee zdyes
koor**ee**t?]

all right хорошо [нarash**o**]

I'm all right со мной всё
в порядке [samn**oy** fsyo
fpar**ya**tkyeh]

are you all right? с вами
всё в порядке? [sv**a**mee fsyo
fpar**ya**tkyeh?]

almond миндаль **m** [meend**a**l]

almost почти [pacht**ee**]

alone (man/woman) один/одна
[ad**ee**n/adn**a**]

alphabet алфавит [alfav**ee**t]

а ah	р er
б beh	с es
в veh	т teh
г geh	у oo
д deh	ф ef
е yeh	х нa
ё yo	ц tseh
ж ʒeh	ч chyeh
з zeh	ш sha
и ee	щ sh-chya
й ee kratka-yeh	ъ tv**yo**rdi znak
к ka	ы iy
л el	ь mya**н**kee znak
м em	э e
н en	ю yoo
о o	я ya
п peh	

already уже [ooʒ**eh**]

also тоже [t**o**ʒeh]

although хотя [нat**ya**]

altogether всего [fsyev**o**]

always всегда [fsyeg**da**]

am*: at seven am в семь часов утра [fsyem chas**of** **oo**tra]

amazing (surprising) удивительный [oodeev**ee**tyelni]
(very good) потрясающий [patryas**a**-yoosh-chee]

ambulance скорая помощь [sk**o**ra-ya p**o**mash-ch]

call an ambulance! вызовите скорую помощь! [**vi**zaveetyeh sk**o**roo-yoo p**o**mash-ch!]

America Америка [am**ye**reeka]

American (adj) американский [amyeree**ka**nskee]

I'm American (man/woman) я американец/американка [ya amyeree**ka**nyets/ amyeree**ka**nka]

among среди [sryed**ee**]

amount количество [kal**ee**chyestva]
(money) сумма [s**oo**m-ma]

amp: 13-amp fuse предохранитель на тринадцать ампер [predaнran**ee**tyel na treen**a**tsat amp**yer**]

and и [ee]

angry сердитый [syerd**ee**ti]

animal животное [Jiv**o**tna-yeh]

ankle лодыжка [lad**iy**shka]

anniversary (wedding) юбилей [yoobeel**yay**]

annoy: this man's annoying me этот человек мне досаждает [**e**tat chyelav**ye**k mn**yeh** dasaJd**a**-yet]

annoying: it's annoying это раздражает [**e**ta razdraJ**a**-yet]

another другой [droog**oy**]

can we have another room? можно другой номер? [m**o**Jna droog**oy** n**o**myer?]

another beer, please ещё одно пиво, пожалуйста [yesh-ch**o** adn**o** p**ee**va, paJ**a**lsta]

antibiotics антибиотики [anteebee-**o**teekee]

antifreeze антифриз [anteefr**ee**s]

antihistamine антигистамин [anteegeestam**ee**n]

antique антиквариат [anteekvaree-**at**]

antique shop антикварный магазин [anteekv**a**rni magaz**ee**n]

antiseptic антисептическое средство [anteesept**ee**chyeska-yeh sr**ye**tstva]

any: have you got any bread/ tomatoes? у вас есть хлеб/ помидоры? [oo vas yest нlyep/ pameed**o**ri?]

do you have any ...? у вас есть ...? [oo vas yest ...?]

sorry, I don't have any извините, у меня нет [eezveen**ee**tyeh, oo men**ya** nyet]

anybody кто-нибудь [kto-neeb**oot**]

does anybody speak English? кто-нибудь говорит по-

английски? [kto-neeboot
gavareet pa-angleeskee?]
there wasn't anybody there
там никого не было [tam
neekavo nyebila]
anything что-нибудь [shto-
neeboot]

dialogues

anything else? что-
нибудь ещё? [shto-neeboot
yesh-cho?]
nothing else, thanks
больше ничего,
спасибо [bolsheh neechyevo,
spaseeba]

would you like anything
to drink? вы хотите
что-нибудь выпить?
[viy Hateetyeh shto-neeboot
viypeet?]
I don't want anything,
thanks спасибо, я
ничего не хочу [spaseeba,
ya neechyevo nyeh Hachoo]

apart from кроме [kromyeh]
apartment квартира
[kvarteera]
apartment block
многоквартирный дом
[mnogakvarteerni dom]
aperitif аперитив [apyereeteef]
apology извинение
[eezveenyenee-yeh]
appendicitis аппендицит
[apyendeetseeyt]

appetizer закуска [zakooska]
apple яблоко [yablaka]
appointment приём
[preeyom]

dialogue

good morning, how can
I help you? доброе
утро, чем я могу вам
помочь? [dobra-yeh ootra,
chyem ya magoo vam
pamoch?]
I'd like to make an
appointment (said by man/
woman) я бы хотел/
хотела записаться на
приём [yabi Hatyel/Hatyela
zapeesatsa na preeyom]
what time would you like?
какое время для вас
удобно? [kako-yeh vryemya
dlya vas oodobna?]
three o'clock в три часа
[ftree chasa]
I'm afraid that's not
possible, is four o'clock
all right? боюсь, что в
три часа не получится,
в четыре вас устроит?
[bayoos, shto ftree chasa nyeh
paloocheetsa, fchyetiyryeh vas
oostro-eet?]
yes, that will be fine да,
это меня устроит [da, eta
myenya oostro-eet]
the name was ...? ваше
имя ...? [vasheh
eemya ...?]

apricot абрикос [abreek**o**s]

April апрель **m** [apr**yel**]

area район [r**i-on**]

area code междугородный код [myeɹdoogar**o**dni kod]

arm рука [r**oo**ka]

arrange: will you arrange it for us? вы организуете это для нас? [viy arganeez**oo**-yetyeh **e**ta dlya nas?]

arrival прибытие [preeb**yi**tee-yeh]

arrive приезжать/приехать [pree-yeɹɹ**at**/pree-**ye**ʜat]

when do we arrive? когда мы приезжаем? [kagd**a** miy pree-yeɹ-J**a**-yem?]

has my fax arrived yet? ещё не пришёл факс для меня? [yesh-ch**o** nyeh preesh**o**l faks dlya men**ya**?]

we arrived today мы приехали сегодня [miy pree-**ye**нalee syev**o**dnya]

art искусство [eesk**oo**stva]

art gallery картинная галерея [kart**ee**n-na-ya galyer**yeh**-ya]

artist художник [ʜood**o**ɹneek]

as: as big as такой же большой как ... [tak**oy**ɹeh balsh**oy** kak ...]

as soon as possible как можно быстрее [kak m**o**ɹna bistr**yeh**-yeh]

ashtray пепельница [p**ye**pyelneetsa]

ask спрашивать/спросить [spr**a**shivat/spras**eet**]

I didn't ask for this (said by man/woman) это не то, что я заказал/заказала [**e**ta nyeh to, shto ya zakaz**a**l/zakaz**a**la]

could you ask him to ...? попросите его, пожалуйста ... [papras**ee**tyeh yev**o**, paɹ**a**lsta ...]

asleep: she's asleep она спит [an**a** speet]

aspirin аспирин [aspeer**ee**n]

asthma астма [**a**stma]

astonishing поразительный [paraz**ee**telni]

at: at the hotel в гостинице [vgast**ee**neetseh]

at the station на станции [na st**a**ntsi-ee]

at six o'clock в шесть часов [fshest chas**of**]

at Sasha's у Саши [oo s**a**shi]

athletics атлетика [atl**ye**teeka]

ATM банкомат [bankam**a**t]

attractive привлекательный [preevlyek**a**tyelni]

aubergine баклажан [baklaɹ**a**n]

August август [**a**vgoost]

aunt тётя [t**yo**tya]

Australia Австралия [afstral**ee**-ya]

Australian (adj) австралийский [afstral**ee**skee]

I'm Australian (man/woman) я австралиец/австралийка [ya afstral**ee**-yets/afstral**ee**ka]

Austria Австрия [**a**fstree-ya]

automatic (adj)

автоматический
[aftamateechyeskee]
(noun: car) с автоматической
коробкой передач
[saftamateechyeski karopkı
pyeryedach]
autumn осень f [osyen]
  in the autumn осенью
  [osenyoo]
avenue аллея [alyeh-ya]
average (not good)
посредственный
[pasryetstvyen-ni]
  on average в среднем
  [fsryednyem]
awake: is he awake? он
проснулся? [on prasnoolsya?]
away: go away! уходите!
[ooHadeetyeh!]
  is it far away? это далеко?
  [eta dalyeko?]
awful ужасный [ooJasni]

B

baby ребёнок [ryebyonak]
baby food детское питание
[dyetska-yeh peetanee-yeh]
baby's bottle бутылочка
для кормления ребёнка
[bootiylachka dlya karmlyenee-ya
ryebyonka]
baby-sitter няня [nyanya]
back (of body) спина [speena]
  (back part) задняя часть
  [zadnya-ya chast]
  at the back сзади [z-zadee]
  I'd like my money back (said

by man/woman) я хотел/
хотела бы получить
обратно деньги [ya Hatyel/
Hatyela biy paloocheet abratna
dyengee]
to come back
возвращаться/вернуться
[vazvrash-chatsa/vyernootsa]
to go back (by transport)
уезжать/уехать [oo-yeJ-Jat/
oo-yeHat]
  (on foot)
возвращатьсвернуться
[vazvrash-chatsa/vyernootsa]
backache боль в спине [bol
fspeenyeh]
bacon бекон [byekon]
bad плохой [plaHoy]
  not bad неплохо [nyeploHa]
  a bad headache сильная
  головная боль [seelna-ya
  galavna-ya bol]
badly плохо [ploHa]
bag сумка [soomka]
  (handbag) дамская сумка
  [damska-ya soomka]
  (suitcase) чемодан
  [chyemadan]
baggage багаж [bagash]
baggage checkroom
камера хранения
[kamyera Hranyenee-ya]
baggage claim выдача
багажа [viydacha bagaJa]
bakery булочная [boolachna-
ya]
balcony балкон [balkon]
  a room with a balcony
  номер с балконом [nomyer

zbalk**o**nam]

bald лысый [**liy**si]
ball мяч [myach]
ballet балет [bal**yet**]
ballpoint pen шариковая
ручка [sha**ree**kava-ya r**oo**chka]
banana банан [ban**an**]
band (orchestra) оркестр
[ark**yes**tr]
bandage бинт [beent]
Bandaid® пластырь **m**
[pl**as**tir]
bank (money) банк [bank]
bank account банковский
счёт [b**a**nkofskee sh-chot]
banknote банкнота [bankn**o**ta]
bar бар [bar]
 a bar of chocolate плитка
шоколада [pl**ee**tka shakal**a**da]
barber's парикмахерская
[paree**н**ma**н**yerska-ya]
bargaining

dialogue

 how much is this?
 сколько это стоит?
 [sk**o**lka eta st**o**-eet?]
 100,000 roubles сто
 тысяч рублей [sto t**iy**syach
 roobl**yay**]
 that's too expensive это
 слишком дорого [eta
 sl**ee**shkam d**o**raga]
 how about 70,000? как
 насчёт семидесяти
 тысяч? [kak nash-chot
 syem**ee**dyestee t**iy**syach?]
 I'll let you have it for

 90,000 отдам за
 девяносто тысяч [ad-
 dam za dyevyan**o**sta t**iy**syach]
 can you reduce it a bit
 more?/OK, it's a deal
 сбросьте ещё немного/
 ладно, идёт [sbr**o**styeh
 yesh-cho nyemn**o**ga/l**a**dna,
 eed**yot**]

basket корзина [karz**ee**na]
bath ванна [v**a**n-na]
 can I have a bath? можно
 ли принять ванну?
 [m**o**лnalee preen**ya**t van-n**oo**?]
bathhouse баня [b**a**nya]
bathroom ванная [v**a**n-na-ya]
 with a private bathroom с
 ванной [sv**a**n-nl]
bath towel банное
 полотенце [b**a**n-na-yeh
 palat**ye**ntseh]
bathtub ванна [v**a**n-na]
battery (for radio) батарейка
 [batar**yay**ka]
 (for car) аккумулятор
 [akoomool**ya**tar]
bay бухта [b**oo**нta]
be* быть [biyt]
beach пляж [plyash]
 on the beach на пляже [na
 pl**ya**Jeh]
beach mat пляжная
 подстилка [pl**ya**Jna-ya
 patst**ee**lka]
beach umbrella пляжный
 зонт [pl**ya**Jni zont]
beans фасоль (**f**, sing) [fas**o**l]
 French beans фасоль [fas**o**l]

Be

broad beans бобы [babiy]

beard борода [barada]

beautiful красивый [kraseevi]

because потому что [patamooshta]

because of из-за [eez-za]

bed кровать f [kravat]

I'm going to bed now я ложусь спать [ya laJoos spat]

bed and breakfast проживание и завтрак [praJivanee-yeh ee zaftrak]

bedroom спальня [spalnya]

beef говядина [gavyadeena]

beer пиво [peeva]

two beers, please два пива, пожалуйста [dva peeva, paJalsta]

before перед [pyeryet]

begin начинаться/начаться [nacheenatsa/nachatsa]

when does it begin? когда начало? [kagda nachala?]

beginner (man/woman) начинающий/начинающая [nacheena-yoosh-chee/ nacheena-yoosh-cha-ya]

beginning: at the beginning в начале [vnachalyeh]

behind за [za]

behind me за мной [za mnoy]

Belgium Бельгия [byelgee-ya]

believe верить/поверить [vyereet/pavyereet]

below под [pod]

belt ремень [ryemyen]

bend (in road) поворот [pavarot]

berth (on ship) койка [koyka]

beside: beside the ... рядом с ... [ryadam s ...]

best лучший [loochshi]

better лучше [loochsheh]

are you feeling better? вам лучше? [vam loochsheh?]

between между [myeJdoo]

beyond за [za]

bicycle велосипед [vyelaseepyet]

big большой [balshoy]

too big слишком большой [sleeshkam balshoy]

it's not big enough недостаточно большой [nyedastatachna balshoy]

bike велосипед [vyelaseepyet]

(motorbike) мотоцикл [matatsiykl]

bill счёт [sh-chot]

(US: banknote) банкнота [banknota]

could I have the bill, please? счёт, пожалуйста [sh-chot, paJalsta]

bin мусорное ведро [moosarna-yeh vyedro]

bird птица [pteetsa]

birthday день рождения [dyen raJdyenee-ya]

happy birthday! с днём рождения! [sdnyom raJdyenee-ya!]

biscuit печенье [pyechyenyeh]

bit: a little bit немножко [nyeh-mnoshka]

a big bit большой кусок [balsh**oy** koos**ok**]

a bit of ... кусочек ... [koos**o**chyek ...]

a bit expensive дороговато [daragav**a**ta]

bite (by insect) укус (насекомого) [ook**oo**s (nasyek**o**mava)]

(by dog) укус (собаки) [ook**oo**s (sab**a**kee)]

bitter (taste) горький [**go**rkee]

black чёрный [ch**o**rni]

black market чёрный рынок [ch**o**rni r**i**nak]

Black Sea Чёрное море [ch**o**rna-yeh m**o**ryeh]

blanket одеяло [adyeh-**ya**la]

bleach (for toilet) хлорка [Hl**o**rka]

bless you! будьте здоровы! [b**oo**t-tyeh zdar**o**vi!]

blind слепой [slyep**oy**]

blinds шторы [sht**o**ri]

blocked (road) перегороженный [pyeryegar**o**Jen-ni]

(sink) засоренный [zas**o**ryen-ni]

blond (adj) белокурый [byelak**oo**ri]

blood кровь **f** [krof]

high blood pressure высокое давление [vis**o**ka-yeh davl**ye**nee-yeh]

blouse блузка [bl**oo**ska]

blow-dry укладка феном [ookl**a**tka f**ye**nam]

I'd like a cut and blow-dry пожалуйста, постригите и сделайте укладку феном [pa**J**alsta, pastreeg**ee**tyeh ee sd**ye**lItyeh ooklatk**oo** f**ye**nam]

blue синий [s**ee**nee]

blue eyes голубые глаза [galoob**iy**-yeh gl**a**za]

blusher румяна pl [room**ya**na]

boarding pass посадочный талон [pas**a**dachni tal**o**n]

boat лодка [l**o**tka]

(for passengers) корабль **m** [kar**a**bl]

when is the next boat to ...? когда следующий рейс в ...? [kagd**a** sl**ye**doo-sh-chee r**ya**ys v ...?]

body тело [t**ye**la]

boil: do we have to boil the water? нужно ли кипятить воду? [n**oo**Jnalee keepyat**ee**t vod**oo**?]

boiled egg варёное яйцо [var**yo**na-yeh yIts**o**]

boiled water кипячёная вода [keepyach**o**na-ya vad**a**]

boiler кипятильник [keepyat**ee**lneek]

bone кость [kost]

bonnet (of car) капот [kap**o**t]

book (noun) книга [kn**ee**ga]

(verb) заказывать/заказать [zak**a**zivat/zakaz**a**t]

can I book a seat? могу ли я заказать билет [mag**oo**lee ya zakaz**a**t beel**ye**t?]

dialogue

I'd like to book a table for two (said by man/woman) я хотел/хотела бы заказать столик на двоих [ya hat**yel**/hat**yela** biy zakaz**at** st**o**leek na dva-**ee**н]

what time would you like it booked for? на какое время? [na kak**o**-yeh vr**ye**mya?]

half past seven на половину восьмого [na palav**ee**noo vasm**o**va]

that's fine хорошо [нarash**o**]

and your name? ваше имя? [**v**asheh **ee**mya?]

родилась в тысяча девятьсот шестидесятом году [ya rad**ee**lsa/rad**ee**las ft**iy**syacha dyevyatsot shesteedyes**ya**tam gad**oo**]

borrow занимать/занять [zaneem**at**/zan**yat**]

may I borrow ...? вы не одолжите ...? [viy nyeh adalJ**iy**teh ...?]

both оба [**o**ba]

bother: sorry to bother you извините за беспокойство [eezveen**ee**tyeh za byespak**oy**stva]

bottle бутылка [boot**iy**lka]

a bottle of vodka бутылка водки [boot**iy**lka v**o**tkee]

bottle-opener открывалка [atkriv**a**lka]

bottom (of person) зад [zat]

at the bottom of ... (street etc) в конце ... (улицы) [fkants**eh** (**oo**leetsi)]

(hill) у подножия ... [oo padn**o**Ji-ya ...]

bouncer вышибала [vishib**a**la]

bowl тарелка [tar**ye**lka]

box коробка [kar**o**pka]

box office театральная касса [tyeh-atr**a**lna-ya k**a**s-sa]

boy мальчик [**m**alcheek]

boyfriend друг [drook]

bra бюстгальтер [byoostg**a**lter]

bracelet браслет [brasl**yet**]

brake тормоз [**t**ormas]

brandy коньяк [kan**yak**]

bread хлеб [н**l**yep]

bookshop, bookstore книжный магазин [kn**ee**Jni magaz**een**]

boot (footwear) ботинок [bat**ee**nak]

(of car) багажник [bag**a**Jneek]

border (of country) граница [gran**ee**tsa]

bored: I'm bored мне скучно [mnyeh sk**oo**shna]

boring скучный [sk**oo**shni]

born: I was born in Manchester (said by man/woman) я родился/родилась в Манчестере [ya rad**ee**lsa/rad**ee**las vmanch**ye**steryeh]

I was born in 1960 (said by man/woman) я родился/

white bread белый хлеб
[b**ye**li Hlyep]

brown bread чёрный хлеб
[ch**o**rni Hlyep]

rye bread ржаной хлеб
[rJan**oy** Hlyep]

wholemeal bread хлеб из
непросеянной муки [Hlyep
eez nyepras**yeh**-yanı mook**ee**]

break (verb) ломать/сломать
[lam**at**/slam**at**]

I've broken the ... (said by man/
woman) я сломал/
сломала ... [ya slam**a**l/slam**a**la]

I think I've broken my wrist
(said by man/woman) кажется,
я сломал/сломала
запястье [k**a**Jetsa, ya slam**a**l/
slam**a**la zap**ya**styeh]

break down ломаться/
сломаться [lam**a**tsa/slam**a**tsa]

I've broken down у меня
сломалась машина [oo
men**ya** slam**a**las mash**ı**na]

breakdown поломка
[pal**o**mka]

breakdown service
экстренная техпомощь
[**e**kstryen-na-ya tyeHp**o**mosch-ch]

breakfast завтрак [z**a**ftrak]

break-in: I've had a break-in
мою комнату обокрали
[ma-**yoo** k**o**mnatoo abak**ra**lee]

breast грудь f [grood]

breathe дышать [dish**a**t]

breeze ветерок [vyetyer**o**k]

bribe взятка [vz**ya**tka]

bridge (over river) мост [mosst]

brief краткий [kr**a**tkee]

briefcase портфель m
[partf**ye**l]

bright (light etc) яркий [**ya**rkee]

bright red ярко-красный
[**ya**rka-kr**a**sni]

brilliant (idea, person)
блестящий [blyest**ya**sh-chee]

bring приносить/принести
[preenas**eet**/preenyest**ee**]

I'll bring it back later я верну
это позже [ya vyern**oo e**ta poJ-
Jeh]

Britain Великобритания
[vyeleeka-breet**a**nee-ya]

British британский
[breet**a**nskee]

brochure брошюра
[brash**oo**ra]

broken сломанный [sl**o**man-
ni]

bronchitis бронхит
[branH**eet**]

brooch брошь f [brosh]

broom метла [myetl**a**]

brother брат [brat]

brother-in-law (husband's brother)
деверь [d**ye**vyer]
(wife's brother) шурин
[sh**oo**reen]

brown коричневый
[kar**ee**chnyevi]

brown hair каштановые
волосы [kasht**a**navi-yeh
v**o**lasi]

brown eyes карие глаза
[k**a**ree-yeh glaz**a**]

bruise синяк [seen**ya**k]

brush щётка [sh-ch**o**tka]
(artist's) кисть f [keest]

bucket ведро [vyedro]

buffet (on train etc) буфет [boofyet]
(in restaurant) шведский стол [shvetskee stol]

buggy (for child) детская коляска [dyetska-ya kalyaska]

building здание [zdanee-yeh]

bulb (light bulb) лампочка [lampachka]

Bulgaria Болгария [balgaree-ya]

bumper бампер [bampyer]

bunk койка [koyka]

bureau de change обмен валюты [abmyen valyooti]

burglary ограбление [agrablyenee-yeh]

burn (noun) ожог [aJok]
(verb) гореть/сгореть [garyet/sgaryet]
this is burnt это горелое [eta garyela-yeh]

burst: a burst pipe лопнувшая труба [lopnoofsha-ya trooba]

bus автобус [aftoboos]
what number bus is it to ...? какой автобус идёт до ...? [kakoy aftoboos eedyot da ...?]
when is the next bus to ...? когда следующий автобус до ...? [kagda slyedoosh-chee aftoboos da ...?]
what time is the last bus? когда приходит последний автобус? [kagda preeHodeet paslyednee aftoboos?]

dialogue

does this bus go to ...?
идёт ли этот автобус до ...? [eedyotlee etat aftoboos da ...?]
no, you need a number ...
нет, вам нужен номер ... [nyet, vam nooJen nomyer ...]

business бизнес [beeznes]

bus station автобусная станция [aftoboosna-ya stantsi-ya]

bus stop остановка автобуса [astanofka aftoboosa]

bust бюст [byoost]

busy (restaurant etc) оживлённый [aJivlyon-ni]
I'm busy tomorrow (said by man/woman) я буду занят/занята завтра [ya boodoo zanyat/zanyata zaftra]

but но [no]

butcher's мясной магазин [myasnoy magazeen]

butter масло [masla]

button пуговица [poogaveetsa]

buy покупать/купить [pakoopat/koopeet]
where can I buy ...? где можно купить ...? [gdyeh moJna koopeet ...?]

by: by train/by car/by plane на поезде/на машине/на самолёте [na po-yezdyeh/na mashiynyeh/na samalyotyeh]
the book is written by ...

книга написана ... [**knee**ga na**pee**sana ...]

by the window около окна [**o**kala a**kna**]

by the sea у моря [oo **mo**rya]

by Thursday к четвергу [kchyetvyer**goo**]

bye! пока! [pa**ka**]

C

cabaret кабаре [kabar**eh**]

cabbage капуста [kap**oo**sta]

cabin (on ship) каюта [ka-**yoo**ta]

cable car фуникулёр [fooneekool**yor**]

café кафе [kaf**eh**]

cagoule куртка от дождя [k**oo**rtka ad-da**Jd**ya]

cake торт [tort]

a piece of cake кусок торта [koos**o**k t**o**rta]

cake shop кондитерская [kand**ee**tyerska-ya]

call (verb) звать/позвать [zvat/paz**va**t]

(verb: to phone) звонить/позвонить [zvan**ee**t/pazvan**ee**t]

what's it called? как это называется? [kak **e**ta naz**i**va-yetsa?]

he/she is called ... его/её зовут ... [ye**vo**/ye-**yo** zav**oo**t ...]

please call the doctor вызовите, пожалуйста, врача [**viy**zaveetyeh, paJ**a**lsta, vrach**a**]

please give me a call at 7.30 am tomorrow позвоните мне, пожалуйста, завтра в семь тридцать утра [pazvan**ee**tyeh mnyeh, paJ**a**lsta, z**a**ftra fs**ye**m tr**ee**tsat oot**ra**]

please ask him to call me пожалуйста, попросите его мне позвонить [paJ**a**lsta, papras**ee**tyeh ye**vo** mnyeh pazvan**ee**t]

call back: I'll call back later я вернусь позже [ya vyern**oos** po**J**-Jeh]

(phone back) я перезвоню попозже [ya pyeryezvan**yoo** pap**o**J-Jeh]

call round: I'll call round tomorrow я зайду завтра [ya z**i**doo z**a**ftra]

camcorder видеокамера [v**ee**dyeh-ok**a**myera]

camera фотоаппарат [f**o**ta-apar**a**t]

camera shop магазин кино- и фотоаппаратуры [magaz**ee**n k**ee**na-ee-f**o**ta-aparat**oo**ri]

camp (verb) жить в палатках [J**i**yt fpal**a**tkaH]

can we camp here? можно ли здесь разбить лагерь? [m**o**Jnalee zdyes razb**ee**t l**a**gyer?]

camping gas газовый баллончик [g**a**zavi bal**o**ncheek]

campsite кемпинг [k**ye**mpeeng]

can банка [b**a**nka]

a can of beer банка пива [banka peeva]

can*: can you ...? вы можете ...? [viy mojetyeh ...?]

can you show me ...? вы можете показать мне ...? [viy mojetyeh pakazat mnyeh ...?]

can I have ...? можно мне, пожалуйста ... [mojna mnyeh, pajalsta ...]

I can't ... я не могу ... [ya nyeh magoo ...]

Canada Канада [kanada]

Canadian канадский [kanatskee]

I'm Canadian (man/woman) я канадец/канадка [ya kanadyets/kanatka]

canal канал [kanal]

cancel отменять/отменить [atmyenyat/atmyeneet]

candies конфеты [kanfyeti]

candle свеча [svyecha]

can-opener открывалка [atkrivalka]

cap (hat) шапка [shapka]
(of bottle) крышка [kriyshka]

car машина [mashiyna]
by car на машине [na mashiynyeh]

carafe графин [grafeen]
a carafe of white wine, please графин белого вина, пожалуйста [grafeen byelava veena, pajalsta]

card (birthday etc) открытка [atkriytka]
here's my (business) card моя карточка,

пожалуйста [ma-ya kartachka, pajalsta]

cardigan кофта [kofta]

cardphone телефон, принимающий карточки [tyelyefon, preeneema-yoosh-chee kartachkee]

cards карты [karti]

careful осторожный [astarojni]
be careful! осторожно! [astarojna!]

caretaker (man/woman) сторож [storash]

car ferry автопаром [aftaparom]

car park стоянка [sta-yanka]

carpet ковёр [kavyor]

car rental прокат автомобилей [prakat aftamabeelyay]

carriage (of train) вагон [vagon]

carrier bag сумка [soomka]

carrot морковь f [markof]

carry нести [nyestee]

carry-cot переносная кроватка [pyeryenasna-ya kravatka]

carton пакет [pakyet]

case (suitcase) чемодан [chyemadan]

cash наличные деньги [naleechni-yeh dyengee]
will you cash this for me? (travellers' cheque) обменяйте, пожалуйста, на наличные [abmyenyaytyeh, pajalsta, na naleechni-yeh]

cash desk касса [kas-sa]

cash dispenser банкомат [bankamat]

cassette кассета [kas-syeta]

cassette recorder кассетный магнитофон [kas-syetni magneetafon]

castle замок [zamak]

casualty department палата скорой помощи [palata skori pomash-chee]

cat кошка [koshka]

catch (verb: ball) ловить/ поймать [laveet/pimat]
where do we catch the bus to ...? откуда идёт автобус до ...? [atkooda eedyot aftoboos da ...?]

cathedral собор [sabor]

Catholic (adj) католический [kataleechyeskee]

cauliflower цветная капуста [tsvyetna-ya kapoosta]

cave пещера [pyesh-chyera]

caviar икра [eekra]
red caviar красная икра [krasna-ya eekra]
black caviar чёрная икра [chorna-ya eekra]

ceiling потолок [patalok]

celery сельдерей [syeldyeryay]

cemetery кладбище [kladbeesh-chyeh]

centigrade по Цельсию [pa tselsee-yoo]

centimetre сантиметр [santeemyetr]

central центральный [tsentralni]

central heating центральное отопление [tsentralna-yeh ataplyenee-yeh]

centre центр [tsentr]
how do we get to the city centre? как попасть в центр города? [kak papast ftsentr gorada?]

cereal сухой завтрак [sooHoy zaftrak]

certainly да, конечно [da, kanyeshna]

certainly not ни в коем случае [nee fko-yem sloocha-yeh]

chair стул [stool]

champagne шампанское [shampanska-yeh]

change (noun: money) мелочь [myelach]
(verb: money) обменивать/ обменять [abmyeneevat/ abmyenyat]
can I change this for ...? можно обменять это на ...? [moлna abmyenyat eta na ...?]
I don't have any change у меня нет мелочи [oo menya nyet myelachee]
can you give me change for a 10,000 rouble note? вы не могли бы разменять десять тысяч? [viy nyeh magleebi razmyenyat dyesyat tiysyach?]

dialogue

do we have to change (trains)? нужно ли нам сделать пересадку? [**noo**Jnalee nam zd**ye**lat pyeryes**a**tkoo?]

yes, change at St Petersburg/no, it's a direct train да, сделайте пересадку в Санкт-Петербурге/нет, это прямой поезд [da, zd**ye**lityeh pyeryes**a**tkoo fsankt-peetyerb**oo**rgyeh/nyet, **e**ta pryam**oy** po-yest]

changed: to get changed переодеваться/ переодеться [pyeryeh-ad**ye**vatsa/pyeryeh-ad**ye**tsa]

charge (noun) цена [ts**ena**] (verb) назначать/ назначить цену [naznach**at**/ nazn**a**cheet ts**e**noo]

cheap дешёвый [d**ye**shovi]

do you have anything cheaper? у вас нет ничего подешевле? [oo vas nyet neech**e**vo padyesh**e**vlyeh?]

check (US: bill) счёт [sh-ch**yot**] (US: cheque) чек [chyek]

check (verb) проверять/ проверить [pravver**ya**t/ pravv**ye**reet]

could you check the ..., please? проверьте ..., пожалуйста [pravv**ye**rtyeh ...,

paJ**a**lsta]

check in регистрироваться/ зарегистрироваться [ryegeestr**ee**ravatsa/ zaryegeestr**ee**ravatsa]

where do we have to check in? где проходит регистрация? [gdyeh praH**o**deet ryegeestr**a**tsi-ya?]

check-in регистрация [ryegeestr**a**tsi-ya]

cheek щека [sh-chyek**a**]

cheerio! пока! [pak**a**!]

cheers! (toast) ваше здоровье! [**va**sheh zdar**o**vyeh!]

cheese сыр [siyr]

chemist's аптека [apt**ye**ka]

cheque чек [chyek]

do you take cheques? вы принимаете чеки? [viy preen**ee**ma-yetyeh ch**ye**kee?]

cheque book чековая книжка [ch**ye**kava-ya kn**ee**shka]

cheque card чековая карточка [ch**ye**kava-ya k**a**rtachka]

cherry вишня [v**ee**shnya]

chess шахматы [sh**a**Hmati]

chest грудь f [grood]

chewing gum жвачка [J**va**chka]

chicken цыплёнок [tsipl**yo**nak]

chickenpox ветрянка [vyetr**ya**nka]

child ребёнок [ryeb**yo**nak]

children дети [d**ye**tee]

child minder няня [n**ya**nya]

children's pool бассейн для
детей [basayn dlya dyetyay]
children's portion детская
порция [dyetska-ya portsi-ya]
chin подбородок [padbarodak]
China Китай [Keetl]
Chinese (adj) китайский
[keetlskee]
chips картофель фри
[kartofyel free]
(US: crisps) чипсы [cheepsi]
chocolate шоколад [shakalat]
milk chocolate молочный
шоколад [malochni shakalat]
plain chocolate шоколад
[shakalat]
hot chocolate горячий
шоколад [garyachee shakalat]
choose выбирать/выбрать
[vibeerat/viybrat]
Christian name имя [eemya]
Christmas Рождество
[raJdyestvo]
Christmas Eve канун
рождества [kanoon raJdyestva]
merry Christmas!
счастливого Рождества!
[sh-chasleevava raJdyestva!]
church церковь f [tserkaf]
cider сидр [seedr]
cigar сигара [seegara]
cigarette сигарета [seegaryeta]
(Russian non-filter) папироса
[papeerosa]
cigarette lighter зажигалка
[zaJigalka]
cinema кино [keeno]
circle круг [krook]
(in theatre) ярус [yaroos]

CIS СНГ [es-en-geh]
city город [gorat]
city centre центр города
[tsentr gorada]
clean (adj) чистый [cheesti]
can you clean these for me?
вы можете почистить это
[viy moJetyeh pacheesteet eta?]
cleaning solution (for contact
lenses) раствор для линз
[rastvor dlya leenz]
cleansing lotion
очищающий лосьон
[acheesh-cha-yoosh-chee lasyon]
clear (obvious) ясный [yasni]
clever умный [oomni]
cliff скала [skala]
climbing альпинизм
[alpeeneezm]
clinic клиника [kleeneeka]
cloakroom (for coats) гардероб
[gardyerop]
clock часы [chasiy]
close (verb) закрывать/
закрыть [zakrivat/zakriyt]

dialogue

what time do you close?
когда вы закрываетесь?
[kagda viy zakriva-yetyes?]
we close at 8pm on
weekdays and 6pm
on Saturdays мы
закрываемся в восемь
в будние дни и в шесть
по субботам [miy zakriva-
yemsya vvosyem vboodnee-yeh
dnee ee fshest pa soobotam]

CI

47

do you close for lunch?
у вас есть обеденный
перерыв? [oo vas yest
abyedyen-ni pyeryeriyf?]
yes, between 1 and 2pm
да, с часу до двух [da,
schasoo da dvooн]

closed закрыто [zakriyta]
cloth (fabric) ткань **f** [tkan]
(for cleaning etc) тряпка
[tryapka]
clothes одежда [adyeJda]
cloud облако [oblaka]
cloudy облачный [oblachni]
clutch сцепление
[stseplyenee-yeh]
coach междугородный
автобус [myeJdoo-garodni
aftoboos]
(on train) вагон [vagon]
coach trip автобусная
экскурсия [aftoboosna-ya
ekskoorsee-ya]
coast берег [byeryek]
on the coast на побережье
[na pabyeryeJeh]
coat пальто [palto]
(jacket) куртка [koortka]
coathanger вешалка
[vyeshalka]
cockroach таракан [tarakan]
cocoa какао [kaka-o]
code (for phoning) код [kod]
**what's the (dialling) code for
Moscow?** какой код для
Москвы? [kakoy kod dlya
maskviy?]
coffee кофе **m** [kofyeh]

two coffees, please две
чашки кофе, пожалуйста
[dvyeh chashkee kofyeh, paJalsta]
coin монета [manyeta]
Coke® Кока-кола [koka-kola]
cold холодный [нalodni]
(noun) простуда [prastooda]
I'm cold мне холодно
[mnyeh нolodna]
I have a cold у меня
простуда [oo menya prastooda]
collapse: **he's collapsed** он
потерял сознание [on
patyeryal saznanee-yeh]
collar воротник [varatneek]
collect: **I've come to collect ...**
(said by man/woman) я
пришёл/пришла за ... [ya
preeshol/preeshla za ...]
collect call звонок с
оплатой вызываемым
абонентом [zvanok saplati
visiva-yemim abanyentam]
college колледж [kaledJ]
colour цвет [tsvyet]
**do you have this in other
colours?** у вас есть это
другого цвета? [oo vas yest
eta droogova tsvyeta?]
colour film цветная плёнка
[tsvyetna-ya plyonka]
comb расчёска [rash-choska]
come приходить/прийти
[preeнadeet/preetee]

dialogue

where do you come from?
вы откуда? [viy atkooda?]

I come from Edinburgh
я из Эдинбурга [ya eez edeenboorga]

come back возвращаться/
вернуться [vazvrash-chatsa/
vyernootsa]
I'll come back tomorrow я
вернусь завтра [ya vyernoos
zaftra]
come in входить/войти
[fHadeet/vitee]
comfortable удобный
[oodobni]
communism коммунизм
[kamooneezm]
communist (adj)
коммунистический
[kamooneesteechyeskee]
Communist party
коммунистическая
партия [kamooneesteechyeska-
ya partee-ya]
compact disc компакт-диск
[kampakt-deesk]
company (business) компания
[kampanee-ya]
compartment (on train) купе
[koopeh]
complain жаловаться/
пожаловаться [Jalavatsa/
paJalavatsa]
complaint жалоба [Jalaba]
I have a complaint у меня
есть жалоба [oo myenya yest
Jalaba]
completely совершенно
[savyershen-na]
computer компьютер

[kampyooter]
concert концерт [kantsert]
concierge (in hotel) дежурная
[dyeJoorna-ya]
conditioner (for hair)
опаласкиватель m
[apalaskeevatyel]
condom презерватив
[pryezyervateef]
conference конференция
[kanfyeryentsi-ya]
confirm подтверждать/
подтвердить [patvyerJdat/
patverdeet]
congratulations!
поздравляю! [pazdravlya-
yoo!]
connecting flight
стыковочный рейс
[stikovachni ryays]
connection (transport)
пересадка [pyeryesatka]
conscious в сознании
[fsaznanee-ee]
constipation запор [zapor]
consulate консульство
[konsoolstva]
contact (verb) связаться с
[svyazatsa s]
contact lenses контактные
линзы [kantaktni-yeh leenzi]
contraceptive
противозачаточное
средство [proteevazachatochna-
yeh sryetstva]
convenient удобный [oodobni]
that's not convenient это не
удобно [eta nyeh oodobna]
cook (verb) готовить/

приготовить [gatoveet/
preegatoveet]

the meat is not cooked мясо
не прожарено [myasa nyeh
praJaryena]

cooker плита [pleeta]

cookie печенье [pyechyenyeh]

cooking utensils кухонная
посуда [kooHan-na-ya pasooda]

cool прохладный [praHladni]

cork пробка [propka]

corkscrew штопор [shtopar]

corner: on the corner на углу
[na oogloo]

in the corner в углу [voogloo]

cornflakes кукурузные
хлопья [kookooroozni-yeh
Hlopya]

correct (right) правильный
[praveelni]

corridor коридор [kareedor]

cosmetics косметика
[kasmyeteeka]

cost (noun) стоимость f [sto-
eemast]

how much does it cost?
сколько это стоит? [skolka
eta sto-eet?]

cot детская кроватка
[dyetska-ya kravatka]

cottage (in the country) дача
[dacha]

cotton хлопок [Hlopak]

cotton wool вата [vata]

couch (sofa) диван [deevan]

couchette спальное место
[spalna-yeh myesta]

cough (noun) кашель m
[kashel]

cough medicine средство от
кашля [sryedstva at kashlya]

could: could you ...? вы
не могли бы ..? [viy nyeh
magleebi ...?]

could I have ...? можно
мне ...? [moJna mnyeh ...?]

country страна [strana]

(countryside) деревня
[dyeryevnya]

in the country за городом
[zagaradam]

countryside деревня
[dyeryevnya]

couple (two people) пара [para]

a couple of hours пару
часов [paroo chasof]

courgette кабачок [kabachok]

courier курьер [kooryer]

course (main course etc) блюдо
[blyooda]

of course конечно
[kanyeshna]

of course not конечно, нет
[kanyeshna, nyet]

cousin (male/female) кузен/
кузина [koozen/koozeena]

cow корова [karova]

cracker крекер [krekyer]

craft shop художественный
салон [HoodoJestvyen-ni salon]

crash (noun) авария [avaree-ya]

I've had a crash (said by man/
woman) я попал/попала
в аварию [ya papal/papala
vavaree-yoo]

crazy сумасшедший
[soomashetshi]

cream (in coffee etc) сливки pl

[sleefkee]
(in cake, lotion) крем [kryem]
(colour) кремовый [kryemavi]
soured cream сметана
[smyetana]
creche ясли pl [yaslee]
credit card кредитная
карточка [kryedeetna-ya
kartachka]

do you take credit cards? вы
принимаете кредитные
карточки? [viy preeneema-
yetyeh kryedeetni-yeh kartachkee?]

dialogue

can I pay by credit card?
могу ли я заплатить
кредитной карточкой?
[magoolee ya zaplateet kryedeetni
kartachki?]
which card do you want to
use? какой карточкой вы
хотите заплатить? [kakoy
kartachki viy нateetyeh zaplateet?]
Mastercard/Visa
yes, sir да, пожалуйста
[da, paJalsta]
what's the number? какой
номер? [kakoy nomyer?]
and the expiry date? когда
истекает срок действия?
[kagda eesteyka-yet srok
dyeystvee-ya?]

Crimea Крым [kriym]
crisps хрустящий
картофель [Hroostyash-chee
kartofyel]

crockery посуда [pasooda]
crossing (by sea, across river)
переправа [pyeryeprava]
crossroads перекрёсток
[pyeryekryostak]
crowd толпа [talpa]
crowded переполненный
[pyeryepolnyen-ni]
crown (on tooth) коронка
[karonka]
cruise круиз [kroo-ees]
crutches костыли [kastilee]
cry (verb) плакать/заплакать
[plakat/zaplakat]
cucumber огурец [agooryets]
pickled cucumber солёный
огурец [salyoni agooryets]
cup чашка [chashka]
a cup of tea, please чашку
чая, пожалуйста [chashkoo
cha-ya, paJalsta]
cupboard шкаф [shkaf]
cure (verb) лечить/вылечить
[lyecheet/viylyecheet]
curly кудрявый [koodryavi]
current (electrical) ток [tok]
curtains занавески
[zanavyeskee]
cushion подушка [padooshka]
custom обычай [abiychee]
Customs таможня [tamoJnya]
Customs form таможенная
декларация [tamoJen-na-ya
dyeklaratsi-ya]
cut (noun) порез [paryes]
(verb) резать/разрезать
[ryezat/razryezat]
I've cut myself (said by man/
woman) я порезался/

порезалась [ya par**ye**zalsa/
par**ye**zalas]

cutlery столовые приборы
[st**a**lovi-yeh preeb**o**ri]

cycling велоспорт [vyelasp**o**rt]

cyclist (man/woman)
велосипедист/
велосипедистка
[vyelaseepyed**ee**st/
vyelaseepyed**ee**stka]

Czech Republic Чешская
республика [ch**ye**shska-ya
ryesp**oo**bleeka]

D
—

dad папа [p**a**pa]

daily ежедневно [yeJedn**ye**vna]
(adj) ежедневный
[yeJedn**ye**vni]

damage (verb) повреждать/
повредить [pavryeJd**a**t/
pavryed**ee**t]
it's damaged это
повреждено [**e**ta
pavryeJdyen**o**]
I'm sorry, I've damaged this
(said by man/woman) извините,
я повредил/
повредила это
[eezveen**ee**tyeh, ya pavryed**ee**l/
pavryed**ee**la **e**ta]

damn! чёрт! [chort!]

damp сырой [sir**oy**]

dance (noun) танец [t**a**nyets]
(verb) танцевать [tantsev**a**t]
would you like to dance?
можно пригласить вас на

танец? [m**o**Jna preeglas**ee**t vas
na t**a**nyets?]

dangerous опасный [ap**a**sni]

Danish (adj) датский
[d**a**tskee]

dark (adj: colour) тёмный
[t**yo**mni]
dark green тёмно-зелёный
[t**yo**mna-zyely**o**ni]
it's getting dark темнеет
[tyemn**yeh**-yet]

date*: what's the date today?
какое сегодня число?
[kak**o**-yeh syev**o**dnya chees**lo**?]
let's make a date for next
Monday договоримся на
следующий понедельник
[dagavar**ee**msya na sl**ye**doosh-chee
panyed**ye**lneek]

dates (fruit) финики
[f**ee**neekee]

daughter дочь [doch]

daughter-in-law невестка
[nyev**ye**stka]

dawn рассвет [ras-sv**yet**]
at dawn на рассвете [na ras-
sv**ye**tyeh]

day день m [dyen]
the day before накануне
[nakan**oo**nyeh]
the day after tomorrow
послезавтра [p**o**slyeh-z**a**ftra]
the day before yesterday
позавчера [pazafchyer**a**]
next day на следующий
день [na sl**ye**doosh-chee dyen]
every day каждый день
[k**a**Jdi dyen]
all day весь день [vyes dyen]

in two days' time через два дня [chyeryes dva dnya]

have a nice day всего хорошего! [fsyevo Harosheva!]

day trip однодневная экскурсия [adnadnyevna-ya ekskoorsee-ya]

dead мёртвый [myortvi]

deaf глухой [glooHoy]

deal (business) сделка [zdyelka]

it's a deal (said by man/woman) согласен/согласна [saglasyen/saglasna]

death смерть f [smyert]

decaffeinated coffee кофе без кофеина [kofyeh byes kafyeh-eena]

December декабрь m [dyekabr]

decide решать/решить [ryeshat/ryeshiyt]

we haven't decided yet мы ещё не решили [miy yesh-cho nyeh ryeshiylee]

decision решение [ryeshenee-yeh]

deck (on ship) палуба [palooba]

deckchair шезлонг [shezlong]

deep глубокий [gloobokee]

definitely: we'll definitely come мы обязательно придём [miy abyazatyelna preedyom]

it's definitely not possible это совершенно невозможно [eta savyershen-na nyevazmoJna]

degree (qualification) диплом [deeplom]

delay (noun) задержка [zadyershka]

delay: the flight was delayed рейс задержался [ryays zadyerJalsa]

deliberately умышленно [oomiyshlen-na]

delicatessen кулинария [kooleenaree-ya]

delicious вкусный [fkoosni]

deliver доставлять/доставить [dastavlyat/dastaveet]

delivery (of mail) доставка [dastafka]

democratic демократический [dyemakrateechyeskee]

Denmark Дания [danee-ya]

dental floss нитка для чистки зубов [neetka dlya cheestkee zoobof]

dentist зубной врач [zoobnoy vrach]

dialogue

> it's this one here вот этот [vot etat]
> this one? этот? [etat?]
> no that one нет, вот этот [nyet, vot etat]
> here здесь [zdyes]
> yes да [da]

dentures зубной протез [zoobnoy prates]

deodorant дезодорант [dyezadarant]

department отдел [ad-dyel]

department store универмаг

[ooneevyermak]

departure (train) отправление [atpravlyenee-yeh]

(plane) вылет [viylyet]

departure lounge зал ожидания [zal aJidanee-ya]

depend: it depends как сказать [kak skazat]

it depends on ... это зависит от ... [eta zaveeseet at ...]

deposit (as security) задаток [zadatak]

(as part payment) взнос [vznos]

dessert десерт [dyesyert]

destination: what's your destination? куда вы едете? [kooda viy yedeetyeh?]

develop проявлять/ проявить [pra-yavlyat/pra-yaveet]

dialogue

could you develop these films? вы можете проявить эти плёнки? [viy moJetyeh pra-yaveet etee plyonkee?]

yes, certainly да, конечно [da, kanyeshna]

when will they be ready? когда они будут готовы? [kagda anee boodoot gatovi?]

tomorrow afternoon завтра днём [zaftra dnyom]

how much is the four-hour

service? сколько стоит проявить за четыре часа? [skolka sto-eet pra-yaveet za chyetiyryeh chasa?]

diabetic (noun) диабетик [dee-abyeteek]

dial (verb) набирать/набрать номер [nabeerat/nabrat nomyer]

dialling code код [kod]

diamond бриллиант [breeleeant]

diaper пелёнка [pyelyonka]

diarrhoea понос [panos]

do you have something for diarrhoea? у вас есть что-нибудь от поноса? [oo vas yest shto-neeboot at panosa?]

diary (for personal experiences) дневник [dnyevneek]

(business) записная книжка [zapeesna-ya kneeshka]

dictionary словарь m [slavar]

didn't*

see not

die умирать/умереть [oomeerat/oomyeryet]

diesel дизельное топливо [deezyelna-yeh topleeva]

diet диета [dee-yeta]

I'm on a diet я на диете [ya na dee-yetyeh]

I have to follow a special diet (said by man/woman) я должен/ должна соблюдать особую диету [ya dolJen/dalJna sablyoodat asoboo-yoo dee-yetoo]

difference разница [razneetsa]

what's the difference? в чём разница? [fchom razneetsa?]

different разный [razni]

they are different они разные [anee razni-yeh]

a different table другой столик [droogoy stoleek]

difficult трудный [troodni]

difficulty трудность f [troodnast]

dining room столовая [stalova-ya]

dinner (evening meal) ужин [ooJin]

to have dinner ужинать/поужинать [ooJinat/paooJinat]

direct (adj) прямой [pryamoy]

is there a direct train? есть ли прямой поезд? [yestlee pryamoy po-yest?]

direction направление [napravlyenee-yeh]

which direction is it? в каком это направлении? [fkakom eta napravlyenee-ee?]

is it in this direction? это в этом направлении? [eta vetam napravlyenee-ee?]

directory enquiries справочная [spravachna-ya]

dirt грязь f [gryas]

dirty грязный [gryazni]

disabled инвалид [eenvaleet]

is there access for the disabled? есть ли доступ для инвалидов? [yestlee dostoop dlya eenvaleedaf?]

disappear исчезать/исчезнуть [eeschyezat/eeschyeznoot]

my watch has disappeared мои часы пропали [ma-ee cha-siy prapalee]

disappointed: I am disappointed (said by man/woman) я разочарован/разочарована [ya razacharovan/razacharovana]

disappointing неважный [nyevaJni]

disaster катастрофа [katastrofa]

disco дискотека [deeskatyeka]

discount скидка [skeetka]

is there a discount? нет ли скидки? [nyetlee skeetkee?]

disease болезнь f [balyezn]

disgusting отвратительный [atvrateetyelni]

dish блюдо [blyooda]

dishcloth кухонное полотенце [kooHan-na-yeh palatyentseh]

disinfectant дезинфицирующее средство [dyezeen-feetsiyroo-yoosh-chyeh-yeh sryetstva]

disk (for computer) диск [deesk]

disposable diapers/nappies одноразовые пелёнки [adnarazavi-yeh pyelyonkee]

distance расстояние [rasta-yanee-yeh]

in the distance на расстоянии [na rasta-yanee-ee]

district район [ri-on]

disturb беспокоить [byespako-eet]

diversion (detour) объезд
[abyest]
divorced: I'm divorced (said by
man/woman) я разведён/
разведена [ya razvyedyon/
razvyedyena]
dizzy: I feel dizzy у меня
кружится голова [oo
myenya krooJitsa galava]
do делать/сделать [dyelat/
sdyelat]
  what shall we do? что нам
  делать? [shto nam dyelat?]
  how do you do it? как это
  делается? [kak eta dyela-
  yetsa?]
  will you do it for me?
  пожалуйста, сделайте это
  для меня [paJalsta, zdyelItyeh
  eta dlya menya]

dialogues

  how do you do?
  здравствуйте!
  [zdrastvooytyeh!]
  nice to meet you
  приятно
  познакомиться [pree-
  yatna paznakomeetsa]
  what do you do? (work)
  кем вы работаете? [kyem
  viy rabota-yetyeh?]
  I'm a teacher, and you?
  (said by man/woman) я
  учитель/учительница,
  а вы? [ya oocheetyel/
  oocheetyelneetsa, aviy?]
  I'm a student (said by man/

woman) я студент/
студентка [ya stoodyent/
stoodyentka]
what are you doing this
evening? что вы делаете
сегодня вечером? [shto
viy dyela-yetyeh syevodnya
vyechyeram?]
we're going out for a drink,
do you want to join us?
мы идём куда-нибудь
выпить, не хотите
пойти с нами? [miy
eedyom kooda-neeboot viypeet,
nyeh Hateetyeh pItee snamee?]

do you want cream? вы
хотите сливки? [viy
Hateetyeh sleefkee?]
I do, but she doesn't я да,
а она нет [ya da, a ana nyet]

doctor врач [vrach]
(title) доктор [doktar]
we need a doctor нам
нужен врач [nam nooJen
vrach]
please call a doctor
вызовите, пожалуйста,
врача [viyzaveetee, paJalsta,
vracha]

dialogue

  where does it hurt? где у
  вас болит? [gdyeh oo vas
  baleet?]
  right here здесь [zdyes]
  does that hurt now? а

теперь больно? [atyep**yer bo**lna?]

yes да [da]

take this to the chemist
получите это в аптеке
[paloo**chee**tyeh **e**ta vapt**ye**kyeh]

document документ
[dakoom**ye**nt]

dog собака [sa**ba**ka]

doll кукла [**koo**kla]

domestic flight внутренний
рейс [v**noo**tryen-nee ryays]

don't!* (to adult/child)
перестаньте/перестань!
[pyeryest**a**ntyeh/pyeryest**a**n!]

don't do that! (to adult/child) не
делайте/делай этого! [nyeh
d**ye**lityeh/d**ye**li **e**tava!]

door дверь f [dvyer]

doorman швейцар
[shv**ya**yts**a**r]

double двойной [dvin**oy**]

double bed двуспальная
кровать [dvoosp**a**lna-ya krav**a**t]

double room двухместный
номер [dvoo**Hmye**sni **no**myer]

doughnut пончик [**po**ncheek]

down вниз [vnees]

put it down over there
положите там [pala**Ji**ytyeh
tam]

it's down there on the right
это там, справа [**e**ta tam,
sp**ra**va]

it's further down the road
это дальше по дороге [**e**ta
d**a**lsheh pa dar**o**gyeh]

downmarket (restaurant etc)

дешёвый [dyesh**o**vi]

downstairs внизу [vneez**oo**]

dozen дюжина [d**yoo**Jina]

half a dozen полдюжины
[pold**yoo**Jini]

draught beer бочковое пиво
[bach**ko**va-yeh p**ee**va]

draughty: it's draughty дует
[d**oo**-yet]

drawer ящик [**ya**sh-cheek]

drawing рисунок [rees**oo**nak]

dreadful ужасный [ooJ**a**sni]

dream сон [son]
(aspiration) мечта [my**ech**ta]

dress (noun) платье [p**la**tyeh]

dressed: to get dressed
одеваться/одеться
[adyev**a**tsa/ad**ye**tsa]

dressing (for cut) перевязка
[pyeryev**ya**ska]
(for salad) приправа
[preep**ra**va]

dressing gown халат [Hal**a**t]

drink (noun) напиток
[nap**ee**tak]
(verb) пить/выпить [peet/
viypeet]

a cold drink
прохладительный
напиток [praHlad**ee**tyelni
nap**ee**tak]

can I get you a drink? не
хотите ли что-нибудь
выпить? [nyeh Hat**ee**tyehlee
sht**o**-neeboot **viy**peet?]

what would you like (to
drink)? что бы вы хотели
(выпить)? [sht**o**bi viy Hat**ye**lee
(**viy**peet)?]

no thanks, I don't drink
спасибо, я не пью
[spaseeba, ya nyeh pyoo]

I'll just have a drink of water
стакан воды, пожалуйста
[stakan vadiy, paJalsta]

drinking water питьевая
вода [peetyeva-ya vada]

is this drinking water?
это питьевая вода? [eta
peetyeva-ya vada?]

drive водить машину
[vadeet mashiynoo]

we drove here мы
приехали сюда на
машине [miy pree-yeHalee
syooda na mashiynyeh]

I'll drive you home я отвезу
вас домой [ya atvezoo vas
damoy]

driver водитель m [vadeetyel]

driving licence водительские
права [vadeetyelskee-yeh prava]

drop: just a drop, please
(of drink) чуть-чуть,
пожалуйста [choot-choot,
paJalsta]

drug (medical) лекарство
[lyekarstva]

drugs (narcotics) наркотики
[narkoteekee]

drunk (adj) пьяный [pyani]

dry (adj) сухой [sooHoy]

dry-cleaner's химчистка
[Heemcheestka]

duck утка [ootka]

due: he was due to arrive
yesterday он должен был
приехать вчера [on doljen

biyl pree-yeнat fchyera]

when is the train due? когда
приходит поезд? [kagda
preeнodeet po-yest?]

dull (pain) тупой [toopoy]
(weather) пасмурный
[pasmoorni]

dummy (baby's) пустышка
[poostiyshka]

during в течение
[ftyechyenee-yeh]

dust пыль [piyl]

dustbin мусорный ящик
[moosarni yash-cheek]

dusty пыльный [piylni]

duty-free беспошлинный
[byesposhleen-ni]

duty-free shop магазин
беспошлинной торговли
[magazeen byesposhleen-ni
targovlee]

duvet одеяло [adye-yala]

E

each (every) каждый [kaJdi]
how much are they each?
сколько стоит каждый?
[skolka sto-eet kaJdi?]

ear ухо [ooнa]

earache: I have earache у
меня болит ухо [oo menya
baleet ooнa]

early рано [rana]
early in the morning рано
утром [rana ootram]

I called by earlier (said by man/
woman) я заходил/

заходила раньше [ya zaнadeel/zaнadeela ransheh]

earrings серьги [syergee]

east восток [vastok]
 in the east на востоке [na vastokyeh]

Easter Пасха [pasнa]

eastern восточный [vastochni]

Eastern Europe Восточная Европа [vastochna-ya yevropa]

easy лёгкий [lyoнkee]

eat есть/поесть [yest/pa-yest]
 we've already eaten, thanks мы уже поели, спасибо [miy ooJeh pa-yelee, spaseeba]

eau de toilette туалетная вода [too-alyetna-ya vada]

economy class экономический класс [ekanameechyeskee klass]

Edinburgh Эдинбург [edeenboork]

egg яйцо [yitso]

eggplant баклажан [baklaJan]

either: either ... or ... или ... или ... [eelee ... eelee ...]
 either of them любой из них [lyooboy eez neeн]

elastic (noun) резинка [ryezeenka]

elastic band резинка [ryezeenka]

elbow локоть **m** [lokat]

electric электрический [elyektreechyeskee]

electrical appliances электрические приборы [elyektreechyeskee-yeh preebori]

electric fire электрокамин [elyektrakameen]

electrician электрик [elyektreek]

electricity электричество [elyektreechyestva]

elevator лифт [leeft]

else: something else что-то другое [shto-ta droogo-yeh]
 somewhere else где-нибудь в другом месте [gdyeh-neeboot vdroogom myestyeh]

dialogue

> would you like anything else? вы хотите ещё что-нибудь? [viy нateetyeh yesh-cho shto-neeboot?]
> no, nothing else, thanks нет, спасибо, больше ничего [nyet, spaseeba, bolsheh neechyevo]

e-mail (noun) электронная почта [elyektronnaya pochta]

embassy посольство [pasolstva]

emergency критическая ситуация [kreeteechyeska-ya seetoo-atsi-ya]
 this is an emergency! требуется неотложная помощь! [tryeboo-yetsa nyeh-atloJna-ya pomash-ch!]

emergency exit запасной выход [zapasnoy viyнat]

empty пустой [poostoy]

end (noun) конец [kanyets]

at the end of the street в
конце улицы [fkantseh
ooleetsi]

when does it end? когда это
заканчивается?
заканчивается? [kagda eta
zakancheeva-yetsa?]

engaged (toilet/telephone)
занято [zanyata]
(to be married: man/woman)
помолвлен/помолвлена
[pamolvlyen/pamolvlyena]

engine (car) двигатель m
[dveegatyel]

England Англия [anglee-ya]

English (adj) английский
[angleeskee]
(language) английский язык
[angleeskee yaziyk]
I'm English (man/woman) я
англичанин/англичанка
[ya angleechaneen/angleechanka]
do you speak English? вы
говорите по-английски?
[vi gavareet-yeh pa-angleeskee?]

enjoy: to enjoy oneself
хорошо проводить/
провести время [Harasho
pravadeet/pravyestee vryemya]

dialogue

how did you like the film?
вам понравился фильм?
[vam panraveelsya feelm?]
I enjoyed it very much, did
you enjoy it? мне очень
понравился, а вам?
[mnyeh ochyen panraveelsa,
a vam?]

enjoyable приятный [pree-
yatni]

enlargement (of photo)
увеличение
[oovyeleechyenee-yeh]

enormous огромный
[agromni]

enough достаточно
[dastatachna]
that's enough достаточно
[dastatachna]
that's not enough этого
недостаточно [etava
nyedastatachna]
it's not big enough это не
достаточно большое [eta
nyeh dastatachna balsho-yeh]

entrance вход [fHot]
(to house) подъезд [padyest]

envelope конверт
[kanvyert]

epileptic эпилептик
[epeelyepteek]

equipment оборудование
[abaroodavanee-yeh]
(for climbing etc) снаряжение
[snaryaJenee-yeh]
(for photography)
фотоаппаратура [fota-ap-
paratoora]

error ошибка [ashiypka]

escalator эскалатор
[eskalatar]

especially особенно [asobyen-
na]

essential основной
[asnavnoy]
it is essential that ...
необходимо, чтобы ...

[nyeh-apHadeema, shtobi ...]

ethnic (restaurant, dress etc)
национальный [natsi-analni]

EU Европейский Союз
[yevrapyayskee sa-yoos]

Europe Европа [yevropa]

European (adj) европейский
[yevrapyayskee]

even даже [daJeh]
even if ... даже если [daJeh
yeslee]

evening вечер [vyechyer]
this evening сегодня
вечером [syevodnya
vyechyeram]
in the evening вечером
[vyechyeram]

evening meal ужин [ooJin]

eventually в конце концов
[fkantseh kantsof]

ever когда-нибудь [kagda-
neeboot]

dialogue

have you ever been to
Novgorod? вы когда-
нибудь были в
Новгороде? [viy kagda-
neeboot biylee vnovgaradyeh?]
yes, I was there two years
ago (said by man/woman) да,
я там был/была два
года назад [da, ya tam biyl/
bila dva goda nazat]

every каждый [kaJdi]
every day каждый день
[kaJdi dyen]

everyone все [fsyeh]

everything всё [fsyo]

everywhere везде [vyezdyeh]

exactly! совершенно верно
[savyershen-na vyerna]

exam экзамен [ekzamyen]

example пример [preemyer]
for example например
[napreemyer]

excellent отличный
[atleechni]
excellent! отлично!
[atleechna!]

except кроме [kromyeh]

excess baggage излишек
багажа [eezleeshek bagaJa]

exchange rate обменный
курс [abmyen-ni koors]

exciting увлекательный
[oovlyekatyelni]

excuse me (to get past, to say
sorry) извините!
[eezveeneetyeh!]
(to get attention) простите!
[prasteetyeh!]
(addressing someone with
question) извините,
пожалуйста ...
[eezveeneetyeh, paJalsta ...]

exhausted: I'm exhausted
(said by man/woman) я очень
устал/устала [ya ochyen
oostal/oostala]

exhaust pipe выхлопная
труба [viHlapna-ya trooba]

exhibition выставка [viystafka]

exit выход [viyHat]
where's the nearest exit? где
ближайший выход? [gdyeh

bleeɈishi **viy**нat?]

expect ожидать [aɈi**dat**]

expensive дорогой [dara**goy**]

experienced опытный
[**o**pitni]

explain объяснять/
объяснить [abyasn**yat**/
abyas**neet**]

can you explain that? вы
можете это объяснить?
[viy **mo**Ɉetyeh **e**ta abyas**neet**?]

express (mail) срочное
письмо [**sro**chna-yeh pees**mo**]
(train, bus) экспресс [eks**pres**]

extension (telephone)
добавочный (номер)
[da**ba**vachni (**no**myer)]

extension 221, please
добавочный двести
двадцать один,
пожалуйста [da**ba**vachni
dvyestee **dva**tsat a**deen**, paɈal**sta**]

extension lead удлинитель
[oodleen**ee**tyel]

extra: can we have an extra
one? можно ещё один?
[**mo**Ɉna yesh-**cho** a**deen**?]

do you charge extra
for that? вы берёте
дополнительную плату
за это? [viy byer**yo**tyeh
dapalneetyelnoo-yoo **pla**too za **e**ta?]

extraordinary удивительный
[oodeev**ee**tyelni]

extremely крайне [**krı**nyeh]

eye глаз [glas]

will you keep an eye on my
suitcase for me?
присмотрите,

пожалуйста, за моим
чемоданом [preesmat**ree**tyeh,
paɈal**sta**, za ma-**eem**
chyema**da**nam]

eyebrow pencil карандаш
для бровей [karan**da**sh dlya
brav**vay**]

eye drops глазные капли
[glaz**niy**-yeh **ka**plee]

eyeglasses очки [ach**kee**]

eyeliner карандаш для глаз
[karan**da**sh dlya glas]

eye shadow тени для век pl
[**tye**nee dlya vyek]

F
━

face лицо [leet**so**]

factory фабрика [**fa**breeka]

faint (verb) падать/упасть
в обморок [**pa**dat/oo**past**
vobmarak]

she's fainted она упала
в обморок [a**na** oo**pa**la
vobmarak]

I feel faint мне дурно [mnyeh
doorna]

fair (funfair) парк
аттракционов [park at-
traktsi-**onaf**]
(trade) выставка [**viy**stafka]
(adj: just) справедливый
[sprav-yedl**ee**vi]

fairly довольно [da**vol**na]

fake подделка [pad-**dye**lka]

fall (verb) падать/упасть
[**pa**dat/oo**past**]

she's had a fall она упала

[ana oopala]

fall (US: autumn) осень f [osyen]

in the fall осенью [osyenyoo]

false ложный [loJni]

family семья [syemya]

famous знаменитый [znamyeneeti]

fan (electrical) вентилятор [vyenteelyatar]

(sport: man/woman) любитель/любительница [lyoobeetyel/lyoobeetyelneetsa]

fantastic замечательный [zamyechatyelni]

far далеко [dalyeko]

dialogue

is it far from here? это далеко отсюда? [eta dalyeko atsyooda?]

no, not very far нет, не очень далеко [nyet, nyeh ochyen dalyeko]

well how far? как далеко? [kak dalyeko?]

it's about 20 kilometres примерно двадцать километров [preemyerna dvatsat keelamyetraf]

fare стоимость f проезда [sto-eemast pra-yezda]

farm ферма [fyerma]

fashionable модный [modni]

fast быстрый [biystri]

fat (person) толстый [tolsti]

(on meat) жир [Jir]

father отец [atyets]

father-in-law (wife's father) тесть [tyest]

(husband's father) свёкор [svyokar]

faucet кран [kran]

fault (mechanical) неисправность f [nyeh-eespravnast]

sorry, it was my fault извините, это моя вина [eezveeneetyeh, eta ma-ya veena]

it's not my fault это не моя вина [eta nyeh ma-ya veena]

faulty: this is faulty это не работает [eta nyeh rabota-yet]

favourite любимый [lyoobeemi]

fax (noun) факс [faks]

(verb) посылать/послать по факсу [pasilat/paslat pa faksoo]

I want to send a fax Я хочу послать факс [ya Hachoo paslat faks]

fax (machine) факс [faks]

February февраль m [fyevral]

feel чувствовать/почувствовать [choostvavat/pachoostvavat]

I feel hot мне жарко [mnyeh Jarka]

I feel unwell мне нехорошо [mnyeh nyeh-Harasho]

I feel like going for a walk мне хочется прогуляться [mnyeh Hochyetsa pragoolyatsa]

how are you feeling? как вы себя чувствуете? [kak viy syebya choostvoo-yetyeh?]

I'm feeling better мне
лучше [mnyeh **loo**chsheh]

felt-tip (pen) фломастер
[fla**ma**styer]

fence забор [za**bo**r]

fender (of car) бампер
[**bam**pyer]

ferry паром [pa**ro**m]

festival фестиваль m
[fyes**tee**val]

fetch: I'll fetch him я схожу
за ним [ya sнa**joo** za neem]

will you come and fetch me
later? вы зайдёте за мной
попозже? [viy zíd**yo**tyeh za
mnoy papo**J**-Jeh?]

feverish: I'm feverish меня
лихорадит [myen**ya**
leeнa**ra**deet]

few: a few несколько
[**nye**skalka]

a few days несколько дней
[**nye**skalka dnyay]

fiancé жених [Jeneeн]

fiancée невеста [nyev**ye**sta]

field поле [**po**lyeh]

fight (noun) драка [**dra**ka]

figs инжир [eenJ**iy**r]

fill in заполнять/заполнить
[zapaln**ya**t/za**po**lneet]

do I have to fill this in? мне
нужно это заполнить?
[mnyeh **noo**Jna eta za**po**lneet?]

fill up наполнять/
наполнить [napaln**ya**t/
na**po**lneet]

fill it up, please полный
бак, пожалуйста [**po**lni bak,
pa**Ja**lsta]

filling (in cake, sandwich)
начинка [na**chee**nka]
(in tooth) пломба [**plo**mba]

film (movie) фильм [feelm]
(for camera) плёнка [pl**yo**nka]

dialogue

do you have this kind of
film? у вас есть такая
плёнка? [oo vas yest taka-ya
pl**yo**nka?]
yes, how many exposures?
да, на сколько кадров?
[da, na sk**o**lka k**a**draf?]
36 тридцать шесть
[**tree**tsat shest]

film processing проявление
плёнки [pra-yavl**ye**nee-yeh
pl**yo**nkee]

filthy грязный [**grya**zni]

find (verb) находить/найти
[naнa**dee**t/n**ítee**]

I can't find it я не могу это
найти [ya nyeh mag**oo** eta n**ítee**]

I've found it (said by man/
woman) я нашёл/нашла это
[ya nash**o**l/nash**la e**ta]

find out узнавать/узнать
[oozna**va**t/ooz**na**t]

could you find out for me?
вы не могли бы узнать
для меня [viy nyeh mag**lee**bi
ooz**na**t dlya myen**ya**?]

fine (weather) хороший
[на**ro**shi]
(punishment) штраф [shtraf]

dialogues

finger палец [palyets]
finish (verb) заканчивать/закончить [zakancheevat/zakoncheet]
I haven't finished yet (said by man/woman) я ещё не закончил/закончила [ya yesh-cho nyeh zakoncheel/zakoncheela]
when does it finish? когда это заканчивается? [kagda eta zakancheeva-yetsa?]
Finland Финляндия [feenlyandee-ya]
fire (in hearth) огонь **m** [agon]
(campfire) костёр [kastyor]
(blaze) пожар [paJar]
fire! пожар! [paJar!]
can we light a fire here? здесь можно разложить костёр? [zdyes moJna razlaJiyt kastyor?]
my room is on fire! в моём номере пожар! [vma-yom nomyeryeh paJar!]
fire alarm пожарная тревога [paJarna-ya tryevoga]

fire brigade пожарная команда [paJarna-ya kamanda]
fire escape пожарная лестница [paJarna-ya lyesneetsa]
fire extinguisher огнетушитель **m** [agnyetooshiytyel]
first первый [pyervi]
I was first (said by man) я был первым [ya biyl pyervim] (said by woman) я была первой [ya biyla pyervi]
at first сначала [snachala]
the first time первый раз [pyervi ras]
first turn on the left первый поворот налево [pyervi pavarot nalyeva]
first aid первая помощь **f** [pyerva-ya pomash-ch]
first-aid kit походная аптечка [paHodna-ya aptyechka]
first class (travel etc) первым классом [pyervim klasam]
first floor второй этаж [ftaroy etash]
(US) первый этаж [pyervi etash]
first name имя [eemya]
fish (noun) рыба [riyba]
fit (attack) приступ [preestoop]
fit: it doesn't fit me это мне не по размеру [eta mnyeh nyeh pa razmyeroo]
fitting room примерочная [pryemyerachna-ya]
fix (verb: arrange) чинить/

починить [cheeneet/pacheeneet]

can you fix this? (repair) вы можете это починить? [viy moJetyeh eta pacheeneet?]

fizzy газированный [gazeerovan-ni]

flag флаг [flag]

flash (for camera) вспышка [fspiyshka]

flat (noun: apartment) квартира [kvarteera]
(adj) плоский [ploskee]

I've got a flat tyre у меня спустила шина [oo menya spoosteela shiyna]

flavour вкус [fkoos]

flea блоха [blaнa]

flight рейс [ryays]

flight number номер рейса [nomyer ryaysa]

flood наводнение [navadnyenee-yeh]

floor (of room) пол [pol]
(storey) этаж [etash]

on the floor на полу [na paloo]

florist цветочный магазин [tsvyetochni magazeen]

flour мука [mooka]

flower цветок [tsvyetok]

flu грипп [greep]

fluent: he speaks fluent Russian он бегло говорит по-русски [on byegla gavareet pa-rooskee]

fly (noun) муха [mooнa]
(verb) лететь/полететь [lyetyet/palyetyet]

can we fly there? туда можно полететь? [tooda moJna palyetyet?]

fog туман [tooman]

foggy туманный [tooman-ni]

folk dancing народные танцы pl [narodni-yeh tantsi]

folk music народная музыка [narodna-ya moozika]

follow следовать/последовать [slyedavat/paslyedavat]

follow me следуйте за мной [slyedooyteh za mnoy]

food еда [yeda]

food poisoning пищевое отравление [peesh-chyevo-yeh atravlyenee-yeh]

food shop/store гастроном [gastranom]

foot (of person) ступня [stoopnya]

on foot пешком [pyeshkom]

football (game) футбол [footbol]
(ball) футбольный мяч [footbolni myach]

football match футбольный матч [footbolni match]

for: do you have something for a headache/diarrhoea? у вас есть что-то от головной боли/поноса? [oo vas yest shto-ta at galavnoy bolee/panosa?]

dialogues

who's the chicken Kiev for? для кого котлеты

по-Киевски? [dlya kavo
katl**ye**ti pa-**kee**-yefskee?]
that's for me это для
меня [**e**ta dlya men**ya**]
and this one? a это? [a
eta?]
that's for her это для неё
[**e**ta dlya nyeh-**yo**]

where do I get the bus
for Belorussky station?
откуда идёт автобус до
Белорусского вокзала?
[atk**oo**da eed**yo**t aft**o**boos da
byelar**oo**skava vakz**a**la?]
the bus for the railway
station leaves from
Tverskaya street автобус
до вокзала идёт с
Тверской улицы [aft**o**boos
da vakz**a**la eed**yo**t stvyersk**oy**
ooleetsi]

how long have you
been here? вы давно
приехали? [viy davn**o** pree-
yeHalee?]
I've been here for two
days, how about you? я
здесь уже два дня, а
вы? [ya zdyes oo**Jeh** dva dnya,
a viy?]
I've been here for a week
я здесь уже неделю [ya
zdyes oo**Jeh** nyed**ye**lyoo]

forehead лоб [lop]
foreign иностранный
[eenastr**a**n-ni]

foreigner (man/woman)
иностранец/иностранка
[eenastr**a**nyets/eenastr**a**nka]
forest лес [lyes]
forget забывать/забыть
[zabiv**a**t/zab**iy**t]
I forget, I've forgotten (said by
man/woman) я забыл/забыла
[ya zab**iy**l/zab**iy**la]
fork (for eating) вилка [**vee**lka]
form (document) бланк [blank]
formal (dress) вечерний
[vyech**ye**rnee]
fortnight две недели [dvyeh
nyed**ye**lee]
fortunately к счастью [ksh-
ch**a**styoo]
forward: could you forward
my mail? вы не могли бы
переслать мне мою почту
[viy nyeh magl**ee**bi pyeresl**a**t
mnyeh ma-**yoo** p**o**chtoo]
forwarding address адрес
для пересылки [**a**dryes dlya
pyeryes**iy**lkee]
foundation (make-up)
тональный крем [tan**a**lni
kryem]
fountain фонтан [fant**a**n]
foyer (hotel, theatre) фойе [fay-
yeh]
fracture перелом [pyerel**o**m]
France Франция [fr**a**ntsi-ya]
free (no charge) бесплатный
[byespl**a**tni]
is it free (of charge)? это
бесплатно? [**e**ta byespl**a**tna?]
freeway автострада
[aftastr**a**da]

English → Russian

Fr

freezer морозилка [mar**a**zeelka]
French (adj, language) французский [frants**oo**skee]
French fries картофель фри [kart**o**fyel free]
frequent частый [ch**a**sti]
how frequent is the bus to Suzdal? как часто ходят автобусы в Суздаль? [kak ch**a**sta н**o**dyat aft**o**boosi fs**oo**zdal?]
fresh (weather, breeze) прохладный [pra**н**ladni] (fruit etc) свежий [sv**ye**ji]
fresh orange juice свежий апельсиновый сок [sv**ye**ji apyels**ee**navi sok]
Friday пятница [p**ya**tneetsa]
fridge холодильник [**н**alad**ee**lneek]
fried жареный [**J**aryeni]
fried egg яичница [ya-**ee**shneetsa]
friend (male/female) друг/ подруга [drook/padr**oo**ga]
friendly дружеский [dr**oo**Jeskee]
from: when does the next train from Yaroslavl arrive? когда приходит следующий поезд из Ярославля? [kagd**a** pree**н**odeet sl**ye**doosh-chee p**o**-yest eez yarasl**a**vlya?]
from Monday to Friday с понедельника до пятницы [spanyed**ye**lneeka da p**ya**tneetsi]
from Moscow to Tver от

Москвы до Твери [at maskv**i**y da tv**ye**ree]

dialogue

where are you from? вы откуда? [viy atk**oo**da?]
I'm from England я из англии [ya eez **a**nglee-ee]

front передняя часть [pyer**ye**dnya-ya chast]
in front впереди [fpyeryed**ee**]
in front of the hotel перед гостиницей [p**ye**ryed gast**ee**neetsay]
at the front спереди [sp**ye**ryedee]
frost мороз [mar**o**s]
frozen замёрзший [zam**yo**rshi]
frozen food замороженные продукты [zamar**o**Jeni-yeh prad**oo**kti]
fruit фрукты [fr**oo**kti]
fruit juice фруктовый сок [fr**oo**ktovi sok]
frying pan сковородка [skavar**o**tka]
FSS ФСБ (Федеральная Служба Безопасности) [ef-es-b**eh** (fyedyer**a**lna-ya sl**oo**Jba byezap**a**snastee)]
full полный [p**o**lni]
this fish is full of bones в этой рыбе одни кости [v**e**ti r**i**ybyeh adn**ee** k**o**stee]
I'm full (said by man/woman) я наелся/наелась [ya na-**ye**lsya/ na-**ye**las]

68

full board полный пансион [**po**lni pansee-**o**n]

fun: it was fun было весело [**bi**yla v**ye**syela]

funeral похороны pl [**po**Harani]

funny (strange) странный [**stran**-ni]

(amusing) забавный [zab**a**vni]

fur мех [myeн]

fur hat меховая шапка [myeн**a**va-ya sh**a**pka]

furniture мебель **f** [m**ye**byel]

further дальше [**da**lsheh]

it's further down the road это дальше по улице [**e**ta d**a**lsheh pa **oo**leetseh]

dialogue

how much further is it to Klin? далеко ли ещё до Клина? [dalyek**o**lee yesh-ch**o** da kl**ee**na?]

about 5 kilometres около пяти километров [**o**kala pyat**ee** keelam**ye**traf]

fuse предохранитель **m** [pryedaнran**ee**tyel]

the lights have fused свет перегорел [svyet pyeryegar**yel**]

fuse wire проволока для предохранителя [**pro**valaka dlya pryedaнran**ee**tyelya]

future будущее [b**oo**doosh-chyeh-yeh]

in future в будущем [vb**oo**doosh-chyem]

G

game (cards etc) игра [**ee**gra]

(match) матч [match]

(meat) дичь **f** [deech]

garage (for fuel) бензоколонка [byenzakal**o**nka]

(for repairs) станция техобслуживания [**stan**tsi-ya tyeнaps**loo**Jivanee-ya]

(for parking) гараж [gar**ash**]

garden сад [sat]

garlic чеснок [chyesn**o**k]

gas газ [gas]

(US: petrol) бензин [byenz**een**]

gas cylinder (camping gas) газовый баллон [**ga**zavi bal**on**]

gas-permeable lenses газопроницаемые линзы [gazapraneets**a**-yemi-yeh l**ee**enzi]

gas station бензоколонка [byenzakal**o**nka]

gate ворота [var**o**ta]

(at airport) выход [**viy**нat]

gay гомосексуалист [gomaseksoo-al**ee**st]

gay bar бар для гомосексуалистов [bar dlya gomaseksoo-al**ee**staf]

gear передача [pyeryed**a**cha]

gearbox коробка передач [kar**o**pka pyeryed**ach**]

general (adj) общий [**o**psh-chee]

general delivery до востребования

[da vastr**ye**bavanee-ya]

gents' toilet мужской
туалет [mooshsk**oy** too-al**yet**]

genuine (antique etc)
подлинный [p**o**dleen-ni]

German (adj) немецкий
[nyem**ye**tskee]

Germany Германия
[gyerm**a**nee-ya]

get (fetch) приносить/
принести [preenas**ee**t/
preenyest**ee**]

could you get me another
one, please? принесите,
пожалуйста, ещё один
[preenyes**ee**tyeh, pa**J**alsta, yesh-ch**o**
ad**een**]

how do I get to ...? как
попасть в ...? [kak pap**a**st
v ...?]

do you know where I can get
them? вы не знаете, где я
могу их достать [viy nyeh
zna-yetyeh, gdyeh ya mag**oo** ee**н**
dast**a**t?]

dialogue

can I get you a drink?? что
вы будете пить? [shto viy
b**oo**dyetyeh peet?]

no, I'll get this one, what
would you like? нет,
позвольте мне, что бы
вы хотели? [nyet, pazv**o**ltyeh
mnyeh, shto biy viy наt**ye**lee?]

a glass of red wine бокал
красного вина [bak**a**l
kr**a**snava veen**a**]

get back (return)
возвращаться/вернуться
[vazvrash-ch**a**tsa/vyern**oo**tsa]

get in (arrive) приезжать/
приехать [pree-ye**J**-**J**at/pree-
yeнаt]

get off выходить/выйти
[vih**a**deet/**viy**tee]

where do I get off? где мне
выходить? [gdyeh mnyeh
vih**a**deet?]

get on (to train etc) садиться/
сесть [sad**ee**tsa/syest]

get out (of car etc) выходить/
выйти [vih**a**deet/**viy**tee]

get up (in the morning)
вставать/встать [fstav**a**t/
fstat]

gift подарок [pad**a**rak]

gift shop магазин
сувениров [magaz**ee**n
soovyen**ee**raf]

gin джин [djin]

a gin and tonic, please джин
с тоником, пожалуйста
[djin st**o**neekam, pa**J**alsta]

girl (child) девочка [d**ye**vachka]
(young woman) девушка
[d**ye**vooshka]

girlfriend подруга [padr**oo**ga]

give давать/дать [dav**a**t/dat]

can you give me
some change? вы не
разменяете? [viy nyeh
razmyen**ya**-yetyeh?]

I gave it to him (said by man/
woman) я отдал/отдала ему
это [ya ad-d**a**l/ad-dal**a** yem**oo** eta]

will you give this to ...?

передайте это, пожалуйста, ... [pyeryedItyeh eta, paJalsta, ...]

dialogue

how much do you want for this? сколько вы хотите за это? [skolka viy Hateetyeh za eta?]
40,000 roubles сорок тысяч рублей [sorak tiysyach rooblyay]
I'll give you 30,000 я дам вам тридцать тысяч [ya dam vam treetsat tiysyach]

give back возвращать/ вернуть [vazvrash-chat/ vernoot]
glad: I'm glad (said by man/ woman) я рад/рада [ya rat/ rada]
glass (material) стекло [styeklo]
(for drinking) стакан [stakan]
a glass of wine бокал вина [bakal veena]
glasses очки [achkee]
gloves перчатки [pyerchatkee]
glue (noun) клей [klyay]
go (on foot) идти/пойти [eet-tee/pitee]
(by transport) ехать/поехать [yeHat/pa-yeHat]
we'd like to go to the Kremlin мы хотели бы сходить в Кремль [miy Hatyeleebi sHadeet fkryeml]
where are you going?

куда вы идёте? [kooda viy eedyotyeh?]
where does this bus go? куда идёт этот автобус? [kooda eedyot etat aftoboos?]
let's go! пойдемте! [pIdyomtyeh!]
she's gone (left) она ушла [ana ooshla]
where has he gone? куда он ушёл? [kooda on ooshol?]
I went there last week (said by man/woman) я там был/была на прошлой неделе [ya tam biyl/bila na proshli nyedyelyeh]
hamburger to go гамбургер на вынос [gamboorgyer na viynas]
go away уходить/уйти [ooHadeet/ooytee]
go away! уходите! [ooHadeetyeh!]
go back (return) возвращаться/вернуться [vazvrash-chatsa/vyernootsa]
go down (the stairs etc) спускаться/спуститься [spooskatsa/spoosteetsa]
go in входить/войти [fHadeet/vItee]
go out: do you want to go out tonight? вы не хотите куда-нибудь пойти сегодня вечером? [viy nyeh Hateetyeh kooda-neebood pitee syevodnya vyechyeram?]
go through проходить/ пройти [praHadeet/pritee]
go up (the stairs etc)

подниматься/подняться
[padneematsa/padnyatsa]

goat коза [kaza]

God бог [boh]

goggles защитные очки
[zash-cheetni-yeh achkee]

gold золото [zolata]

good хороший [Haroshi]
good! хорошо! [Harasho!]
it's no good это не годится
[eta nyeh gadeetsa]

goodbye до свидания [da
sveedanya]

good evening добрый вечер
[dobri vyechyer]

Good Friday Страстная
Пятница [strasna-ya
pyatneetsa]

good morning доброе утро
[dobra-yeh ootra]

good night (leaving) до
свидания [da sveedanya]
(when going to bed) спокойной
ночи [spakoyni nochee]

goose гусь **m** [goos]

got: we've got to leave нам
нужно идти [nam nooJna
eet-tee]
have you got any ...? у вас
есть ... [oo vas yest ...]

government правительство
[praveetyelstva]

gradually постепенно
[pastyepyen-na]

gram(me) грамм [gram]

grammar грамматика [gram-
mateeka]

granddaughter внучка
[vnoochka]

grandfather дедушка
[dyedooshka]

grandmother бабушка
[babooshka]

grandson внук [vnook]

grapefruit грейпфрут
[gryaypfroot]

grapefruit juice
грейпфрутовый сок
[gryaypfrootavi sok]

grapes виноград [veenagrat]

grass трава [trava]

grateful благодарный
[blagadarni]

gravy соус [so-oos]

great (excellent)
замечательный
[zamyechatyelni]
that's great! здорово!
[zdorava!]
a great success большой
успех [balshoy oospyeH]

Great Britain
Великобритания
[vyeleekabreetanee-ya]

Greece Греция [gryetsi-ya]

greedy жадный [Jadni]

green зелёный [zyelyoni]

greengrocer's овощной
магазин [avash-chnoy
magazeen]

grey серый [syeri]

grilled жареный на
рашпере [Jaryeni na
rashpyeryeh]

grocer's бакалейный
магазин [bakalyayni magazeen]

ground: on the ground на
земле [na zyemlyeh]

ground floor первый этаж [p**ye**rvi et**a**sh]

group группа [gr**oo**p-pa]

guarantee (noun) гарантия [garant**ee**-ya]

guest (man/woman) гость/гостья [gost/g**o**stya]

guesthouse дом для приезжих [dom dlya pree**ye**J-JiH]

guide (noun: man/woman) гид [geet]

guidebook путеводитель **m** [pooteevad**ee**tyel]

guided tour экскурсия с гидом [eksk**oo**rsee-ya zg**ee**dam]

guitar гитара [geet**a**ra]

gum (in mouth) десна [dyesn**a**]

gun (pistol) пистолет [peestal**yet**]
(rifle) ружье [rooj**yo**]

gym спортзал [sportz**a**l]

gymnastics гимнастика [geemn**a**steeka]

H

hair волосы pl [v**o**lasi]

hairbrush щётка для волос [sh-ch**o**tka dlya val**o**s]

haircut стрижка [str**ee**shka]

hairdresser's парикмахерская [pareeHm**a**Hyerska-ya]

hairdryer фен [fyen]

hair gel гель для волос **m** [gyel dlya val**o**s]

hair grips шпильки

[shp**ee**lkee]

hairspray лак для волос [lak dlya val**o**s]

half* половина [palav**ee**na]

half an hour полчаса [p**o**lchas**a**]

half a litre пол-литра [p**o**l-l**ee**tra]

about half that примерно половина от этого [preem**ye**rna palav**ee**na at **e**tava]

half board полупансион [p**o**loo-pansee-**o**n]

half-bottle полбутылки [polboot**i**ylkee]

half fare половинный тариф [palav**ee**n-ni tar**ee**f]

half-price полцены [pol-tsen**i**y]

ham ветчина [vyetcheen**a**]

hamburger гамбургер [g**a**mboorger]

hand рука [rook**a**]

handbag сумочка [s**oo**machka]

handbrake ручной тормоз [roochn**oy** t**o**rmas]

handkerchief носовой платок [nasav**oy** plat**o**k]

handle (on door, suitcase etc) ручка [r**oo**chka]

hand luggage ручная кладь **f** [roochn**a**-ya klat]

hangover похмелье [paHm**ye**lyeh]

I've got a hangover я с похмелья [ya sraHm**ye**lya]

happen случаться/случиться [sloochatsa/sloocheetsa]

what's happening? что нового? [shto novava?]

what has happened? что случилось? [shto sloocheelas?]

happy счастливый [sh-chastleevi]

I'm not happy about this мне это не нравится [mnyeh eta nyeh nraveetsa]

harbour порт [port]

hard твёрдый [tvyordi] (difficult) трудный [troodni]

hard-boiled egg яйцо вкрутую [yıtso fkrootoo-yoo]

hard currency валюта [valyoota]

hard lenses жёсткие линзы [Joskee-yeh leensi]

hardly едва [yedva]

hardly ever очень редко [ochyen ryetka]

hardware shop хозяйственный магазин [Hazyıstvyen-ni magazeen]

hat шляпа [shlyapa] (with flaps) шапка [shapka]

hate (verb) ненавидеть [nyenaveedyet]

have* иметь [eemyet]

can I have ...? можно, пожалуйста ...? [moJna, paJalsta ...?]

do you have ...? у вас есть ...? [oo vas yest ...?]

what'll you have? что бы вы хотели? [shto biy viy Hatyelee?]

I have to leave now мне нужно идти [mnyeh nooJna eet-tee]

do I have to ...? нужно ли мне ...? [nooJnalee mnyeh ...?]

can we have some ...? можно, пожалуйста ...? [moJna, paJalsta ...?]

hayfever сенная лихорадка [syen-naya leeHaratka]

hazelnuts фундук [foondook]

he* он [on]

head голова [galava]

headache головная боль f [galavna-ya bol]

headlights фары [fari]

healthy здоровый [zdarovi]

hear слышать/услышать [sliyshat/oosliyshat]

dialogue

can you hear me? вы меня слышите? [viy myenya sliyshityeh?]
I can't hear you, could you repeat that? я вас не слышу, повторите, пожалуйста [ya vas nyeh sliyshoo, paftareetyeh, paJalsta]

hearing aid слуховой аппарат [slooHavoy aparat]

heart сердце [syertseh]

heart attack сердечный приступ [syerdyechni preestoop]

heartburn изжога [eezJoga]

heat жара [Jara]

heater (in room, car) обогреватель [abagryevatyel]

heating отопление

[ataplyenee-yeh]

heavy тяжёлый [tyeжoli]

heel (of foot) пятка [pyatka]
  (of shoe) каблук [kablook]
  please could you heel these?
  вы можете поставьте
  сюда набойки? [viy moжetyeh
  pastaveet syooda naboykee?]

heelbar мастерская по
  ремонту обуви [mastyerska-
  ya pa ryemontoo oboovee]

height (of person) рост [rost]
  (of mountain, building etc)
  высота [visata]

helicopter вертолёт
  [vyertalyot]

hello здравствуйте
  [zdrastvooytyeh]
  (answer on phone) алло [allo]

helmet (for motorcycle) шлем
  [shlyem]

help (noun) помощь f [pomash-
  ch]
  (verb) помогать/помочь
  [pamagat/pamoch]
  help! помогите!
  [pamageetyeh!]
  can you help me? вы
  можете мне помочь? [viy
  moжetyeh mnyeh pamoch?]
  thank you very much for your
  help большое спасибо за
  помощь [balsho-yeh spaseeba
  za pomash-ch]

helpful полезный [palyezni]

hepatitis гепатит [gyepateet]

her*: I haven't seen her (said by
  man/woman) я её не видел/
  видела [ya yeh-yo nyeh veedyel/

veedyela]
  to her ей [yay]
  with her с ней [snyay]
  for her для неё [dlya nyeh-yo]
  that's her это она [eta ana]
  that's her towel это её
  полотенце [eta yeh-yo
  palatyentseh]

herbal tea травяной чай
  [travyanoy chI]

herbs кухонные травы
  [kooHan-ni-yeh travi]

here здесь [zdyes]
  here is/are ... вот ... [vot...]
  here you are вот,
  пожалуйста [vot, paжalsta]

hers* её [yeh-yo]
  that's hers это её [eta yeh-yo]

hey! эй! [ay!]

hi! (hello) привет! [preevyet!]

hide (verb) прятаться/
  спрятаться [pryatatsa/
  spryatatsa]

high высокий [visokee]

highchair высокий детский
  стул [visokee dyetskee stool]

highway (US) автострада
  [aftastrada]

hill холм [Holm]

him*: I haven't seen him
  (said by man/woman) я его не
  видел/видела [ya yevo nyeh
  veedyel/veedyela]
  to him ему [yemoo]
  with him с ним [sneem]
  for him для него [dlya nyevo]
  that's him это он [eta on]

hip бедро [byedro]

hire брать/взять напрокат

[brat/vzyat naprakat]
for hire напрокат [naprakat]
where can I hire a bike? где
я могу взять напрокат
велосипед? [gdyeh ya magoo
vzyat naprakat vyelaseepyet?]
his*: it's his car это его
машина [eta yevo mashiyna]
that's his это его [eta yevo]
hit (verb) ударять/ударить
[oodaryat/oodareet]
hitch-hike путешествовать
автостопом [pootyeshestvavat
aftastopam]
hobby хобби n [Hob-bee]
hockey хоккей m [Hakyay]
hold (verb) держать/
подержать [dyerJat/padyerJat]
hole дыра [dira]
holiday праздник [prazneek]
on holiday в отпуске
[votpooskyeh]
Holland Голландия [galandee-
ya]
home дом [dom]
at home (in my house etc) дома
[doma]
(in my country) на родине [na
rodeenyeh]
we go home tomorrow мы
едем домой завтра [miy
yedyem damoy zaftra]
honest честный [chyesni]
honey мёд [myot]
honeymoon медовый месяц
[myedovi myesyats]
hood (US: of car) капот [kapot]
hope (verb) надеяться
[nadyeh-yatsa]

I hope so надеюсь, что да
[nadyeh-yoos, shto da]
I hope not надеюсь, что
нет [nadyeh-yoos, shto nyet]
hopefully надо надеяться
[nada nadyeh-yatsa]
horn (of car) гудок [goodok]
horrible ужасный [ooJasni]
horse лошадь f [loshat]
horse riding верховая езда
[vyerHava-ya yezda]
hospital больница
[balneetsa]
hospitality гостеприимство
[gastyepree-eemstva]
thank you for your hospitality
спасибо за ваше
гостеприимство [spaseeba
za vasheh gastyepree-eemstva]
hot (water, food) горячий
[garyachee]
(weather) жаркий [Jarkee]
(spicy) острый [ostri]
I'm hot мне жарко [mnyeh
Jarka]
it's hot today сегодня
жарко [syevodnya Jarka]
hotel гостиница
[gasteeneetsa]
hotel room номер [nomyer]
hour час [chas]
house дом [dom]
hovercraft судно на
воздушной подушке
[soodna na vazdooshni
padooshkyeh]
how как [kak]
how many? сколько?
[skolka?]

76

how do you do?
здравствуйте [zdrastvooytyeh]

dialogues

how are you? как дела?
[kak dyela?]
fine, thanks, and you?
хорошо, спасибо, а у
вас? [Harasho, spaseeba, a
oo vas?]

how much is it? сколько
это стоит? [skolka eta
sto-eet?]
10,500 roubles десять
тысяч пятьсот рублей
[dyesyat tiysyach pyatsot
rooblyay]
I'll take it я возьму это
[ya vazmoo eta]

humid влажный [vlaJni]
Hungary Венгрия [vyengree-ya]
hungry голодный [galodni]
are you hungry? вы
голодны? [viy goladni?]
hurry (verb) спешить
[spyeshiyt]
I'm in a hurry я спешу [ya
spyeshoo]
there's no hurry это не к
спеху [eta nyeh kspyeHoo]
hurry up! быстрее! [bistryeh-yeh]
hurt (verb) причинять/
причинить боль
[preecheenyat/preecheeneet bol]

it hurts больно [bolna]
it really hurts очень больно
[ochyen bolna]
husband муж [moosh]
hydrofoil судно на
подводных крыльях
[soodna na padvodniH kriylyaH]

I

I* я [ya]
ice лёд [lyot]
with ice со льдом [saldom]
no ice, thanks безо льда,
пожалуйста [byezalda,
paJalsta]
ice cream мороженое
[maroJena-yeh]
ice-cream cone рожок [raJok]
ice lolly эскимо [eskeemo]
ice rink каток [katok]
ice skates коньки [kankee]
ice skating катание на
коньках [katanee-yeh na
kankaH]
icon икона [eekona]
icy ледяной [lyedyanoy]
idea идея [eedyeh-ya]
idiot идиот [eedee-ot]
if если [yeslee]
ignition зажигание [zaJiganee-yeh]
ill: he/she is ill он болен/она
больна [on bolyen/ona balna]
I feel ill мне плохо [mnyeh
ploHa]
illness болезнь f [balyezn]
imitation (leather)

искусственный
[eeskoostvyen-ni]

(jewellery) подделка [pad-dyelka]

immediately немедленно
[nyemyedlyen-na]

important важный [vaɹni]

it's very important это очень
важно [eta ochyen vaɹna]

it's not important это не
важно [eta nyeh vaɹna]

impossible: it's impossible
это невозможно [eta
nyevazmoɹna]

impressive впечатляющий
[fpyechatlya-yoosh-chee]

improve улучшать/
улучшить [ooloochshat/
ooloochshit]

in: it's in the centre это в
центре [eta ftsentryeh]

in my car в моей машине
[vma-yay mashiynyeh]

in Moscow в Москве
[vmaskvyeh]

in two days from now через
два дня [chyeryez dva dnya]

in five minutes через пять
минут [chyeryes pyat meenoot]

in May в мае [vma-yeh]

in English по-английски
[pa-angleeskee]

in Russian по-русски [pa-rooskee]

include включать/
включить [fklyoochat/
fklyoocheet]

does that include meals? в
это входит стоимость

питания? [veta fнodeet sto-eemast peetanee-ya?]

is that included? это
включено в стоимость?
[eta fklyoochyeno fsto-eemast?]

inconvenient неудобный
[nyeh-oodobni]

incredible поразительный
[parazeetyelni]

Indian (adj) индийский
[eendeeskee]

indicator указатель m
[ookazatyel]

indigestion несварение
[nyesvaryenee-yeh]

indoor pool закрытый
бассейн [zakriyti bassyayn]

indoors в помещении
[fpamyesh-chyenee-ee]

inexpensive дешёвый
[dyeshovi]

infection инфекция
[eenfyektsi-ya]

infectious инфекционный
[eenfyektsi-on-ni]

inflammation воспаление
[vaspalyenee-yeh]

informal неофициальный
[nyeh-afeetsi-alni]

information информация
[eenfarmatsi-ya]

do you have any information
about ...? у вас есть какая-
то информация о ...? [oo
vas yest kaka-ya-ta eenfarmatsi-ya
a...?]

information desk
справочный стол
[spravachni stol]

injection инъекция [eenyektsiya]

injured раненый [ranyeni]
  she's been injured она
  ранена [ana ranyena]

innocent: I'm innocent (said by
  man/woman) я не виновен/
  виновна [ya nyeh veenovyen/
  veenovna]

insect насекомое
  [nasyekoma-yeh]

insect bite укус насекомого
  [ookoos nasyekomava]
  do you have anything
  for insect bites? у вас
  есть что-то от укусов
  насекомых? [oo vas yest shto-
  ta at ookoosaf nasyekomiн?]

insect repellent средство
  от насекомых [sryetstva at
  nasyekomiн]

inside внутри [vnootree]
  inside the hotel в
  гостинице [vgasteeneetseh]
  let's sit inside давайте
  сядем внутри [daviteh
  syadyem vnootree]

insist настаивать [nasta-eevat]
  I insist я настаиваю [ya
  nasta-eeva-yoo]

instant coffee растворимый
  кофе m [rastvareemi kofyeh]

instead вместо [vmyesta]
  give me that one instead
  дайте мне это взамен
  [diteh mnyeh eta vzamyen]
  instead of ... вместо ...
  [vmyesta ...]

insurance страховка
  [straнofka]

intelligent умный [oomni]

interested: I'm interested in ...
  меня интересует ... [myenya
  eentyeryesoo-yet ...]

interesting интересный
  [eentyeryesni]
  that's very interesting это
  очень интересно [eta ochyen
  eentyeryesna]

international
  международный
  [myeждoonarodni]

Internet Интернет [eenternet]

interpreter (man/woman)
  переводчик/переводчица
  [pyeryevotcheek/
  pyeryevotcheetsa]

intersection перекрёсток
  [pyeryekryostak]

interval (at theatre) антракт
  [antrakt]

into в [v]
  I'm not into ... я не
  увлекаюсь ... [ya nyeh
  oovlyeka-yoos ...]

Intourist Интурист
  [eentooreest]

introduce знакомить/
  познакомить [znakomeet/
  paznakomeet]
  may I introduce ...?
  разрешите представить ...
  [razryeshiytyeh pryetstaveet...]

invitation приглашение
  [preeglashenee-yeh]

invite приглашать/
  пригласить [preeglashat/
  preeglaseet]

Ireland Ирландия [eerlandee-ya]

Irish ирландский [eerlantskee]

I'm Irish (man/woman) я ирландец/ирландка [ya eerlandyets/eerlantka]

iron (for ironing) утюг [ootyook]

can you iron these for me? вы не могли бы погладить это? [viy nyeh magleebi pagladeet eta?]

island остров [ostraf]

it* это [eta]

it is ... это ... [eta ...]

is it ...? это ...? [eta ...?]

where is it? где это? [gdyeh eta?]

it's him это он [eta on]

Italian (adj) итальянский [eetalyanskee]

Italy Италия [eetalee-ya]

itch: it itches чешется [chyeshetsa]

J

jack (for car) домкрат [damkrat]

jacket куртка [koortka]
(tailored) пиджак [peedjak]

jam варенье [varyenyeh]

jammed: it's jammed заело [za-yela]

January январь m [yanvar]

jar (noun) банка [banka]

jaw челюсть f [chyelyoost]

jazz джаз [djaz]

jealous ревнивый [ryevneevi]

jeans джинсы [djinsi]

jellyfish медуза [myedooza]

jersey джерси n [djersee]

jetty пристань f [preestan]

jeweller's ювелирный магазин [yoovyeleerni magazeen]

jewellery ювелирные изделия pl [yoovyeleerni-yeh eezdyelee-ya]

Jewish еврейский [yevrayskee]

job работа [rabota]

jogging бег трусцой [byek troostsoy]

to go jogging бегать трусцой [byegat troostsoy]

joke шутка [shootka]

journey путешествие [pootyeshestvee-yeh]

have a good journey! счастливого пути! [sh-chasleevava pootee!]

jug кувшин [koofshiyn]

a jug of water кувшин воды [koofshiyn vadiy]

juice сок [sok]

July июль m [ee-yool]

jump (verb) прыгать/прыгнуть [priygat/priygnoot]

jumper джемпер [djempyer]

junction (of roads) перекрёсток [pyeryekryostak]
(on motorway) развилка [razveelka]

June июнь m [ee-yoon]

just (only) только [tolka]

just two только два [tolka dva]

just for me только для меня [tolka dlya myenya]

just here именно здесь [eemyen-na zdyes]

not just now не сейчас [nyeh syechas]

we've just arrived мы только что приехали [miy tolka shto pree-yeHalee]

K

keep (verb) оставлять/ оставить [astavlyat/astaveet]

keep the change сдачи не надо [zdachee nyeh nada]

can I keep it? я могу оставить это себе? [ya magoo astaveet eta seebyeh?]

please keep it пожалуйста, оставьте это себе [paJalsta, astaftyeh eta seebyeh]

ketchup кетчуп [kyetchoop]

kettle чайник [chIneek]

key ключ [klyooch]

the key for room 201, please ключ от номера двести один, пожалуйста [klyooch at nomyera dvyestee adeen, paJalsta]

keyring кольцо для ключей [kaltso dlya klyoochyay]

kidneys почки [pochkee]

kill (verb) убивать/убить [oobeevat/oobeet]

kilo килограмм [keelagram]

kilometre километр [keelamyetr]

how many kilometres is it to ...? сколько километров до ... [skolka keelamyetraf da ...]

kind (generous) добрый [dobri]

that's very kind вы очень любезны [viy ochyen lyoobyezni]

dialogue

> **which kind do you want?** какой именно вы хотите? [kakoy eemyen-na viy HateetyeH?]
> **I want this/that kind** вот этот/тот, пожалуйста [vot etat/tot, paJalsta]

kiosk киоск [kee-osk]

kiss (noun) поцелуй m [patselooy]
(verb) целовать/ поцеловать [tselavat/ patselavat]

kitchen кухня [kooHnya]

Kleenex® бумажный носовой платок [boomaJni nasavoy platok]

knee колено [kalyena]

knickers трусики [trooseekee]

knife нож [nosh]

knock (verb) стучать/ постучать [stoochat/ pastoochat]

knock down сбивать/сбить [zbeevat/zbeet]

he's been knocked down by a car его сбила машина [yevo zbeela mashiyna]

knock over (object) опрокидывать/опрокинуть [aprakeedivat/aprakeenoot]

(pedestrian) сбивать/сбить с ног [zbeevat/zbeet snok]

know (somebody, something, a place) знать [znat]

I don't know я не знаю [ya nyeh zna-yoo]

I didn't know that (said by man/woman) я этого не знал/знала [ya etava nyeh znal/znala]

do you know where I can find ...? вы не знаете, где я могу найти ...? [viy nyeh zna-yetyeh, gdyeh ya magoo nitee ...?]

Kremlin Кремль **m** [kryeml]

L

label ярлык [yarliyk]

ladies' room, ladies' toilets женский туалет [Jenskee too-alyet]

ladies' wear женская одежда [Jenska-ya adyeJda]

lady дама [dama]

lager светлое пиво [svyetla-yeh peeva]

lake озеро [ozyera]

lamb (meat) баранина [baraneena]

lamp лампа [lampa]

lane (narrow street) переулок [pyeryeh-oolak]

(country road) дорожка [daroshka]

(motorway) ряд [ryat]

language язык [yaziyk]

language course курсы иностранного языка [koorsi eenastran-nava yazika]

large большой [balshoy]

last последний [paslyednee]

last week на прошлой неделе [na proshli nyedyelyeh]

last Friday в прошлую пятницу [fproshloo-yoo pyatneetsoo]

last night (evening) вчера вечером [fchyera vyechyeram]

what time is the last train to Omsk? когда отходит последний поезд в Омск? [kagda atHodeet paslyednee po-yest vomsk?]

late: sorry I'm late извините за опоздание [eezveeneeetyeh za apazdanee-yeh]

the train was late поезд опоздал [po-yest apazdal]

we must go, we'll be late нам нужно идти, а то опоздаем [nam nooJna eet-tee, a to apazda-yem]

it's getting late становится поздно [stanoveetsa pozna]

later позже [poJ-Jeh]

I'll come back later я вернусь попозже [ya vyernoos papoJ-Jeh]

see you later пока! [paka!]

later on потом [patom]

latest последний [paslyednee]

by Wednesday at the latest не позднее среды [nyeh paznyeh-yeh sryediy]

laugh (verb) смеяться/ засмеяться [smyeh-yatsa/ zasmyeh-yatsa]

launderette, laundromat прачечная самообслуживания [prachyechna-ya sama-apsloojivanee-ya]

laundry (clothes) бельё [byelyo]
(place) прачечная [prachyechna-ya]

lavatory туалет [too-alyet]

law закон [zakon]

lawn газон [gazon]

lawyer юрист [yooreest]

laxative слабительное [slabeetyelna-yeh]

lazy ленивый [lyeneevi]

lead (electrical) провод [provat]
(verb) вести/привести [vyestee/preeveestee]

where does this lead to? куда это ведёт? [kooda eta vyedyot?]

leaf лист [leest]

leaflet брошюрка [brashoorka]

leak течь f [tyech]

the roof leaks крыша течёт [kriysha tyechot]

learn учиться [oocheetsa]

least: not in the least нисколько [neeskolka]

at least по крайней мере [pa kriynyay myeryeh]

leather кожа [koʒa]

leave (verb: by transport) уезжать/уехать [oo-yeʒ-ʒat/ oo-yeʜat]
(on foot) уходить/уйти [ooʜadeet/ooytee]

I am leaving tomorrow я уезжаю завтра [ya oo-yeʒʒa-yoo zaftra]

he left yesterday он уехал вчера [on oo-yeʜal fchyera]

may I leave this here? можно это здесь оставить? [moʒna eta zdyes astaveet?]

I left my coat in the bar (said by man/woman) я оставил/ оставила пальто в баре [ya astaveel/astaveela palto vbaryeh]

when does the bus for Vladimir leave? когда отходит автобус во Владимир? [kagda atʜodeet aftoboos va vladeemeer?]

leek лук-порей m [look-paryay]

left-handed левша [lyefsha]

left левый [lyevi]

on the left слева [slyeva]

to the left налево [nalyeva]

turn left поверните налево [pavyerneetyeh nalyeva]

there's none left ничего не осталось [neechyevo nyeh astalas]

left luggage (office) камера

хранения [**k**amyera нranyenee-ya]

leg нога [nag**a**]

lemon лимон [l**ee**mon]

lemonade лимонад [leeman**a**t]

lemon tea чай с лимоном **m** [chi sleem**o**nam]

lend одолжить [adalJ**iy**t]

will you lend me your pen? одолжите, пожалуйста, вашу ручку [adalJ**iy**tyeh, paJ**a**lsta, vash**oo** r**oo**chkoo]

lens (of camera) объектив [abyekt**ee**f]

lesbian лесбиянка [lyezbee-**ya**nka]

less меньше [m**ye**nsheh]

less than меньше, чем [m**ye**nsheh, chyem]

less expensive менее дорогой [m**ye**nyeh-yeh darag**oy**]

lesson урок [oor**o**k]

let (allow) позволять/ позволить [pazval**ya**t/ pazv**o**leet]

will you let me know? вы мне дадите знать? [viy mnyeh dad**ee**tyeh znat?]

I'll let you know я дам вам знать [ya dam vam znat]

let's go for something to eat пойдёмте поедим [pidy**o**mtyeh pa-yed**ee**m]

to let сдаётся [sda-**yo**tsa]

let off высаживать/ высадить [vis**a**Jivat/v**iy**sadeet]

let me off at the corner я выйду на углу [ya v**iy**doo na

oogl**oo**]

letter письмо [peesm**o**]

do you have any letters for me? есть ли для меня письма? [**ye**stlee dlya myen**ya** p**ee**sma?]

letterbox почтовый ящик [pacht**o**vi **ya**sh-cheek]

lettuce салат [sal**a**t]

lever (noun) рычаг [rich**a**k]

library библиотека [beeblee-at**ye**ka]

licence (driver's) водительские права pl [vad**ee**tyelskee-yeh prav**a**] (permit) лицензия [leets**e**nzee-ya]

lid крышка [kr**iy**shka]

lie (verb: tell untruth) лгать/ солгать [lgat/salg**a**t]

lie down лежать/лечь [lyeJ**a**t/ lyech]

life жизнь **f** [Jizn]

lifebelt спасательный пояс [spas**a**tyelni p**o**-yas]

lifeguard (man/woman) спасатель [spas**a**tyel]

life jacket спасательный жилет [spas**a**tyelni Jil**ye**t]

lift (in building) лифт [leeft]

could you give me a lift? вы не могли бы меня подвезти? [viy nyeh magl**ee**bi men**ya** padvyest**ee**?]

would you like a lift? вас подвезти? [vas padvyest**ee**?]

light (noun) свет [svyet] (not heavy) лёгкий [l**yo**нkee]

do you have a light? (for

cigarette) нет ли у вас огонька? [nyetlee oo vas aganka?]

light green светло-зелёный [svyetla-zyelyoni]

light bulb лампочка [lampachka]

I need a new light bulb мне нужна новая лампочка [mnyeh noozhna nova-ya lampachka]

lighter (cigarette) зажигалка [zazhigalka]

lightning молния [molnee-ya]

like: I like it мне это нравится [mnyeh eta nraveetsa]

I like going for walks я люблю гулять [ya lyooblyoo goolyat]

I like you вы мне нравитесь [viy mnyeh nraveetyes]

I don't like it мне это не нравится [mnyeh eta nyeh nraveetsa]

do you like ...? вам нравится ...? [vam nraveetsa ...?]

I'd like a beer (said by man/woman) я бы выпил/выпила кружку пива [ya biy viypeel/viypeela krooshkoo peeva]

I'd like to go swimming (said by man/woman) я бы хотел/хотела поплавать [ya biy Hatyel/Hatyela paplavat]

would you like a drink? не хотите что-нибудь

выпить? [nyeh Hateetyeh shto-neeboot viypeet?]

would you like to go for a walk? не хотите прогуляться? [nyeh Hateetyeh pragoolyatsa?]

what's it like? на что это похоже? [na shto eta paHozheh?]

I want one like this я такой же хочу [ya takoyzheh Hachoo]

lime лайм [lim]

line линия [leenee-ya]

lips губы [goobi]

lip salve гигиеническая помада [geegee-yeneechyeska-ya pamada]

lipstick губная помада [goobna-ya pamada]

liqueur ликёр [leekyor]

listen слушать [slooshat]

litre литр [leetr]

a litre of milk литр молока [leetr malaka]

little маленький [malyenkee]

just a little, thanks чуть-чуть, спасибо [choot-choot, spaseeba]

a little milk немного молока [nyemnoga malaka]

a little bit more ещё немного [yesh-cho nyemnoga]

live (verb) жить [Jit]

we live together мы живём вместе [miy Jivyom vmyestyeh]

dialogue

where do you live? где вы живёте? [gdyeh viy

Jiv**yo**tyeh?]
I live in London я живу
в Лондоне [ya Jiv**oo**
vl**o**ndanyeh]

lively оживлённый [aJivl**yo**n-
ni]
liver (in body, food) печень **f**
[p**ye**chyen]
loaf буханка [boo**нa**nka]
lobby (in hotel) вестибюль **m**
[vyesteeby**oo**l]
lobster омар [am**a**r]
local местный [m**ye**sni]
can you recommend a local
restaurant? вы можете
порекомендовать
местный ресторан? [viy
mo**J**etyeh paryekamyendav**a**t
m**ye**sni ryestar**a**n?]
lock (noun) замок [zam**o**k]
(verb) запирать/запереть
[zapeer**a**t/zapyer**ye**t]
it's locked это заперто [**e**ta
z**a**pyerta]
lock in запирать/запереть
[zapeer**a**t/zapyer**ye**t]
lock out: I've locked myself
out (said by man/woman) я
случайно захлопнул/
захлопнула дверь [ya
slooch**i**na za**нl**opnool/za**нl**opnoola
dvyer]
locker шкафчик [shk**a**fcheek]
(for luggage etc)
автоматическая камера
хранения [aftamat**ee**chyeska-
ya k**a**myera **н**ran**ye**nee-ya]
lollipop леденец [lyedeen**ye**ts]

London Лондон [l**o**ndan]
long длинный [d**ee**n-ni]
how long will it take to fix it?
сколько времени займёт
починка? [sk**o**lka vr**ye**meenee
zim**yo**t pach**ee**nka?]
how long does it take?
сколько времени это
занимает? [sk**o**lka vr**ye**meenee
eta zan**ee**ma-yet?]
a long time долго [d**o**lga]
one day/two days longer
ещё один день/два дня
[yesh-ch**o** ad**ee**n dyen/dva dnya]
long-distance call
междугородный
разговор [mye**J**doogar**o**dni
razgav**o**r]
look: I'm just looking, thanks я
просто смотрю, спасибо
[ya pr**o**sta smatr**yoo**, spas**ee**ba]
you don't look well вы
неважно выглядите [viy
nyeh va**J**na v**i**yglyadeetyeh]
look out! осторожно!
[astar**o**Jna!]
can I have a look? можно
мне взглянуть? [m**o**Jna
mnyeh vzglyan**oo**t?]
look after ухаживать за
[oo**нa**Jivat za]
look at смотреть/
посмотреть на [smatr**ye**t/
pasmatr**ye**t na]
look for искать/поискать
[eesk**a**t/pa-eesk**a**t]
I'm looking for ... я ищу ...
[ya eesh-ch**oo** ...]
look forward to с

нетерпением ждать
[snyetyerp**ye**nee-yem Jd**a**t]
I'm looking forward to it я с
нетерпением жду этого
[ya snyetyerp**ye**nee-yem Jdoo
etava]
loose (handle etc)
расшатанный [rassh**a**tan-ni]
lorry грузовик [gr**oo**zav**ee**k]
lose терять/потерять
[tyer**ya**t/patyer**ya**t]
I've lost my way (said by
man/woman) я заблудился/
заблудилась [ya
zabl**oo**deelsya/zabl**oo**deelas]
**I'm lost, I want to get
to ...** (said by man/woman) я
заблудился/заблудилась,
мне нужно добраться
до ... [ya zabl**oo**deelsa/
zabl**oo**deelas, mnyeh n**oo**Jna
dabr**a**tsa da ...]
I've lost my bag (said by man/
woman) я потерял/потеряла
сумку [ya patyer**ya**l/patyer**ya**la
s**oo**mkoo]
lost property (office) бюро
находок [by**oo**ro nah**o**dak]
lot: a lot, lots много [mn**o**ga]
not a lot немного [nyemn**o**ga]
a lot of people много
народу [mn**o**ga nar**o**doo]
a lot bigger намного
больше [namn**o**ga b**o**lsheh]
I like it a lot мне очень
нравится [mnyeh **o**chyen
nr**a**veetsa]
lotion лосьон [las**yo**n]
loud громкий [gr**o**mkee]

lounge (in house) гостиная
[gast**ee**na-ya]
(in hotel) фойе [fay-**yeh**]
(in airport) зал ожидания [zal
aJid**a**nee-ya]
love (noun) любовь f
[ly**oo**b**o**f]
(verb) любить [ly**oo**b**ee**t]
lovely замечательный
[zamyech**a**tyelni]
low низкий [n**ee**skee]
luck удача [ood**a**cha]
good luck! желаю успеха!
[Jil**a**-yoo oosp**ye**Ha!]
luggage багаж [bag**a**sh]
luggage trolley тележка для
багажа [tyel**ye**shka dlya bagaJ**a**]
lunch обед [ab**ye**t]
lungs лёгкие [l**yo**Hkee-yeh]
luxurious (hotel, furnishings)
роскошный [rask**o**shni]
luxury роскошь f [r**o**skash]

M

machine машина [mash**ee**na]
mad (insane) сумасшедший
[soomash**e**tshi]
(angry) рассерженный
[rass**ye**rJen-ni]
magazine журнал [Joorn**a**l]
maid (in hotel) горничная
[g**o**rneechna-ya]
maiden name девичья
фамилия [d**ye**veechya
fam**ee**lee-ya]
mail (noun) почта [p**o**chta]
(verb) отправлять/

отправить [atpravlyat/
atpraveet]
is there any mail for me?
есть ли для меня почта?
[yestlee dlya myenya pochta?]
mailbox почтовый ящик
[pachtovi yash-cheek]
main главный [glavni]
main course основное
блюдо [asnavno-yeh blyooda]
main post office
главпочтамт [glafpachtamt]
main road (in town) главная
улица [glavna-ya ooleetsa]
(in country) главная дорога
[glavna-ya daroga]
make (brand name) марка
[marka]
(verb) делать/сделать [dyelat/
sdyelat]
I make it 130,000 roubles
по моим расчётам, сто
тридцать тысяч рублей
[pa ma-eem rash-chotam, sto
treetsat tiysyach rooblyay]
what is it made of? из чего
это сделано? [ees chyevo eta
zdyelana?]
make-up косметика
[kasmyeteeka]
man мужчина [moosh-cheena]
manager (of hotel)
администратор
[admeeneestrator]
(of company) менеджер
[menedjer]
can I see the
manager? позовите
администратора,

пожалуйста [pazaveetyeh
admeeneestratara, paJalsta]
manageress (in shop etc)
заведующая
[zavyedoosh-cha-ya]
manual (with manual gears)
с ручной коробкой
передач [sroochnoy karopki
pyeryedach]
many многие [mnogee-yeh]
not many немногие
[nyemnogee-yeh]
map (city plan) план [plan]
(road map, geographical) карта
[karta]
network map схема [sнyema]
March март [mart]
margarine маргарин
[margareen]
market рынок [riynak]
marmalade мармелад
[marmyelat]
married: I'm married (said by a
man/woman) я женат/
замужем [ya Jenat/zamooJem]
are you married? (to man/
woman) вы женаты/
замужем? [viy Jenati/
zamooJem?]
mascara тушь для ресниц
[toosh dlya ryesneets]
match (football etc) матч
[match]
matches спички [speechkee]
material (fabric) ткань f [tkan]
matter: it doesn't matter
неважно [nyevaJna]
what's the matter? в чём
дело? [fchom dyela?]

mattress матрас [matras]

May май **m** [mɪ]

may: may I have another one? можно ещё один, пожалуйста? [**mo**Jna yesh-cho adeen, paJalsta]

may I come in? можно войти? [**mo**Jna vitee?]

may I see it? можно мне взглянуть? [**mo**Jna mnyeh vzglyanoot?]

may I sit here? здесь свободно? [zdyes svabodna?]

maybe может быть [**mo**Jet biyt]

mayonnaise майонез [mɪanes]

me*: that's for me это для меня [**e**ta dlya myen**ya**]

send it to me пошлите это мне [pashl**ee**tyeh **e**ta mnyeh]

me too я тоже [ya to**Jeh**]

meal еда [yeda]

dialogue

did you enjoy your meal? понравилась ли вам еда? [panraveelaslee vam yeda?]

it was excellent, thank you было очень вкусно, спасибо [**biy**la **o**chyen fk**oo**sna, spas**ee**ba]

mean (verb) значить [zn**a**cheet]

what do you mean? что вы имеете в виду? [shto viy eem**yeh**-yetyeh v-veed**oo**?]

dialogue

what does this word mean? что значит это слово? [shto zn**a**cheet **e**ta slova?]

it means ... это значит ... [**e**ta zn**a**cheet ...]

measles корь **f** [kor]

German measles краснуха [krasn**oo**Ha]

meat мясо [**mya**sa]

mechanic механик [myeH**a**neek]

medicine медицина [myedeets**iy**na]

medium (adj: size) средний [sr**ye**dnee]

medium-dry полусухой [poloo-sooH**oy**]

medium-rare немного недожаренный [nyemn**o**ga nyedaJaryen-ni]

medium-sized среднего размера [sr**ye**dnyeva razm**ye**ra]

meet встречаться/ встретиться [fstryech**a**tsa/ fstr**ye**teetsa]

nice to meet you приятно познакомиться [pree-**ya**tna paznak**o**meetsa]

where shall I meet you? где мы встретимся? [gdyeh miy fstr**ye**teemsa?]

meeting встреча [fstr**ye**cha] (business, with more than one person) совещание [savyesh-chanee-yeh]

(gathering) собрание
[sabranee-yeh]
meeting place место для
встречи [myesta dlya
fstryechee]
melon дыня [dinya]
men мужчины [moosh-cheeni]
mend чинить/починить
[cheeneet/pacheeneet]
could you mend this for
me? вы не могли бы это
починить? [viy nyeh magleebi
eta pacheeneet?]
mens' room мужской
туалет [mooshskoy too-alyet]
menswear мужская одежда
[mooshska-ya adyeJda]
mention (verb) упоминать/
упомянуть [oopameenat/
oopameenoot]
don't mention it не за что
[nyeh-za-shta]
menu меню [myenyoo]
may I see the menu,
please? можно меню,
пожалуйста? [moJna
myenyoo, paJalsta]
see menu reader page 204
message сообщение [sa-
apsh-chyenee-yeh]
are there any messages
for me? мне что-нибудь
передавали? [mnyeh shto-
neeboot pyeryedavalee?]
I want to leave a message
for ... вы не могли бы
передать ...? [viy nyeh magleebi
pyeryedat ...?]
metal (noun) металл [myetal]

metre метр [myetr]
microwave oven
высокочастотная печь
[visoka-chastotna-ya pyech]
midday полдень m [poldyen]
at midday в полдень
[fpoldyen]
middle: in the middle в
середине [fsyereedeenyeh]
in the middle of the night
посреди ночи [pasreedee
nochee]
the middle one средний
[sryednee]
midnight полночь f [polnach]
at midnight в полночь
[fpolnach]
might: I might want to stay
another day возможно
я захочу остаться ещё
на один день [vazmoJna ya
zaHachoo astatsa yesh-cho na
adeen dyen]
migraine мигрень f
[meegryen]
mild (weather) тёплый [tyopli]
(taste) неострый [nyeh-ostri]
milk молоко [malako]
milkshake молочный
коктейль m [malochni kaktyayl]
millimetre миллиметр
[meeleemyetr]
minced meat фарш [farsh]
mind: never mind не важно
[nyeh vaJna]
I've changed my mind (said
by man/woman) я передумал/
передумала [ya pyeryedoomal/
pyeryedoomala]

dialogue

do you mind if I open the window? вы не возражаете, если я открою окно? [viy nyeh vazraJa-yetyeh, **yes**lee ya atkro-yoo akn**o**?]
no, I don't mind нет, я не возражаю [nyet, ya nyeh vazraJa-yoo]

mine*: it's mine это моё [**e**ta ma-**yo**]
mineral water минеральная вода [meenyer**a**lna-ya vad**a**]
mints мятные конфеты [**mya**tni-yeh kanf**ye**ti]
minute минута [meen**oo**ta]
  in a minute через минуту [ch**ye**ryez meen**oo**too]
  just a minute минуточку [meen**oo**tachkoo]
mirror зеркало [**zye**rkala]
Miss девушка [**dye**vooshka]
miss: I missed the bus (said by a man/woman) я опоздал/опоздала на автобус [ya apazd**a**l/apazd**a**la na aft**o**boos]
missing: one of my ... is missing пропал один из моих ... [prap**a**l ad**ee**n eez ma-**ee**H ...]
  there's a suitcase missing одного чемодана не хватает [adnav**o** chyemad**a**na nyeh Hvat**a**-yet]
mist туман [toom**a**n]
mistake (noun) ошибка

[ash**iy**pka]
I think there's a mistake мне кажется, здесь ошибка [mnyeh ka**J**etsa, zdyes ash**iy**pka]
sorry, I've made a mistake (said by a man/woman) извините, я ошибся/ошиблась [eezveen**ee**tyeh, ya ash**iy**psya/ash**iy**blas]
mix-up: sorry, there's been a mix-up извините, произошла путаница [eezveen**ee**tyeh, pra-eezashl**a** p**oo**taneetsa]
mobile phone мобильный телефон [mab**ee**lni tyelyef**o**n]
modern современный [savryem**ye**n-ni]
modern art gallery галерея современного искусства [galyer**yeh**-ya savryem**ye**n-nava eesk**oo**stva]
moisturizer увлажняющий крем [oovlaJn**ya**-yoosh-chee kryem]
moment: I won't be a moment минутку [meen**oo**tkoo]
monastery монастырь **m** [manast**iy**r]
Monday понедельник [panyed**ye**lneek]
money деньги pl [**dye**ngee]
month месяц [**mye**syats]
monument памятник [**pa**myatneek]
moon луна [loon**a**]
more* больше [**bo**lsheh]
  can I have some more water, please? можно ещё воды,

пожалуйста [mo**л**na yesh-cho
vad**iy**, pa**л**alsta]
more expensive/interesting
более дорогой/
интересный [b**o**lyeh-yeh
darag**oy**/eentyer**ye**sni]
more than 50 больше
пятидесяти [b**o**lsheh
pyat**ee**dyestee]
more than that более того
[b**o**lyeh-yeh tav**o**]
a lot more гораздо больше
[gar**a**zda b**o**lsheh]

dialogue

> **would you like some
> more?** вы хотите ещё?
> [viy **н**at**ee**tyeh yesh-ch**o**?]
> **no, no more for me, thanks**
> нет, спасибо, мне
> больше не надо [nyet,
> spas**ee**ba, mnyeh b**o**lsheh nyeh
> n**a**da]
> **how about you?** а вы?
> [a viy?]
> **I don't want any more,
> thanks** спасибо, я
> больше не хочу
> [spas**ee**ba, ya b**o**lsheh nyeh
> **н**ach**oo**]

morning утро [**oo**tra]
 this morning сегодня утром
 [syev**o**dnya **oo**tram]
 in the morning утром
 [**oo**tram]
Moscow Москва [mask**va**]
mosquito комар [k**a**mar]

mosquito repellent средство
 от комаров [sry**e**tstva at
 kamar**of**]
**most: I like this one most
 of all** мне больше всего
 нравится вот это [mnyeh
 b**o**lsheh fsyev**o** nrav**ee**tsa vot **e**ta]
most of the time большую
 часть времени [b**o**lshoo-yoo
 chast vr**ye**myenee]
most tourists большинство
 туристов [balshinstv**o**
 too**ree**staf]
mostly главным образом
 [gl**a**vnim **o**brazam]
mother мать [mat]
mother-in-law (wife's mother)
 тёща [t**yo**sh-cha]
 (husband's mother) свекровь
 [svyekr**of**]
motorbike мотоцикл
 [matats**iy**kl]
motorboat моторная лодка
 [mat**o**rna-ya l**o**tka]
motorway автострада
 [aftastr**a**da]
mountain гора [gar**a**]
 in the mountains в горах
 [vgar**a**н]
mountaineering альпинизм
 [alpeen**ee**zm]
mouse мышь **f** [miysh]
moustache усы pl [oos**iy**]
mouth рот [rot]
mouth ulcer язвочка во рту
 [**ya**zvachka vart**oo**]
move (verb) двигать/
 подвинуть [dv**ee**gat/
 padv**ee**noot]

he's moved to another room
он перешёл в другую
комнату [on pyeryeshol
vdroog**oo**-yoo komnatoo]

could you move up a
little? вы не могли бы
подвинуться? [viy nyeh
mag**lee**bi padveen**oo**tsa?]

where has it moved to? где
это теперь находится?
[gdyeh eta tyep**yer** na**ho**deetsa?]

movie кинофильм
[keena**feelm**]

movie theater (US) кинотеатр
[keenatyeh-**atr**]

Mr господин [gaspad**een**]

Mrs/Ms госпожа [gaspaJ**a**]

much много [mn**o**ga]

much better/worse гораздо
лучше/хуже [gar**a**zda
l**oo**chsheh/H**oo**Jeh]

much hotter гораздо жарче
[gar**a**zda J**a**rchyeh]

not much немного
[nyemn**o**ga]

not very much не очень
много [nyeh **o**chyen mn**o**ga]

I don't want very much я не
хочу много [ya nyeh Hach**oo**
mn**o**ga]

mud грязь f [gryas]

mug (for drinking) кружка
[kr**oo**shka]

I've been mugged меня
ограбили [men**ya**
agr**a**beelee]

mum мама [m**a**ma]

mumps свинка [sv**ee**nka]

museum музей m

[mooz**yay**]

mushrooms грибы [greeb**iy**]

music музыка [m**oo**zika]

musician (man/woman)
музыкант/музыкантша
[moozik**a**nt/moozik**a**ntsha]

Muslim (adj) мусульманский
[moosoolm**a**nskee]

mussels мидии [m**ee**dee-ee]

must*: I must (said by a man/
woman) я должен/
должна [ya d**o**lJen/dalJn**a**]

I mustn't drink alcohol мне
не следует пить алкоголь
[mnyeh nyeh sl**ye**doo-yet peet
alkag**o**l]

mustard горчица
[garch**ee**tsa]

my* мой [moy] m, моя [ma-
y**a**] f, моё [ma-**yo**] n, мои
[ma-**ee**] pl

myself: I'll do it myself (said
by a man/woman) я сам/сама
это сделаю [ya sam/sam**a** eta
zd**ye**la-yoo]

by myself (said by man/woman)
один/одна [ad**ee**n/adn**a**]

N

nail (finger) ноготь m [n**o**gat]
(metal) гвоздь m [gvost]

nailbrush щёточка для
ногтей [sh-ch**o**tachka dlya
nakt**yay**]

nail varnish лак для ногтей
[lak dlya nakt**yay**]

name имя n [**ee**mya]

my name's ... меня зовут ... [me**nya** za**voot** ...]

what's your name? как вас зовут? [kak vas za**voot**?]

what is the name of this street? как называется эта улица [kak na**ziva**-yetsa eta **oo**leetsa?]

napkin салфетка [sal**fyet**ka]

nappy пелёнка [pyel**yon**ka]

narrow узкий [**oo**skee]

nasty (weather, person) скверный [skv**yer**ni] (accident) тяжёлый [tya**Jo**li]

national национальный [natsi-a**nal**ni]

nationality национальность [natsi-a**nal**nast]

natural натуральный [natoo**ral**ni]

nausea тошнота [tash**nata**]

navy (blue) тёмно-синий [**tyo**mna-**see**nee]

near рядом [**rya**dam]

is it near the city centre? это недалеко от центра города? [eta nyeda**lyeko** at **tsen**tra ga**rada**?]

do you go near the Winter Palace? вы не проезжаете Зимний дворец? [viy nyeh pra-ye**JJa**-yetyeh **zee**mnee dvar**yets**?]

where is the nearest ...? где ближайший ...? [gdyeh **blee**Jıshi ...?]

nearby поблизости [pa**blee**zastee]

nearly почти [pach**tee**]

necessary необходимый [nyeh-apHa**deemi**]

neck шея [**sheh**-ya]

necklace ожерелье [aJer**yeh**-lyeh]

necktie галстук [**gal**stook]

need: I need ... мне надо ... [mnyeh **nada** ...]

do I need to pay? нужно ли мне заплатить? [**noo**Jnalee mnyeh zapla**teet**?]

needle иголка [ee**gol**ka]

negative (film) негатив [nyega**teef**]

neither: neither (one) of them ни один из них [nee ad**een** eez neeH]

neither ... nor ... ни ... ни ... [nee ... nee ...]

nephew племянник [plyem**yan**-neek]

net (in tennis) сетка [**syet**ka] (in football) ворота [va**rota**]

Netherlands Нидерланды [**needer**landi]

never никогда [neekag**da**]

dialogue

have you ever been to Pskov? вы когда-нибудь были в Пскове? [viy kagda-neebot **biy**lee fpsk**o**vyeh?]

no, never, I've never been there (said by man/woman) нет, я там никогда не был/не была [nyet, ya tam neekag**da nye**bil/nyeh bi**la**]

new новый [**no**vi]
news (radio, TV etc) новости pl [**no**vastee]
newsagent's (kiosk) газетный киоск [gaz**ye**tni kee-**o**sk]
newspaper газета [gaz**ye**ta]
newspaper kiosk газетный киоск [gaz**ye**tni kee-**o**sk]
New Year Новый год [**no**vi got]

Happy New Year! с Новым годом! [s**no**vim **go**dam!]
New Year's Eve новогодняя ночь f [navag**o**dnya-ya noch]
New Zealand Новая Зеландия [**no**va-ya zyel**a**ndee-ya]
New Zealander: I'm a New Zealander (man/woman) я новозеландец/ новозеландка [ya novazyel**a**ndyets/ novazyel**a**ntka]
next следующий [sl**ye**doosh-chee]

the next turning on the left следующий поворот налево [sl**ye**doosh-chee pavar**o**t nal**ye**va]
at the next stop на следующей остановке [na sl**ye**doosh-chyay astan**o**fkyeh]
next week на следующей неделе [na sl**ye**doosh-chyay nyed**ye**lyeh]
next to рядом с [**rya**dam s]
nice (food) вкусный [fk**oo**sni]
(looks, view etc) красивый [kras**ee**vi]

(person) приятный [pree-**ya**tni]
niece племянница [plyemy**an**neetsa]
night ночь f [noch]

at night ночью [**no**chyoo]
good night спокойной ночи [spak**oy**ni **no**chee]

dialogue

> do you have a single room for one night? у вас есть одноместный номер на одни сутки? [oo vas yest adnam**ye**stni **no**myer na adn**ee** s**oo**tkee?]
> yes, madam да, есть [da, yest]
> how much is it per night? сколько это стоит в сутки? [sk**o**lka eta st**o**-eet fs**oo**tkee?]
> it's 300,000 roubles for one night триста тысяч рублей в сутки [tr**ee**sta t**i**ysyach roobl**ya**y fs**oo**tkee]
> OK, I'll take it хорошо, это меня устраивает [Harash**o**, eta myen**ya** oostra-eeva-yet]

nightclub ночной клуб [nachn**oy** kloop]
nightdress ночная рубашка [nachn**a**-ya roob**a**shka]
night porter ночной портье m [nachn**oy** party**eh**]
no нет [nyet]

I've no change у меня нет мелочи [oo myenya nyet myelachee]

there's no ... left ... больше нет [bolsheh nyet]

no way! ни за что! [nee-za-shto!]

nobody никто [neekto]

there's nobody there там никого нет [tam neekavo nyet]

noise шум [shoom]

noisy: it's too noisy слишком шумно [sleeshkam shoomna]

non-alcoholic безалкогольный [byezalkagolni]

none ничего [neechevo]

nonsmoking compartment купе для некурящих [koopeh dlya nekooryash-cheen]

noon полдень m [poldyen]

at noon в полдень [fpoldyen]

no-one никто [neekto]

nor: nor do I я тоже нет [ya toJeh nyet]

normal нормальный [narmalni]

north север [syevyer]

in the north на севере [na syevyeryeh]

to the north на север [na syevyer]

north of Moscow к северу от Москвы [ksyevyeroo at maskviy]

northeast северо-восточный [syevyera-vastochni]

northern северный [syevyerni]

Northern Ireland Северная Ирландия [syevyerna-ya eerlandee-ya]

northwest северо-западный [syevyera-zapadni]

Norway Норвегия [narvyegee-ya]

Norwegian (adj) норвежский [narvyeshskee]

nose нос [nos]

not* не [nyeh]

I'm not hungry (said by man/woman) я не голоден/голодна [ya nyeh goladyen/galadna]

I don't want any, thank you я не хочу, спасибо [ya nyeh Hachoo, spaseeba]

it's not necessary в этом нет необходимости [vetam nyet nyeh-apHadeemastee]

I didn't know that (said by man/woman) я этого не знал/знала [ya etava nyeh znal/znala]

not that one, this one не тот, а этот [nyeh tot, a etat]

note (banknote) банкнота [banknota]

notebook блокнот [blaknot]

notepaper (for letters) почтовая бумага [pachtova-ya boomaga]

nothing ничего [neechevo]

nothing for me, thanks мне ничего, спасибо [mnyeh neechyevo, spaseeba]

nothing else больше ничего [bolsheh neechyevo]

novel роман [raman]

November ноябрь **m** [na-**ya**br]
now сейчас [**see**chas]
number (room, telephone etc)
номер [**no**myer]
(figure) число [chees**lo**]
I've got the wrong number
(said by man/woman) я не туда
попал/попала [ya nyeh too**da**
pa**pal**/pa**pala**]
what is your phone number?
какой ваш номер
телефона? [ka**koy** vash **no**myer
tyelye**fo**na?]
number plate номерной
знак [namyer**noy** znak]
nurse (man/woman) медбрат/
медсестра [myed**brat**/
myet**syestra**]
nut (for bolt) гайка [**gı**ka]
nuts орехи [a**rye**Hee]

O

occupied (toilet/telephone)
занято [**za**nyata]
o'clock*: it's 3 o'clock три
часа [tree cha**sa**]
October октябрь **m** [ak**tya**br]
odd (strange) странный
[**stran**-ni]
of*
off (lights) выключено
[**viy**klyoochyena]
it's just off Pushkin Square
это рядом с Пушкинской
площадью [**e**ta r**ya**dam
s**poo**shkeenskı pl**osh**-chadyoo]
we're off tomorrow мы

уезжаем завтра [miy oo-ye**J**-
Ja-yem za**ftra**]
offensive (language, behaviour)
оскорбительный
[askarb**eet**yelni]
office (place of work) офис
[**o**fees]
often часто [**cha**sta]
not often нечасто
[nye**cha**sta]
how often are the buses? как
часто ходят автобусы?
[kak **cha**sta **Ho**dyat aft**o**boosi?]
oil масло [**ma**sla]
ointment мазь **f** [maz]
OK хорошо [Hara**sho**]
are you OK? с вами всё
в порядке? [s**va**mee fsyo
fpar**ya**tkyeh?]
is that OK with you? вы не
возражаете? [viy nyeh vazraJa-
yetyeh?]
is it OK to ...? можно ...?
[**mo**Jna...?]
that's OK thanks ничего,
спасибо [neechy**evo**,
spas**ee**ba]
I'm OK мне ничего,
спасибо [mnyeh neechy**evo**,
spas**ee**ba]
(I feel OK) со мной всё
в порядке [sa mnoy fsyo
fpar**ya**tkyeh]
is this train OK for ...? этот
поезд идёт до ...? [**e**tat po-
yest eed**yot** da ...?]
I said I'm sorry, OK? (said
by man/woman) я же уже
извинился/извинилась!

[ya Jeh ooJeh eezveeneelsya/
eezveeneelas]
old старый [stari]

dialogue

how old are you? сколько
вам лет? [skolka vam lyet?]
I'm 25 мне двадцать
пять [mnyeh dvatsat pyat]
and you? а вам? [a vam?]

old-fashioned старомодный
[staramodni]
old town (old part of town)
старая часть города [stara-
ya chast gorada]
in the old town в старой
части города [fstari chastee
gorada]
omelette омлет [amlyet]
on* на [na]
on the street/beach на
улице/пляже [na ooleetseh/
plyaJeh]
is it on this road? это на
этой дороге? [eta na eti
darogyeh?]
on the plane на самолёте
[na samalyotyeh]
on Saturday в субботу
[fsoobotoo]
on television по телевизору
[pa tyelyeveezaroo]
I haven't got it on me у меня
его нет с собой [oo menya
yevo nyet s-saboy]
this one's on me (drink) этот
за мой счёт [etat za moy sh-

chot]
the light wasn't on свет не
горел [svyet nyeh garyel]
what's on tonight? что
идёт сегодня? [shto eedyot
syevodnya?]
once (one time) один раз
[adeen ras]
at once (immediately) сразу же
[srazooJeh]
one* один [adeen]
the white one белый [byeli]
one-way ticket билет в один
конец [beelyet vadeen kanyets]
onion лук [look]
only только [tolka]
only one только один [tolka
adeen]
it's only 6 o'clock сейчас
только шесть часов
[syechas tolka shest chasof]
I've only just got here (said
by man/woman) я только что
пришёл/пришла [ya tolka
shto preeshol/preeshla]
on/off switch выключатель
m [viklyoochatyel]
open (adj) открытый [atkriyti]
(verb: door) открывать/
открыть [atkrivat/atkriyt]
when do you open? когда
вы открываетесь? [kagda
viy atkriva-yetyes?]
I can't get it open я не могу
это открыть [ya nyeh magoo
eta atkriyt]
in the open air на
открытом воздухе [na
atkriytam vozdooнyeh]

opening times время
открытия [vr**ye**mya atkr**i**ytee-
ya]

open ticket билет с
открытой датой [beel**ye**t
satkr**i**yti d**a**ti]

opera опера [**o**pyera]

operation (medical) операция
[apyer**a**tsi-ya]

operator (telephone: man/
woman) телефонист/
телефонистка [tyelyefan**ee**st/
tyelyefan**ee**stka]

opposite: in the
opposite direction в
противоположном
направлении
[fprateevapalo**j**nam napravl**ye**nee-
ee]

the bar opposite бар
напротив [bar napr**o**teef]

opposite my hotel напротив
моей гостиницы [napr**o**teef
ma-**yay** gast**ee**neetsi]

optician оптика [**o**pteeka]

or или [**ee**lee]

orange (fruit) апельсин
[apyels**ee**n]

(colour) оранжевый [ar**a**nJevi]

fizzy orange газированный
апельсиновый напиток
[gazeer**o**van-ni apyels**ee**navi
nap**ee**tak]

orange juice апельсиновый
сок [apyels**ee**navi sok]

orchestra оркестр [ark**ye**str]

order: can we order now? (in
restaurant) можно заказать
сейчас? [m**o**Jna zakaz**a**t

syech**a**s?]

I've already ordered, thanks
(said by man/woman) я уже
заказал/заказала, спасибо
[ya ooJ**e** zakaz**a**l/zakaz**a**la,
spas**ee**ba]

I didn't order this (said by
man/woman) я этого не
заказывал/заказывала [ya
etava nyeh zak**a**zival/zak**a**zivala]

out of order не работает
[nyeh rab**o**ta-yet]

ordinary обычный [ab**i**ychni]

Orthodox православный
[pravasl**a**vni]

other другой [droog**oy**]

the other one другой
[droog**oy**]

the other day на днях [na
dny**a**н]

I'm waiting for the others я
жду остальных [ya Jdoo
astaln**i**yн]

do you have any others? у
вас нет других? [oo vas nyet
droog**ee**н?]

otherwise иначе [een**a**chyeh]

our*/ours* наш [nash] **m**,
наша [n**a**sha] **f**, наше
[n**a**sheh] **n**, наши [n**a**shi] pl

out: he's out его нет [yev**o**
nyet]

three kilometres out of town
в трёх километрах от
города [ftry**o**н keelam**ye**traн at
g**o**rada]

outdoors на открытом
воздухе [na atkr**i**ytam
v**o**zdooнyeh]

Ou

99

outside снаружи [snarooJi]
  can we sit outside? можно сесть снаружи? [moJna syest snarooJi?]
oven духовка [dooноfka]
over: over here вот здесь [vot zdyes]
  over there вон там [von tam]
  over 500 свыше пятисот [sviysheh pyateesot]
  our holidays are over наш отпуск кончился [nash otpoosk koncheelsa]
overcharge: you've overcharged me вы с меня слишком много взяли [viy smenya sleeshkam mnoga vzyalee]
overcoat пальто [palto]
overlooking: I'd like a room overlooking the courtyard (said by man/woman) я хотел/хотела бы номер с окнами во двор [ya наtyel/наtyela biy nomyer soknamee va dvor]
overnight (travel) ночной [nachnoy]
overtake обгонять/обогнать [abganyat/abagnat]
owe: how much do I owe you? (said by man/woman) сколько я вам должен/должна? [skolka ya vam dolJen/dalJna?]
own: my own ... мой собственный ... [moy sopstvyen-ni ...]
  are you on your own? (to man/woman) вы один/одна? [viy adeen/adna?]

I'm on my own (said by man/woman) я один/одна [ya adeen/adna]
owner (man/woman) владелец/владелица [vladyelyets/vladyeleetsa]

P

pack (verb) складывать/сложить вещи [skladivat/slaJiyt vyesh-chee]
  a pack of ... пачка ... [pachka]
package (parcel) посылка [pasiylka]
package holiday организованный отдых [arganeezovan-ni oddiн]
packet: a packet of cigarettes пачка сигарет [pachka seegaryet]
padlock висячий замок [veesyachee zamok]
page (of book) страница [straneetsa]
  could you page Mr ...? вызовите, пожалуйста, господина ... [viyzaveetyeh, paJalsta gaspadeena ...]
pain боль [bol]
  I have a pain here у меня здесь болит [oo myenya zdyes baleet]
painful болезненный [balyeznyen-ni]
painkillers болеутоляющие [bolyeh-ootalya-yoosh-chee-yeh]
paint (noun) краска [kraska]

painting (occupation)
живопись f [**j**ivapees]
(picture) картина [kart**ee**na]

pair: a pair of ... пара ...
[**pa**ra ...]

Pakistani (adj) пакистанский
[pakeest**a**nskee]

palace дворец [dvar**y**ets]

pale бледный [bl**ye**dni]

pale blue светло-голубой
[sv**ye**tla-galoob**oy**]

pan кастрюля [kastr**yoo**lya]

pancakes блины [bleen**iy**]

panties (women's) трусики
[tr**oo**seekee]

pants (underwear: men's) трусы
[troos**iy**]
(women's) трусики
[tr**oo**seekee]
(US: trousers) брюки [br**yoo**kee]

pantyhose колготки pl
[kalg**o**tkee]

paper бумага [boom**a**ga]
(newspaper) газета [gaz**ye**ta]

a piece of paper листок
бумаги [leest**o**k boom**a**gee]

paper handkerchiefs
бумажные носовые
платки
[boom**a**Jni-yeh nasav**iy**-yeh
platk**ee**]

parcel посылка [pas**iy**lka]

pardon (me)? (didn't understand/
hear) простите? [prast**ee**tyeh?]

parents родители [rad**ee**tyelee]

park (noun) парк [park]
(verb) парковаться/
припарковаться [parkav**a**tsa/
preeparkav**a**tsa]

can I park here? можно
здесь припарковаться?
[m**o**Jna zdyes preeparkav**a**tsa?]

parking lot стоянка [sta-
yanka]

part часть f [chast]

partner (boyfriend, girlfriend)
друг/подруга [drook/
padr**oo**ga]

party (group) группа
[gr**oo**p-pa]
(celebration) вечеринка
[vyechyer**ee**nka]

pass (in mountains) перевал
[pyeryev**a**l]

passenger (man/woman)
пассажир/пассажирка
[pasaJ**iy**r/pasaJ**iy**rka]

passport паспорт [p**a**spart]

past*: in the past в прошлом
[fpr**o**shlam]

just past the post office
сразу за почтой [sr**a**zoo za
p**o**chti]

path тропинка [trap**ee**nka]

patronymic отчество
[**o**chyestva]

pattern узор [ooz**o**r]

pavement тротуар [tratoo-**a**r]

on the pavement на
тротуаре [na tratoo-**a**ryeh]

pay (verb) платить/
заплатить [plat**ee**t/zaplat**ee**t]

can I pay, please? можно
заплатить? [m**o**Jna
zaplat**ee**t?]

it's already paid for это
уже оплачено [eta ooJ**eh**
apl**a**chyena]

dialogue

who's paying? кто
платит? [kto plateet?]
I'll pay я заплачу [ya
zaplachoo]
no, you paid last time,
it's my turn now нет, вы
платили в прошлый
раз, теперь моя
очередь [nyet, viy plateelee
fproshli ras, tyepyer ma-ya
ochyeryet]

payphone телефон-автомат
[tyelyefon-aftamat]
peaceful мирный [meerni]
peach персик [pyerseek]
peanuts арахис [araHees]
pear груша [groosha]
peas горох [garoH]
peculiar странный [stran-ni]
pedestrian crossing
пешеходный переход
[pyesheHodni pyeryeHot]
peg (for washing) прищепка
[preesh-chyepka]
(for tent) колышек [kolishek]
pen ручка [roochka]
pencil карандаш [karandash]
penfriend (man/woman)
знакомый/знакомая по
переписке [znakomi/
znakoma-ya pa pyeryepeeskyeh]
penicillin пенициллин
[pyeneetsileen]
penknife перочинный
ножик [pyeracheen-ni noJik]
pensioner (man/woman)

пенсионер/пенсионерка
[pyensee-anyer/pyensee-anyerka]
people люди [lyoodee]
the other people in the hotel
другие люди в гостинице
[droogee-yeh lyoodee
vgasteeneetse]
too many people слишком
много народу [sleeshkam
mnoga narodoo]
pepper (spice, vegetable) перец
[pyerets]
peppermint (sweet) мятная
конфета [myatna-ya kanfyeta]
per: per night за ночь [zanach]
how much per day? сколько
стоит в сутки? [skolka sto-eet
fsootkee?]
per cent процент
[pratsent]
perfect идеальный [eedee-
alni]
perfume духи pl [dooHee]
perhaps может быть [moJet
biyt]
perhaps not может быть,
нет [moJet biyt, nyet]
period (of time) период [pyeree-
ot]
(menstruation) месячные pl
[myesyachni-yeh]
perm перманент
[pyermanyent]
permit (noun) разрешение
[razryeshenee-yeh]
person человек [chyelavyek]
personal stereo плейер
[play-yer]
petrol бензин [byenzeen]

petrol can канистра для бензина [kaneestra dlya byenzeena]

petrol station бензоколонка [byenzakalonka]

pharmacy аптека [aptyeka]

phone (noun) телефон [tyelyefon]

(verb) звонить/позвонить [zvaneet/pazvaneet]

phone book телефонный справочник [tyelyefon-ni spravachneek]

phone box телефонная будка [tyelyefon-na-ya bootka]

phone call звонок [zvanok]

phonecard карточка для телефона-автомата [kartachka dlya tyelyefona-aftamata]

phone number номер телефона [nomyer tyelyefona]

photo фотография [fatagrafee-ya]

excuse me, could you take a photo of us? извините, пожалуйста, вы не могли бы нас сфотографировать? [eezveeneetyeh, paJalsta, viy nyeh magleebi nas sfatagrafeeravat?]

phrasebook разговорник [razgavorneek]

piano пианино [pee-aneena]

pickpocket (man/woman) вор/ воровка-карманник [vor/ varofka-karman-neek]

pick up: will you pick me up? вы заедете за мной? [viy za-

yedeetyeh za mnoy?]

picnic пикник [peekneek]

picture (painting) картина [karteena]

(photo) фотография [fatagrafee-ya]

pie пирог [peerok]

piece кусок [koosok]

a piece of ... кусок ... [koosok ...]

pill таблетка [tablyetka]

I'm on the pill я принимаю противозачаточные таблетки [ya preeneema-yoo proteeva-zachatachni-yeh tablyetkee]

pillow подушка [padooshka]

pillow case наволочка [navalachka]

pin булавка [boolafka]

pineapple ананас [ananas]

pineapple juice ананасовый сок [ananasavi sok]

pink розовый [rozavi]

pipe (for smoking) трубка [troopka]

(for water) трубопровод [troobapravot]

pity: it's a pity жаль [Jal]

place (noun) место [myesta]

at your place у вас [oo vas]

at his place у него [oo nyevo]

plain (not patterned) однотонный [adnaton-ni]

plane самолёт [samalyot]

by plane самолётом [samalyotam]

plant растение [rastyenee-yeh]

plasters пластыри [plastiree]

plastic пластмассовый [plasmas-savi]

plastic bag пластиковый пакет [plasteekavi pakyet]

plate тарелка [taryelka]

platform платформа [platforma]

which platform is it for Sergiev Posad? с какой платформы идут поезда до сергиева посада? [skakoy platformi eedoot po-yezda da syergee-yeva pasada?]

play (verb) играть/сыграть [eegrat/sigrat]
(noun: in theatre) пьеса [pyesa]

playground детская площадка [dyetska-ya plash-chatka]

pleasant приятный [pree-yatni]

please пожалуйста [paJalsta]

yes please да, спасибо [da, spaseeba]

could you please ...? вы не могли бы ...? [viy nyeh magleebi ...?]

please don't пожалуйста, не надо [paJalsta, nyeh nada]

pleased: pleased to meet you очень приятно [ochyen pree-yatna]

pleasure: my pleasure пожалуйста [paJalsta]

plenty: plenty of ... много ... [mnoga ...]

we have plenty of time у нас много времени [oo nas mnoga vryemyenee]

that's plenty, thanks достаточно, спасибо [dastatachna, spaseeba]

pliers плоскогубцы [plaskagooptsi]

plug (electrical) штепсельная вилка [shtepsyelna-ya veelka]
(for car) свеча [svyecha]
(in sink) пробка [propka]

plumber сантехник [santyeHneek]

pm*: 2pm два часа дня [dva chasa dnya]

10pm десять часов вечера [dyesyat chasof vyechyera]

poached egg яйцо-пашот [yItso-pashot]

pocket карман [karman]

point: two point five две целых пять десятых [dvyeh tseliH pyat dyesyatiH]

there's no point нет смысла [nyet smiysla]

poisonous ядовитый [yadaveeti]

Poland Польша [polsha]

police милиция [meeleetsi-ya]

call the police! вызовите милицию! [viyzaveetyeh meeleetsi-yoo!]

policeman милиционер [meeleetsi-anyer]

police station отделение милиции [addyelyenee-yeh meeleetsee-ee]

policewoman женщина-милиционер
[Jensh-cheena-meeleetsi-anyer]

Polish польский [polskee]

polish (for shoes) крем для обуви [kryem dlya oboovee]

polite вежливый [vyeJleevi]

polluted загрязнённый
[zagryaznyon-ni]

pool (for swimming) бассейн
[basyayn]

poor (not rich) бедный [byedni]
(quality)
низкокачественный
[neeska-kachyestvyen-ni]

pop music поп-музыка [pop moozika]

pop singer (man/woman) поп-певец/певица [pop pyevvyets/pyeveetsa]

popular популярный
[papoolyarni]

pork свинина [sveeneena]

port (for boats) порт [port]
(drink) портвейн [partvyayn]

porter (in hotel) швейцар
[shvyaytsar]

portrait портрет [partryet]

posh шикарный [shikarni]

possible возможный
[vazmoJni]
is it possible to ...?
возможно ли ...?
[vazmoJnalee]
as soon as possible как можно быстрее [kak moJna bistryeh-yeh]

post (noun: mail) почта
[pochta]

(verb) отправлять/отправить [atpravlyat/atpraveet]
could you post this for me? вы не могли бы отправить это? [viy nyeh magleebi atpraveet eta]

postbox почтовый ящик
[pachtovi yash-cheek]

postcard открытка [atkriytka]

postcode почтовый индекс
[pachtovi eendeks]

poster плакат [plakat]

poste restante до востребования
[da vastryebavanee-ya]

post office почта [pochta]

potato картофель m
[kartofyel]

pots and pans кухонная посуда [koohan-na-ya pasooda]

pottery керамика
[kyerameeka]

pound (money) фунт стерлингов [foont styerleengaf]

power cut отключение электричества
[atklyoochyenee-yeh elyektreechyestva]

power point розетка [razyetka]

practise: I want to practise my Russian я хочу поупражняться в русском языке [ya Hachoo pa-oopraJnyatsa vrooskam yazikyeh]

prawns креветки
[kreevyetkee]

prefer: I prefer ... я
предпочитаю ... [ya
pryetpacheeta-yoo ...]

pregnant беременная
[byeryemyen-na-ya]

prescription (for medicine)
рецепт [ryetsept]

present (gift) подарок
[padarak]

president (of country)
президент [pryezeedyent]

pretty симпатичный
[seempateechni]

it's pretty expensive это
довольно дорого [eta
davolna doraga]

price цена [tsena]

priest священник
[svyash-chyen-neek]

prime minister премьер-
министр [pryemyer meeneestr]

printed matter печатный
материал [pechatni matyeryal]

prison тюрьма [tyoorma]

private частный [chasni]

private bathroom отдельная
ванная [addyelna-ya van-na-ya]

probably вероятно [vyera-
yatna]

problem проблема
[prablyema]

no problem! нет проблем!
[nyet prablyem]

program(me) программа
[pragram-ma]

promise: I promise я обещаю
[ya abyesh-cha-yoo]

pronounce: how is this
pronounced? как это

произносится? [kak eta pra-
eeznoseetsa?]

properly (repaired, locked etc) как
следует [kak slyedoo-yet]

protection factor (of suntan
lotion) защитный фактор
[zash-cheetni faktar]

Protestant протестантский
[pratyestantskee]

public holiday
официальный праздник
[afeetsalni prazneek]

public toilet туалет [too-alyet]

pudding (dessert) десерт
[dyesyert]

pull тянуть/потянуть
[tyanoot/patyanoot]

pullover свитер [sveeter]

puncture (noun) прокол
[prakol]

purple фиолетовый [fee-
alyetavi]

purse (for money) кошелёк
[kashelyok]
(US: handbag) сумочка
[soomachka]

push толкать/толкнуть
[talkat/talknoot]

pushchair детская коляска
[dyetska-ya kalyaska]

put класть/положить [klast/
palaJiyt]

where can I put ...? куда
мне положить ...? [kooda
mnyeh palaJiyt ...?]

could you put us up for the
night? нельзя ли нам
переночевать у вас?
[nyelzyalee nam

pyeryenacheevat oo vas?]
pyjamas пижама [peeJama]

Q

quality качество [kachyestva]
quarantine карантин
[karanteen]
quarter четверть f [chyetvyert]
question вопрос [vapros]
queue (noun) очередь f
[ochyeryet]
quick быстрый [biystri]
  what's the quickest way
  there? как туда побыстрее
  добраться? [kak tooda
  pabistryeh-yeh dabratsa?]
  fancy a quick drink? не
  хотите пропустить
  стаканчик? [nyeh Hateetyeh
  prapoosteet stakancheek?]
quickly быстро [biystra]
quiet (place, hotel) тихий
[teeHee]
  quiet! тише! [teesheh!]
quite: that's quite right
  совершенно верно
  [savyershen-na vyerna]
  quite a lot довольно много
  [davolna mnoga]

R

rabbit кролик [kroleek]
race (for cars) гонки pl [gonkee]
  (for runners) забег [zabyek]
  (for horses) скачки pl

[skachkee]
racket (tennis, squash) ракетка
[rakyetka]
radiator (in room) батарея
[bataryeh-ya]
  (in car) радиатор [radee-atar]
radio радио [radee-o]
  on the radio по радио [pa
  radee-o]
rail: by rail поездом [po-
  yezdam]
railway железная дорога
[Jelyezna-ya daroga]
rain (noun) дождь m [dosht]
  in the rain под дождём [pad
  daJdyom]
  it's raining идёт дождь
  [eedyot dosht]
raincoat плащ [plash-ch]
rape (noun) изнасилование
[eeznaseelavanee-yeh]
rare (uncommon) редкий
[ryetkee]
  (steak) с кровью [skrovyoo]
rash (on skin) сыпь f [siyp]
raspberry малина [maleena]
rat крыса [kriysa]
rate (for changing money) курс
[koors]
rather: it's rather good очень
  неплохо [ochyen nyeploHa]
  I'd rather ... (said by man/woman)
  я предпочёл/предпочла
  бы ... [ya pryetpachol/pryetpachla
  biy ...]
razor бритва [breetva]
razor blades лезвия бритвы
[lyezvee-ya breetvi]
read читать/прочесть

[cheetat/prachyest]

ready готовый [gatovi]

are you ready? вы готовы? [viy gatovi?]

I'm not ready yet (said by man/woman) я ещё не готов/готова [ya yesh-cho nyeh gatof/gatova]

dialogue

when will it be ready? когда это будет готово? [kagda eta boodyet gatova?]

it should be ready in a couple of days это будет готово через пару дней [eta boodyet gatova chyeryes paroo dnyay]

real настоящий [nasta-yash-chee]

really действительно [dyestveetyelna]

I'm really sorry я очень сожалею [ya ochyen saJalyeh-yoo]

that's really great! это замечательно! [eta zamyechatyelna!]

really? (doubt) серьёзно? [syeryozna?]

(polite interest) да? [da?]

rear lights задние фары [zadnee-ee fari]

rearview mirror зеркало заднего вида [zyerkala zadnyeva veeda]

reasonable (prices etc)

умеренный [oomyeryen-ni]

receipt квитанция [kveetantsi-ya]

recently недавно [nyedavna]

reception (in hotel) служба размещения [slooJba razmyesh-chyenee-ya]

at reception в службе размещения [fslooJbyeh razmyesh-chyenee-ya]

reception desk конторка дежурного администратора [kantorka dyeJoornava admeeneestratara]

receptionist дежурный администратор [dyeJoorni admeeneestrator]

recognize узнать [ooznat]

recommend: could you recommend ...? вы можете порекомендовать ...? [viy moJetyeh paryekamyendavat ...?]

record (music) пластинка [plasteenka]

red красный [krasni]

red wine красное вино [krasna-yeh veeno]

refund возмещение [vazmyesh-chyenee-yeh]

can I have a refund? могу я получить обратно деньги? [magoo ya paloocheet abratna dyengee?]

region область f [oblast]

registered: by registered mail заказной почтой [zakaznoy pochtI]

registration number номер машины [nomyer mashIyni]

relative (man/woman)
родственник/
родственница [rotstvyen-
neek/
rotstvyen-neetsa]
religion религия [ryeleegee-ya]
remember: I don't remember я
не помню [ya nyeh pomnyoo]
I remember я помню [ya
pomnyoo]
do you remember? вы
помните? [viy pomneetyeh?]
rent (noun: for apartment)
квартирная плата
[kvarteerna-ya plata]
(verb: car etc) брать/взять
напрокат [brat/vzyat naprakat]
rented car взятая напрокат
машина [vzyata-ya naprakat
mashiyna]
repair (verb) чинить/
починить [cheeneet/
pacheeneet]
can you repair it? вы
можете это починить? [viy
moJetyeh eta pacheeneet?]
repeat повторять/
повторить [paftaryat/
paftareet]
could you repeat that?
повторите, пожалуйста
[paftareetyeh, paJalsta]
reservation
предварительный заказ
[pryedvareetyelni zakas]
I'd like to make a reservation
(at hotel/theatre: said by a man/
woman) я хотел/хотела бы
заказать номер/билет [ya

Hatyel/Hatyela biy zakazat nomyer/
beelyet]

dialogue

I have a reservation
(at hotel/theatre) у меня
заказан номер/билет
[oo myenya zakazan nomyer/
beelyet]
what name please? ваше
имя, пожалуйста [vasheh
eemya, paJalsta]

reserve (verb) заказывать/
заказать заранее [zakazivat/
zakazat zaranyeh-yeh]

dialogue

can I reserve a table for
tonight? могу я заказать
столик на сегодня
вечером? [magoo ya
zakazat stoleek na syevodnya
vyechyeram]
yes madam, for how many
people? да, пожалуйста,
на сколько человек? [da,
paJalsta, na skolka chyelavyek?]
for two на двоих [na
dva-eeH]
and for what time? на
какое время? [na kako-yeh
vryemya?]
for eight o'clock на
восемь часов [na vosyem
chasof]
and could I have your

Re

name please? ваше имя, пожалуйста [vasheh eemya, paJalsta]
see alphabet for spelling

rest: I need a rest мне нужно отдохнуть [mnyeh nooJna ad-daHnoot]
the rest of the group остальные члены группы [astalniy-yeh chlyeni groop-pi]
restaurant ресторан [ryestaran]
restaurant car вагон-ресторан [vagon-ryestaran]
rest room туалет [too-alyet]
retired: I'm retired я на пенсии [ya na pyensee-ee]
return: a return to ... туда и обратно до ... [tooda ee abratna da ...]
return ticket обратный билет [abratni beelyet]
see ticket
reverse charge call разговор, оплачиваемый вызываемым лицом [razgavor, aplacheeva-yemi viziva-yemim leetsom]
reverse gear задний ход [zadnee Hot]
revolting отвратительный [atvrateetyelni]
rib ребро [ryebro]
rice рис [rees]
rich (person) богатый [bagati]
(food) жирный [Jiyrni]
ridiculous нелепый [nyelyepi]
right (correct) правильный

[praveelni]
(not left) правый [pravi]
you were right вы были правы [viy biylee pravi]
that's right правильно [praveelna]
this can't be right не может такого быть [nyeh moJet takova biyt]
right! хорошо [Harasho]
is this the right road for ...? я доеду по этой дороге до ...? [ya da-yedoo pa eti darogyeh da ...?]
on the right справа [sprava]
to the right направо [naprava]
turn right поверните направо [pavyerneetyeh naprava]
right-hand drive вождение по правой стороне [vaJdyenee-yeh pa pravi staranyeh]
ring (on finger) кольцо [kaltso]
I'll ring you я вам позвоню [ya vam pazvanyoo]
ring back перезвонить [pyeryezvaneet]
ripe (fruit) зрелый [zryeli]
rip-off: it's a rip-off это обдираловка [eta abdeeralofka]
rip-off prices грабительские цены [grabeetyelskee-yeh tseni]
risky рискованный [reeskovan-ni]
river река [ryeka]

road дорога [dar**o**ga]
  is this the road for ...? это
  дорога до ... [eta dar**o**ga
  da ...?]
  it's just down the road это
  совсем близко отсюда [eta
  safs**y**em bl**ee**ska ats**yoo**da]
road accident дорожная
  катастрофа [dar**o**ʃna-ya
  katastr**o**fa]
road map дорожная карта
  [dar**o**ʃna-ya k**a**rta]
roadsign дорожный знак
  [dar**o**ʃni znak]
rob: I've been robbed меня
  ограбили [men**ya** agr**a**beelee]
rock скала [sk**a**la]
  (music) рок [rok]
  on the rocks (with ice) со
  льдом [sald**o**m]
roll (bread) булочка [b**oo**lachka]
Romania Румыния
  [room**i**ynee-ya]
roof крыша [kr**i**ysha]
room (in hotel) номер [n**o**myer]
  (in house) комната [k**o**mnata]
  in my room в моём номере
  [vma-**y**om n**o**myeryeh]
room service обслуживание
  в номере [apsl**oo**ʃivanee-yeh
  vn**o**myeryeh]
rope канат [kan**a**t]
rosé (wine) розовое вино
  [r**o**zava-yeh veen**o**]
roughly (approximately)
  приблизительно
  [preebleez**ee**tyelna]
round: it's my round моя
  очередь [m**a**-ya **o**chyeryet]

roundabout (for traffic)
  круговое движение
  [kroogav**o**-yeh dvee**Je**nee-yeh]
route маршрут
  [marshr**oo**t]
  what's the best route to ...?
  как лучше добраться
  до ...? [kak l**oo**chsheh dabr**a**tsa
  da ...?]
rubber (material) резина
  [ryez**ee**na]
  (eraser) ластик [l**a**steek]
rubber band резинка
  [ryez**ee**nka]
rubbish (waste) мусор [m**oo**sar]
  (poor quality goods) барахло
  [baraHl**o**]
rubbish! (nonsense) чепуха!
  [chyepoo**Ha**!]
rucksack рюкзак [ry**oo**kzak]
rude грубый [gr**oo**bi]
ruins развалины [razv**a**leeni]
rum ром [rom]
rum and Coke® кока-кола с
  ромом [k**o**ka-k**o**la sr**o**mam]
run (verb: person) бежать/
  побежать [bye**Ja**t/pabye**Ja**t]
  how often do the buses
  run? как часто ходят
  автобусы? [kak ch**a**sta H**o**dyat
  aft**o**boosi?]
  I've run out of money у меня
  кончились деньги [oo
  men**ya** k**o**ncheelees d**ye**ngee]
Russia Россия [rass**ee**-ya]
Russian (adj, man) русский
  [r**oo**skee]
  (woman) русская [r**oo**ska-ya]
  (language) русский язык

[**roo**skee ya**ziyk**]
the Russians русские
[**roo**skee-yeh]

S

sad грустный [**groo**sni]
saddle (for bike, horse) седло
[**syed**lo]
safe (not in danger) в
безопасности
[vbyezap**a**snastee]
(not dangerous) безопасный
[byezap**a**sni]
safety pin английская
булавка [angl**ee**ska-ya bool**a**fka]
sail (verb) плавать/плыть
[**pla**vat/pliyt]
sailing (sport) парусный
спорт [**pa**roosni sport]
salad салат [sal**a**t]
salad dressing заправка к
салату [za**pra**fka ksal**a**too]
salami салями f [sal**ya**mee]
sale: for sale продаётся
[prada-**yo**tsa]
salmon лосось m [las**o**s]
salt соль f [sol]
same: the same то же самое
[**to**Jeh s**a**ma-yeh]
the same as this такой же
как этот [tak**oy**Jeh kak **e**tat]
the same again, please то
же самое, пожалуйста
[**to**Jeh s**a**ma-yeh, pa**J**alsta]
it's all the same to me мне
всё равно [mnyeh fsyo ravn**o**]
sand песок [pyes**o**k]

sandals сандали [sand**a**lee]
sandwich бутерброд
[booterbr**o**t]
sanitary napkins/towels
гигиенические
прокладки [geegee-
yen**ee**chyeskee-yeh prakl**a**tkee]
Saturday суббота [soob**o**ta]
sauce соус [s**o**-oos]
saucepan кастрюля
[kastr**yoo**lya]
saucer блюдце [bl**yoo**tseh]
sauna сауна [s**a**-oona]
sausage (salami) колбаса
[kalbas**a**]
(frankfurter) сосиска
[sas**ee**ska]
say говорить/сказать
[gavar**ee**t/skaz**a**t]
how do you say ... in
Russian? как по-русски ...?
[kak pa-r**oo**skee ...?]
what did he say? что он
сказал? [shto on skaz**a**l?]
she said ... она сказала ...
[an**a** skaz**a**la ...]
could you say that again?
повторите, пожалуйста
[paftar**ee**tyeh, pa**J**alsta]
scarf (for neck) шарф [sharf]
(for head) платок [plat**o**k]
scenery пейзаж [pyayz**a**sh]
schedule (US: timetable)
расписание [raspeesan**ee**-yeh]
scheduled flight рейсовый
полёт [**ryay**savi pal**yo**t]
school школа [shk**o**la]
scissors: a pair of scissors
ножницы pl [n**o**Jneetsi]

scooter мотороллер [matarol-lyer]

scotch виски **n** [veeskee]

Scotch tape® клейкая лента [klyayka-ya lyenta]

Scotland Шотландия [shatlandee-ya]

Scottish шотландский [shatlantskee]

I'm Scottish (man/woman) я шотландец/шотландка [ya shatlandyets/shatlantka]

scrambled eggs яичница-болтунья [ya-eeshneetsa-baltoonya]

scratch (noun) царапина [tsarapeena]

screw (noun) винт [veent]

screwdriver отвёртка [atvyortka]

sea море [moryeh]

by the sea у моря [oo morya]

seafood морские продукты [marskee-yeh pradookti]

search (verb) искать [eeskat]

seasick: I feel seasick меня укачало [menya ookachala]

I get seasick меня укачивает [menya ookacheeva-yet]

seaside: by the seaside на море [na moryeh]

seat место [myesta]

is this seat taken? это место свободно? [eta myesta svabodna?]

seat belt ремень **m** [ryemyen]

secluded уединённый [oo-yedeenyon-ni]

second (adj) второй [ftaroy]

(in time) секунда [syekoonda]

just a second! секундочку! [syekoondachkoo!]

second class (travel etc) второй класс [ftaroy klas]

second floor третий этаж [tryetee etash]

(US) второй этаж [ftaroy etash]

second-hand подержанный [padyerJan-ni]

second-hand bookshop букинистический магазин [bookeeneesteechyeskee magazeen]

see видеть/увидеть [veedyet/ooveedyet]

can I see? можно посмотреть? [moJna pasmatryet?]

have you seen ...? вы не видели ...? [viy nyeh veedyelee ...?]

I saw him this morning (said by man/woman) я видел/видела его сегодня утром [ya veedyel/veedyela yevo syevodnya ootram]

see you! пока! [paka!]

I see (I understand) понятно [panyatna]

self-service самообслуживание [sama-apslooJivanee-yeh]

sell продавать/продать [pradavat/pradat]

do you sell ...? у вас продаётся ...? [oo vas prada-**yo**tsa ...?]

Sellotape® клейкая лента [kl**yay**ka-ya l**ye**nta]

send посылать/послать [pasi**lat**/pas**lat**]

I want to send this to England я хочу послать это в Англию [ya нa**choo** pas**lat** eta **van**glee-yoo]

senior citizen (man/woman) пожилой человек/ пожилая женщина [paji**loy** chyela**vyek**/paji**la**-ya **j**ensh-cheena]

separate (adj) отдельный [ad-**dyel**ni]

separated: we're separated мы разошлись [miy razash**lees**]

separately (pay, travel) отдельно [ad-**dyel**na]

September сентябрь m [syent**yabr**]

septic септический [syept**ee**chyeskee]

serious серьёзный [syer**yoz**ni] (illness) опасный [a**pas**ni]

service charge плата за обслуживание [**pl**ata za apsl**oo**jivanee-yeh]

service station (for repairs) станция техобслуживания [st**a**ntsi-ya tyeнapsl**oo**jivanee-ya] (for petrol) бензоколонка [byenzaka**lon**ka]

serviette салфетка [salf**ye**tka]

set menu комплексный обед [**k**omplyeksni ab**yet**]

several несколько [**nye**skolka]

sew шить/сшить [shiyt/s-shiyt]

could you sew this back on? вы не могли бы пришить это [viy nyeh magl**ee**bi preesh**iyt** et**a**]

sex секс [seks]

sexy привлекательный [preevlyeka**tyel**ni]

shade: in the shade в тени [ftyen**ee**]

shake: to shake hands пожимать/пожать руку [paji**mat**/pa**jat** r**oo**koo]

shallow мелкий [**myel**kee]

shame: what a shame! как жаль! [kak **J**al!]

shampoo шампунь m [sham**poon**]

shampoo and set мытьё и укладка волос [mit**yo** ee ookl**a**tka val**os**]

share: to share a room жить в одной комнате [jiyt vadn**oy** k**om**natyeh]

to share a table сидеть за одним столом [seed**yet** za adn**eem** stal**om**]

sharp острый [**os**tri]

shattered: I'm shattered я совершенно без сил [ya savyersh**en**-na byes seel]

shaver бритва [**bree**tva]

shaving foam пена для бритья [**pye**na dlya breet**ya**]

shaving point розетка для

электробритвы [razyetka
dlya elyektrabreetvi]
shawl шаль **f** [shal]
she* она [ana]
  is she here? она здесь? [ana
  zdyes?]
sheet (for bed) простыня
[prastinya]
shelf полка [polka]
shellfish моллюск [malyoosk]
sherry херес [Hyeryes]
ship корабль **m** [karabl]
  by ship на корабле [na
  karablyeh]
shirt рубашка [roobashka]
shit! чёрт! [chort!]
shock шок [shok]
  I got an electric shock меня
  ударило током [menya
  oodareela tokom]
shocking ужасный [ooJasni]
shoe (man's/woman's) ботинок/
туфля [bateenak/tooflya]
  a pair of shoes ботинки/
  туфли [bateenkee/tooflee]
shoelaces шнурки
[shnoorkee]
shoe polish крем для обуви
[kryem dlya oboovee]
shoe repairer's мастерская
по ремонту обуви
[mastyerska-ya pa ryemontoo
oboovee]
shop магазин [magazeen]
shopping: I'm going shopping
я иду за покупками [ya
eedoo za pakoopkamee]
shopping centre торговый
центр [targovi tsentr]

shop window витрина
[veetreena]
shore берег [byeryek]
short (person) невысокий
[nyevisokee]
  (time, journey) короткий
  [karotkee]
shortcut кратчайший путь
[kratchIshi poot]
shorts шорты [shorti]
should: what should I do?
что мне делать? [shto mnyeh
dyelat?]
  you should ... вам
  следует ... [vam slyedoo-yet ...]
  you shouldn't ... вам не
  следует ... [vam nyeh slyedoo-
  yet ...]
  he should be back soon он
  должен скоро вернутся
  [on dolJen skora vyernootsa]
shoulder плечо [plyecho]
shout (verb) кричать/
крикнуть [kreechat/kreeknoot]
show (in theatre)
представление
[pryetstavlyenee-yeh]
  could you show me?
  покажите, пожалуйста
  [pakaJiytyeh, paJalsta]
shower (of rain) ливень **m**
[leevyen]
  (in bathroom) душ [doosh]
  with shower с душем
  [sdooshem]
shower gel гель для душа **m**
[gyel dlya doosha]
shut (verb) закрывать/
закрыть [zakrivat/zakriyt]

when do you shut? когда вы закрываетесь? [kagda viy zakriva-yetyes?]

they're shut они закрыты [anee zakriyti]

I've shut myself out я не могу попасть внутрь [ya nyeh magoo papast vnootr]

shut up! замолчите! [zamalcheetyeh!]

shutter (on camera) затвор [zatvor]

(on window) ставень m [stavyen]

shy застенчивый [zastyencheevi]

sick (ill) больной [balnoy]

I'm going to be sick (vomit) меня сейчас стошнит [myenya syechas stashneet]

I feel sick меня тошнит [menya tashneet]

side сторона [starana]

on the other side of the street на другой стороне улицы [na droogoy staranyeh ooleetsi]

side lights подфарники [patfarneekee]

side street переулок [pyeryeh-oolak]

sidewalk тротуар [tratoo-ar]

on the sidewalk на тротуаре [na tratoo-aryeh]

sight: the sights of ... достопримечательности ... [dastapreemyechatyelnastee ...]

sightseeing: we're going sightseeing мы идём осматривать

достопримечательности [miy eedyom asmatreevat dastapreemyechatyelnastee]

sightseeing tour экскурсия [ekskoorseeya]

sign (roadsign etc) знак [znak]

signature подпись f [potpees]

signpost указатель m [ookazatyel]

silence тишина [teeshina]

silk шёлк [sholk]

silly глупый [gloopi]

silver серебро [syeryebro]

similar похожий [pahoJi]

simple (easy) простой [prastoy]

since: since last week с прошлой недели [sproshli nyedyelee]

since I got here (said by man/woman) с тех пор, как я приехал/приехала [styeн por, kak ya pree-yeHal/pree-yeHala]

sing петь/спеть [pyet/spyet]

singer (man/woman) певец/певица [pyevyets/pyeveeetsa]

single: a single to ... билет в один конец до ... [beelyet vadeen kanyets da ...]

I'm single (said by man/woman) я не женат/замужем [ya nyeh Jenat/zamooJem]

single bed односпальная кровать [adnaspalna-ya kravat]

single room одноместный номер [adnamyesni nomyer]

single ticket билет в один конец [beelyet vadeen kanyets]

sink (in kitchen) раковина [**ra**kaveena]

sister сестра [syest**ra**]

sister-in-law (wife's sister) своячениица [sva-**ya**chyeneetsa] (husband's sister) золовка [za**lo**fka]

sit: can I sit here? можно здесь сесть? [**mo**Jna zdyes syest?]

is anyone sitting here? здесь кто-нибудь сидит? [zdyes kto-neeboot seed**ee**t?]

sit down садится/сесть [sad**ee**tsa/syest]

please, sit down садитесь, пожалуйста [sad**ee**tyes, paJalsta]

size размер [razm**yer**]

skate (verb) кататься на коньках [ka**ta**tsa na kank**a**H]

skates коньки [kank**ee**]

skating rink каток [ka**tok**]

ski (verb) кататься на лыжах [ka**ta**tsa na **liy**JaH]

skin кожа [**ko**Ja]

skinny тощий [**tosh**-chee]

skirt юбка [**yoo**pka]

skis лыжи [**liy**Ji]

sky небо [**nye**ba]

sleep (verb) спать/поспать [spat/paspat]

did you sleep well? вам хорошо спалось? [vam Harash**o** spal**os**?]

sleeper (on train) спальный вагон [**spa**lni vag**on**]

sleeping bag спальный

мешок [**spa**lni myesh**ok**]

sleeping car спальный вагон [**spa**lni vag**on**]

sleeping pills снотворные таблетки [snatv**o**rni-yeh tabl**yet**kee]

sleepy: I'm feeling sleepy меня клонит ко сну [myen**ya** kl**o**neet ka snoo]

sleeve рукав [**roo**kaf]

slide (photographic) слайд [slId]

slippers тапочки [**ta**pachkee]

slippery скользкий [**skol**skee]

Slovakia Словакия [slav**a**kee-ya]

slow медленный [**mye**dlyen-ni]

slow down! помедленнее, пожалуйста [pam**ye**dleen-nyeh-yeh, paJalsta]

slowly медленно [**mye**dlyen-na]

very slowly очень медленно [**o**chyen m**ye**dlyen-na]

could you speak more slowly? вы не могли бы говорить помедленнее? [viy nyeh mag**lee**bi gavar**ee**t pam**ye**dleenyeh-yeh?]

small маленький [**ma**lyenkee]

smell: it smells (smells bad) плохо пахнет [pl**o**Ha pa**H**nyet]

smile (verb) улыбаться/ улыбнуться [**oo**lib**a**tsa/ oolibn**oo**tsa]

smoke (noun) дым [diym]

do you mind if I smoke? вы не возражаете, если я

закурю? [viy nyeh vazraJa-
yetyeh, **yes**lee ya zakoor**yoo**?]

I don't smoke я не курю [ya
nyeh koor**yoo**]

do you smoke? вы курите?
[viy **koo**reetyeh?]

snack: I'd just like a snack
(said by man/woman) я хотел/
хотела бы слегка
перекусить [ya hat**yel**/hat**yel**a
biy sl**yeH**ka pyeryekoos**eet**]

sneeze (verb) чихать/
чихнуть [cheeH**at**/cheeH**noot**]

snorkel дыхательная
трубка [diH**at**yelna-ya tr**oo**pka]

snow снег [snyek]

it's snowing снег идёт [snyek
eed**yot**]

snowstorm метель **f** [myet**yel**]

so так [tak]

this wine is so good очень
хорошее вино [**o**chyen
Har**o**sheh-ye veen**o**]

it's so expensive это так
дорого [**e**ta tak d**o**raga]

not so much не так много
[nyeh tak mn**o**ga]

not so bad не так уж плохо
[nyeh tak oosh pl**o**Ha]

so am I, so do I я тоже [ya
t**o**Jeh]

so-so так себе [tak seeb**yeh**]

soaking solution (for contact
lenses) раствор для линз
[rastv**o**r dlya leenz]

soap мыло [**miy**la]

soap powder стиральный
порошок [steer**al**ni parash**o**k]

sober трезвый [tr**ye**zvi]

sock носок [nas**o**k]

socket (electrical) розетка
[raz**ye**tka]

soda (water) газированная
вода [gazeer**o**van-na-ya vad**a**]

sofa диван [deev**a**n]

soft (material etc) мягкий
[**mya**Hkee]

soft-boiled egg яйцо
всмятку [yits**o** fsm**ya**tkoo]

soft drink безалкогольный
напиток [byezalkag**o**lni
nap**ee**tak]

soft lenses мягкие линзы
[**mya**Hkee-yeh **lee**nzi]

soldier солдат [sald**a**t]

sole (of foot) ступня [stoopn**ya**]
(of shoe) подошва [pad**o**shva]

**could you put new soles on
these?** вы не могли бы
поставить сюда новые
подмётки? [viy nyeh magl**ee**bi
past**a**veet syood**a** n**o**vi-yeh
padm**yo**tkee?]

some: can I have some?
дайте мне, пожалуйста
[**di**tyeh mnyeh, paJ**a**lsta]

**can I have some water/
bread?** дайте мне,
пожалуйста воды/хлеба
[**di**tyeh mnyeh, paJ**a**lsta, vad**iy**/
Hl**ye**ba]

somebody, someone кто-то
[kt**o**-ta]

something что-нибудь [sht**o**-
neeb**oo**t]

something to eat что-
нибудь поесть [sht**o**-neeboot
pa-**ye**st]

sometimes иногда [eenagda]
somewhere где-нибудь [gdyeh-neeboot]
son сын [siyn]
song песня [pyesnya]
son-in-law зять [zyat]
soon скоро [skora]
  I'll be back soon я скоро вернусь [ya skora vyernoos]
  as soon as possible как можно скорее [kak moJna skaryeh-yeh]
sore: it's sore болит [baleet]
sore throat: I've got a sore throat у меня болит горло [oo myenya baleet gorla]
sorry: I'm sorry прошу прощения [prashoo prash-chyenee-ya]
  sorry! извините! [eezveeneetyeh!]
  sorry? (didn't understand) простите? [prasteet-yeh?]
sort: what sort of ...? какой ...? [kakoy ...?]
  this sort такой [takoy]
soup суп [soop]
sour (taste) кислый [keesli]
soured cream сметана [smyetana]
south юг [yook]
  in the south на юге [na yoogyeh]
South Africa Южная Африка [yooJna-ya afreeka]
South African (adj) южно-африканский [yooJna-afreekanskee]
  I'm South African я из Южной Африки [ya eez yooJni afreekee]
southeast юго-восточный [yooga-vastochni]
southern южный [yooJni]
southwest юго-западный [yooga-zapadni]
souvenir сувенир [soovyeneer]
Soviet советский [savyetskee]
Soviet Union Советский Союз [savyetskee sa-yoos]
spade лопата [lapata]
Spain Испания [eespanee-ya]
Spanish (adj) испанский [eespanskee]
spanner гаечный ключ [ga-yechni klyooch]
spare part запчасть f [zapchast]
spares запчасти [zapchastee]
spare tyre запасная шина [zapasna-ya shiyna]
speak: do you speak English? вы говорите по-английски? [viy gavareetyeh pa-angleeskee?]
  I don't speak Russian я не говорю по-русски [ya nyeh gavaryoo pa-rooskee]

dialogue

  can I speak to Nikolai? можно Николая, пожалуйста? [moJna neekala-ya, paJalsta?]
  who's calling? кто говорит? [kto gavareet?]
  it's Patricia это Патриша

[eta patreesha]
I'm sorry, he's not in,
can I take a message?
извините, его нет, вы
хотите что-нибудь
передать? [eezveeneetyeh,
yevo nyet, viy Hateetyeh shto-
neeboot pyeryedat?]
no thanks, I'll call back
later нет, спасибо, я
перезвоню попозже
[nyet, spaseeba, ya
pyeryezvanyoo papoJ-Jeh]
please tell him I called
пожалуйста, передайте
ему, что я звонила
[paJalsta, pyeryedıtyeh yemoo,
shto ya zvaneela]

spectacles очки [achkee]
speed (noun) скорость **f**
[skorast]
speed limit максимальная
скорость [makseemalna-ya
skorast]
spell: how do you spell it? как
это пишется по буквам?
[kak eta peeshetsa pa bookvam?]
see alphabet
spend тратить/потратить
[trateet/patrateet]
spider паук [pa-ook]
spin-dryer центробежная
сушилка [tsentrabyeJna-ya
sooshiylka]
spoon ложка [loshka]
sport спорт [sport]
sprain: I've sprained my ...
(said by man/woman) я

растянул/растянула ... [ya
rastyanool/rastyanoola ...]
spring (of car, seat) рессора
[ryes-sora]
(season) весна [vyesna]
in the spring весной
[vyesnoy]
square (in town) площадь **f**
[plosh-chat]
stairs лестница [lyesneetsa]
stale несвежий [nyesvyeJi]
stalls партер [parter]
stamp (noun) марка [marka]

dialogue

how much is a stamp for
England? сколько стоит
марка для Англии?
[skolka sto-eet marka dlya
anglee-ee?]
what are you sending? что
вы посылаете [shto viy
pasila-yetyeh?]
this postcard эту
открытку [etoo atkriytkoo]

star звезда [zvyezda]
start (noun) начало [nachala]
(verb) начинать/начать
[nacheenat/nachat]
when does it start? когда
начало? [kagda nachala?]
my car won't start моя
машина не заводится [ma-
ya mashiyna nyeh
zavodeetsa]
starter (food) закуска
[zakooska]

starving: I'm starving я
умираю от голода [ya
oomeera-yoo at golada]

state (country) государство
[gasoodarstva]

(adj) государственный
[gasoodarstvyen-ni]

the States штаты [shtati]

station (rail) вокзал [vakzal]
(underground, bus) станция
[stantsi-ya]

stationery канцелярские
принадлежности
[kantselyarskee-yeh
preenadlyeJnastee]

statue статуя [statoo-ya]

stay: where are you staying?
где вы остановились?
[gdyeh viy astanaveelees?]

I'm staying at ... (said by man/
woman) я остановился/
остановилась в ... [ya
astanaveelsa/astanaveelas v ...]

I'd like to stay another two
nights (said by man/woman) я
бы хотел/хотела остаться
ещё на пару суток [yabi
Hatyel/Hatyela astatsa yesh-cho na
paroo sootak]

steak бифштекс [beefshteks]

steal красть/украсть [krast/
ookrast]

my bag has been stolen у
меня украли сумку [oo
menya ookralee soomkoo]

steep (hill) крутой [krootoy]

step: on the steps на
ступеньках [na stoopyenkaн]

stereo стерео [styereh-o]

sterling фунт стерлингов
[foont styerleengaf]

steward (on plane) стюард
[styoo-art]

stewardess стюардесса
[styoo-ardes-sa]

still: I'm still here я ещё здесь
[ya yesh-cho zdyes]

is he still there? он ещё
здесь? [on yesh-cho zdyes?]

keep still! не двигайтесь!
[nyeh dveegityes!]

sting: I've been stung by a
wasp меня укусила оса
[menya ookooseela asa]

stockings чулки [choolkee]

stomach желудок [Jeloodak]

stomach ache: I have stomach
ache у меня болит живот
[oo menya baleet Jivot]

stone (rock) камень m
[kamyen]

stop (verb) останавливать/
остановить [astanavleevat/
astanaveet]

stop here, please (to taxi
driver etc) пожалуйста,
остановитесь здесь
[paJalsta, astanaveetyes zdyes]

do you stop near ...? вы
останавливаетесь у ...? [viy
astanavleeva-yetyes oo ...?]

stop it! прекратите!
[pryekrateetyeh!]

stopover остановка (в
пути) [astanofka (fpootee)]

storm буря [boorya]

St Petersburg Санкт-
Петербург [sankt-

peetyerb**oork**]
straight прямой [pryam**oy**]
(whisky etc) неразбавленный
[nyerazbavlyen-ni]
it's straight ahead это
прямо [eta pry**a**ma]
straightaway немедленно
[nyem**ye**dlyen-na]
strange (odd) странный
[str**a**n-ni]
stranger (man/woman)
незнакомец/незнакомка
[nyeznak**o**myets/nyeznak**o**mka]
I'm a stranger here (said by
man/woman) я здесь чужой/
чужая [ya zdyes chooJ**oy**/
chooJ**a**-ya]
strap (on watch, suitcase)
ремешок [ryemyesh**o**k]
(on dress) бретелька
[bryet**e**lka]
strawberry клубника
[kloobn**ee**ka]
stream ручей m [rooch**ay**]
street улица [**oo**leetsa]
on the street на улице [na
ooleetseh]
streetmap план города [plan
g**o**rada]
string верёвка [vyery**o**fka]
strong (person, material, taste)
сильный [**see**lni]
(drink) крепкий [kr**ye**pkee]
stuck: it's stuck застряло
[zastr**ya**la]
student (male/female) студент/
студентка [stood**ye**nt/
stood**ye**ntka]
stupid глупый [gl**oo**pi]

suburb пригород [pr**ee**garat]
subway подземный
переход [padz**ye**mni pyerye**н**ot]
(US: underground) метро
[myetr**o**]
suede замша [z**a**msha]
sugar сахар [s**a**нar]
suit (noun) костюм [kast**yoo**m]
it doesn't suit me (jacket etc)
мне это не идёт [mnyeh eta
nyeh eedy**o**t]
it suits you вам это идёт
[vam eta eedy**o**t]
suitcase чемодан [chyemad**a**n]
summer лето [l**ye**ta]
in the summer летом [l**ye**tam]
sun солнце [s**o**ntseh]
in the sun на солнце [na
s**o**ntseh]
out of the sun в тени
[vtyen**ee**]
sunbathe загорать [zagar**a**t]
sunblock средство против
загара [sr**ye**tstva pr**o**teef zag**a**ra]
sunburn солнечный ожог
[s**o**lnyechni aJ**o**k]
sunburnt (burnt) обгорелый
[abgar**ye**li]
Sunday воскресенье
[vaskryes**ye**nyeh]
sunglasses очки от солнца
[achk**ee** at s**o**ntsa]
sunny: it's sunny солнечно
[s**o**lnyechna]
sunset закат [zak**a**t]
sunshade зонтик от солнца
[z**o**nteek at s**o**ntsa]
sunshine солнечный свет
[s**o**lnyechni svyet]

sunstroke солнечный удар
[**so**lnyechni oo**dar**]

suntan загар [za**gar**]

suntan lotion лосьон для
загара [las**yon** dlya za**gar**a]

suntanned загорелый
[zagar**ye**li]

suntan oil масло для загара
[**mas**la dlya za**gar**a]

super замечательный
[zamyecha**tye**lni]

supermarket универсам
[ooneev**yer**sam], супермаркет
[soopyer**mar**kyet]

supper ужин [**oo**Jin]

supplement (extra charge)
доплата [dap**la**ta]

sure: are you sure? вы
уверены? [viy oov**ye**ryeni?]

I'm sure (said by man/woman)
я уверен/уверена [ya
oov**ye**ryen/oov**ye**ryena]

sure! конечно! [kan**ye**shna!]

surname фамилия [fa**mee**lee-
ya]

sweater свитер [**svee**ter]

sweatshirt спортивная
майка [spart**ee**vna-ya m**i**ka]

Sweden Швеция [shv**ye**tsi-ya]

Swedish (adj) шведский
[shv**ye**tskee]

sweet (taste) сладкий [**sla**tkee]
(noun: dessert) десерт
[dyes**ye**rt]

sweets конфеты [kanf**ye**ti]

swelling опухоль f [**o**poonal]

swim (verb) плавать/
поплавать [**pla**vat/pap**la**vat]

I'm going for a swim я иду

плавать [ya eed**oo** pl**a**vat]

let's go for a swim пойдём
поплаваем [pid**yo**m papl**a**va-
yem]

swimming costume
купальник [koop**al**neek]

swimming pool бассейн
[bas**ya**yn]

swimming trunks плавки
[**plaf**kee]

Swiss швейцарский
[shv**ye**tsarskee]

switch (noun) выключатель
m [viklyooch**a**tyel]

switch off выключать/
выключить [viklyooch**at**/
v**i**yklyoocheet]

switch on включать/
включить [fklyooch**at**/
fklyooch**ee**t]

Switzerland Швейцария
[shv**ye**tsaree-ya]

swollen распухший
[rasp**oo**Hshi]

T

table стол [stol]

a table for two столик на
двоих [st**o**leek na dva-**ee**H]

tablecloth скатерть f [sk**a**tyert]

table tennis настольный
теннис [nast**o**lni ten**ee**s]

table wine столовое вино
[stal**o**va-yeh veen**o**]

tailor портной [partn**oy**]

take (verb: lead) брать/взять
[brat/vzyat]

(accept) принимать/
принять [preeneemat/preenyat]
can you take me to the ...?
вы можете отвезти меня
в ...? [viy moJetyeh atvyestee
menya v ...?]
do you take credit cards? вы
принимаете кредитные
карточки? [viy
preeneema-yetyeh kryedeetni-yeh
kartachkee?]
fine, I'll take it хорошо,
я возьму это [Harasho, ya
vazmoo eta]
can I take this? (leaflet etc)
можно это взять? [moJna
eta vzyat?]
how long does it take?
сколько времени это
займёт? [skolka vryemyenee eta
zimyot?]
it takes three hours это
займёт три часа [eta zimyot
tree chasa]
is this seat taken? это
место свободно? [eta myesta
svabodna?]
hamburger to take away
гамбургер на вынос
[gamboorgyer na viynas]
can you take a little off here?
(to hairdresser) вы можете
немного подстричь здесь
[viy moJetyeh nyemnoga patstreech
zdyes?]
talcum powder тальк [tallk]
talk (verb) говорить/
поговорить [gavareet/
pagavareet]

tall высокий [visokee]
tampons тампоны [tamponi]
tan загар [zagar]
  to get a tan загореть
  [zagaryet]
tap кран [kran]
tape measure рулетка
  [roolyetka]
tape recorder магнитофон
  [magneetafon]
taste (noun) вкус [fkoos]
  can I taste it? можно
  попробовать? [moJna
  paprobavat?]
taxi такси n [taksee]
  will you get me a taxi?
  вызовите для меня такси,
  пожалуйста [viyzaveetyeh dlya
  myenya taksee, paJalsta]
  where can I find a taxi? где
  можно поймать такси?
  [gdyeh moJna pimat taksee?]

dialogue

> **to the airport/to the ...**
> **Hotel, please** в аэропорт/
> в гостиницу ...,
> пожалуйста [va-eraport/
> vgasteeneetsoo ..., paJalsta]
> **how much will it be?**
> сколько это будет
> стоить? [skolka eta boodyet
> sto-eet?]
> **60,000 roubles**
> шестьдесят тысяч
> рублей [shezdyesyat tiysyach
> rooblyay]
> **that's fine right here thanks**

я выйду здесь, спасибо [ya **viy**doo zdyes, spas**ee**ba]

taxi driver таксист [taks**ee**st]

taxi rank стоянка такси [sta-**ya**nka taks**ee**]

tea (drink) чай **m** [chɪ]

one tea/two teas, please один чай/два чая, пожалуйста [ad**ee**n chɪ/dva cha-ya, paJ**a**lsta]

tea with milk чай с молоком [chɪ smalak**o**m]

tea with lemon чай с лимоном [chɪ sleem**o**nam]

teabags чайные пакетики [ch**ɪ**ni-yeh pak**ye**teekee]

teach: could you teach me? вы могли бы меня научить ...? [viy magl**ee**bi men**ya** na-ooch**ee**t ...?]

teacher (man/woman) учитель/ учительница [ooch**ee**tyel/ ooch**ee**telneetsa]

team команда [kam**a**nda]

teaspoon чайная ложка [ch**ɪ**na-ya l**o**shka]

tea towel чайное полотенце [ch**ɪ**na-yeh palat**ye**ntseh]

teenager подросток [padr**o**stak]

telephone телефон [tyelyef**o**n]

see phone

television (set) телевизор [tyelyev**ee**zar]

(medium) телевидение [tyelyev**ee**dyenyeh]

tell: could you tell him ...? скажите ему, пожалуйста ... [skaJ**iy**tyeh yemoo, paJ**a**lsta ...]

could you tell me where ...? вы не скажете, где ...? [viy nyeh skaJ**i**tyeh, gdyeh ...?]

temperature (weather) температура [tyempyerat**oo**ra]

tennis теннис [t**e**n-nees]

tent палатка [pal**a**tka]

term (at university, school) семестр [syem**ye**str]

terminus (rail, underground) конечная станция [kan**ye**chna-ya st**a**ntsi-ya] (bus, tram) конечная остановка [kan**ye**chna-ya astan**o**fka]

terrible ужасный [ooJ**a**sni]

terrific замечательный [zamyech**a**tyelni]

text (message) смс [es-em-es]

than* чем [chyem]

smaller than ... меньше, чем ... [**my**ensheh, chyem ...]

thank: thank you/thanks спасибо [spas**ee**ba]

thank you very much большое спасибо [balsh**o**-yeh spas**ee**ba]

thanks for the lift спасибо, что подвезли [spas**ee**ba, shto padvyezl**ee**]

no, thanks нет, спасибо [nyet, spas**ee**ba]

dialogue

thanks спасибо [spas**ee**ba]
that's OK, don't mention it
не за что [**nye**zashto]

that* тот **m** [tot], та **f** [ta], то
n [to]
that boy тот мальчик [tot
m**a**lcheek]
that girl та девочка [ta
d**ye**vachka]
that one тот **m** [tot], та **f** [ta],
то **n** [to]
I hope that ... я надеюсь,
что ... [ya nad**yeh**-yoos, shto ...]
that's great отлично
[atl**ee**chna]
is that ...? это ...? [**eta** ...?]
that's it (that's right) точно
[**to**chna]
thaw (noun) оттепель **f** [**ot**-
tyepyel]
the*
theatre театр [tyeh-**a**tr]
their*/theirs* их [eeн]
them*: I'll tell them я им
скажу [ya eem ska**Joo**]
I know them я их знаю [ya
eeн zn**a**-yoo]
for them для них [dlya neeн]
with them с ними [sn**ee**mee]
to them им [eem]
who? -- them кто? – они
[kto? - an**ee**]
then (at that time) тогда [tagd**a**]
(after that) потом [pat**om**]
there там [tam]
over there вон там [von tam]

up there там, наверху [tam,
navyerн**oo**]
is there/are there ...? есть
ли ...? [**ye**stlee ...?]
there you are (giving something)
вот, пожалуйста [vot,
pa**J**alsta]
thermometer термометр
[tyerm**o**myetr]
Thermos® flask термос
[**te**rmas]
these* эти [**e**tee]
I'd like these (said by man/
woman) я бы хотел/хотела
вот эти [**ya**bi нat**ye**l/нat**ye**la vot
etee]
they* они [an**ee**]
thick густой [goost**oy**]
(stupid) тупой [toop**oy**]
thief (man/woman) вор/
воровка [vor/var**o**fka]
thigh бедро [byedr**o**]
thin (person) худой [нood**oy**]
(thing) тонкий [**to**nkee]
thing вещь **f** [vyesh-ch]
my things мои вещи [ma-**ee**
v**ye**sh-chee]
think думать/подумать
[d**oo**mat/pad**oo**mat]
I think so думаю, да [d**oo**ma-
yoo, da]
I don't think so я так не
думаю [ya tak nyeh
d**oo**ma-yoo]
I'll think about it я подумаю
об этом [ya pad**oo**ma-yoo ab
etam]
third третий [tr**ye**tee]
thirsty: I'm thirsty мне

Th

хочется пить [mnyeh нochyetsa peet]

this* этот **m** [etat], эта **f** [eta], это **n** [eto]

this boy этот мальчик [etat malcheek]

this girl эта девочка [eta dyevachka]

this one этот **m** [etat], эта **f** [eta], это **n** [eta]

this is my wife это моя жена [eta ma-ya Jena]

is this ...? это ...? [eta ...?]

those* те [tyeh]

which ones? – those какие? – те [kakee-yeh? – tyeh]

thread (noun) нитка [neetka]

throat горло [gorla]

throat pastilles пастилки для горла [pasteelkee dlya gorla]

through через [chyeryes]

does it go through ...? (train, bus) он проезжает через ...? [on pra-yeJ-Ja-yet chyeryes ...?]

throw бросать/бросить [brasat/broseet]

throw away выбрасывать/ выбросить [vibrasivat/ viybraseet]

thumb большой палец [balshoy palyets]

thunderstorm гроза [graza]

Thursday четверг [chyetvyerk]

ticket билет [beelyet]
(for bus) талон [talon]

dialogue

a return to Sergiev Posad обратный билет до сергиева посада [abratni beelyet da syergee-yeva pasada]

coming back when? когда обратно? [kagda abratna?]

today/next Tuesday сегодня/в следующий вторник [syevodnya/ fslyedoosh-chee ftorneek]

that will be 10,000 roubles (это будет) десять тысяч рублей [(eta boodyet) dyesyat tiysyach rooblyay]

ticket office билетная касса [beelyetna-ya kas-sa]

ticket punch компостер [kampostyer]

tie (necktie) галстук [galstook]

tight (clothes etc) тесный [tyesni]

it's too tight тесновато [tyesnavata]

tights колготки [kalgotkee]

till касса [kas-sa]

time* время [vryemya]

what's the time? который час? [katori chas?]

this time в этот раз [vetat ras]

last time в прошлый раз [fproshli ras]

next time в следующий раз [fslyedoosh-chee ras]

127

three times три раза [tree raza]

timetable расписание [raspeesanee-yeh]

tin (can) консервная банка [kanservna-ya banka]

tinfoil оловянная фольга [alavyan-na-ya falga]

tin-opener консервный нож [kanservni nosh]

tiny крошечный [kroshechni]

tip (to waiter etc) чаевые pl [cha-yeviy-yeh]

tired усталый [oostali]

I'm tired (said by man/woman) я устал/устала [ya oostal/oostala]

tissues бумажные носовые платки [boomaJni-yeh nasaviy-yeh platkee]

to: to Moscow/London в Москву/в Лондон [vmaskvoo/vlondan]

to Russia/England в Россию/Англию [vrassee-yoo/vanglee-yoo]

to the post office на почту [na pochtoo]

toast (bread) гренок [gryenok]

tobacco табак [tabak]

today сегодня [syevodnya]

toe палец ноги [palyets nagee]

together вместе [vmyestyeh]

we're together (in shop etc) мы вместе [miy vmyestyeh]

toilet туалет [too-alyet]

where is the toilet? где туалет? [gdyeh too-alyet?]

I have to go to the toilet мне нужно в туалет [mnyeh nooJna ftoo-alyet]

toilet paper туалетная бумага [too-alyetna-ya boomaga]

token жетон [Jeton]

tomato помидор [pameedor]

tomato juice томатный сок [tamatni sok]

tomato ketchup кетчуп [kyetchoop]

tomorrow завтра [zaftra]

tomorrow morning завтра утром [zaftra ootram]

the day after tomorrow послезавтра [poslyezaftra]

toner (cosmetic) тонизирующий лосьон [taneezeeroo-yoosh-chee lasyon]

tongue язык [yaziyk]

tonic (water) тоник [toneek]

tonight сегодня вечером [syevodnya vyechyeram]

tonsillitis тонзиллит [tanzeeleet]

too (excessively) слишком [sleeshkam]

(also) тоже [toJeh]

too hot слишком жарко [sleeshkam Jarka]

too much слишком много [sleeshkam mnoga]

me too я тоже [ya toJeh]

tooth зуб [zoop]

toothache зубная боль f [zoobna-ya bol]

toothbrush зубная щётка [zoobna-ya sh-chotka]

toothpaste зубная паста
[zoobna-ya pasta]

top: on top of ... на ... [na ...]

at the top наверху
[navyerнoo]

top floor верхний этаж
[vyerнnee etash]

topless с обнажённой
грудью [sabnaJon-nı groodyoo]

torch фонарик [fanareek]

total (noun) итог [eetog]

tour (noun) экскурсия
[ekskoorsee-ya]

is there a tour of ...? есть ли
экскурсия по ...? [yestlee
ekskoorsee-ya pa ...?]

tour guide (man/woman)
экскурсовод [ekskoorsavot]

tourist (man/woman) турист/
туристка [tooreest/tooreestka]

tour operator бюро
путешествий [byooro
pootyeshestvee]

towards к [k]

towel полотенце
[palatyentseh]

town город [gorat]

in town в городе [vgoradyeh]

just out of town за городом
[zagaradam]

town centre центр города
[tsentr gorada]

town hall мэрия [meree-ya]

toy игрушка [eegrooshka]

track (US: platform) платформа
[platforma]

tracksuit тренировочный
костюм [tryeneerovachni
kastyoom]

traditional традиционный
[tradeetsi-on-ni]

traffic движение [dveeJenee-
yeh]

traffic jam пробка [propka]

traffic lights светофор
[svyetafor]

train поезд [po-yest]

by train поездом [po-yezdam]

dialogue

is this the train for Ufa?
это поезд до Уфы? [eta
po-yest da oofiy?]
sure да [da]
**no, you want that platform
there** нет, вам нужна
та платформа [nyet, vam
nooJna ta platforma]

trainers (shoes) кроссовки
[krasofkee]

train station
железнодорожная
станция [JelyeznadaroJna-ya
stantsi-ya]

tram трамвай **m** [tramvı]

translate переводить/
перевести [pyeryevadeet/
pyeryeh-vyestee]

**would you translate
that?** переведите это,
пожалуйста [pyeryeh-
vyedeetyeh eta, paJalsta]

translator (man/woman)
переводчик/переводчица
[pyeryevotcheek/pyeryevotcheetsa]

trash мусор [moosar]

trash can мусорное ведро [**moo**sarna-yeh vyed**ro**]

travel путешествовать [pootyeshestvavat]

we're travelling around мы путешествуем [miy pootyesh**estvoo**-yem]

travel agent's бюро путешествий [byoo**ro** pootyesh**estvee**]

traveller's cheque дорожный чек [dar**o**Jni chyek]

tray поднос [padn**os**]

tree дерево [d**ye**ryeva]

tremendous (large) огромный [agr**o**mni]
(splendid) замечательный [zamyech**a**tyelni]

trendy модный [**mo**dni]

trim: just a trim please (to hairdresser) немного подровняйте, пожалуйста [n**ye**mn**o**ga padravn**y**Ityeh, paJ**a**lsta]

trip (excursion) экскурсия [eksk**oo**rsee-ya]
I'd like to go on a trip to ... я хочу съездить в ...[ya Hach**oo** s**ye**zdeet v ...]

trolley тележка [tyel**ye**shka]

trolley bus троллейбус [tral**yay**boos]

trouble неприятность [nyepree-**ya**tnast]
I'm having trouble with ... у меня проблемы с ... [oo men**ya** prabl**ye**mi s ...]

trousers брюки [br**yoo**kee]

true верно [v**ye**rna]

that's not true это неправда [**e**ta nyepr**a**vda]

trunk (US: of car) багажник [bag**a**Jneek]

trunks (swimming) плавки [pl**a**fkee]

try (verb) пробовать/ попробовать [pr**o**bavat/ papr**o**bavat]
can I try it? можно я попробую [m**o**Jna ya papr**o**boo-yoo]

try on мерить/померить [m**ye**reet/pam**ye**reet]
can I try it on? можно померить? [m**o**Jna pam**ye**reet?]

T-shirt футболка [footb**o**lka]

Tuesday вторник [ft**o**rneek]

tuna тунец [toon**ye**ts]

tunnel туннель **m** [toon**e**l]

turn: turn left/right повернуть налево/ направо [pavyern**oot** nal**ye**va/ napr**a**va]

turn off: where do I turn off? где мне надо свернуть? [gdyeh mnyeh n**a**da svyern**oot**?]
can you turn the heating off? вы можете выключить отопление? [viy m**o**Jetyeh v**iy**klyoocheet atapl**ye**nee-yeh?]

turn on: can you turn the heating on? вы можете включить отопление? [viy m**o**Jetyeh fklyoocheet atapl**ye**nee-yeh?]

turning (in road) поворот [pavar**ot**]

TV (set) телевизор [tyelyeveezar]
(medium) телевидение [tyelyeveedyenyeh]
tweezers пинцет [peentset]
twice дважды [dvaJdi]
  twice as much в два раза больше [vdva raza bolsheh]
twin beds две односпальные кровати [dvyeh adnaspalni-yeh kravatee]
twin room номер с двумя кроватями [nomyer sdvoomya kpavatyemee]
twist: I've twisted my ankle (said by man/woman) я подвернул/подвернула ногу [ya padvyernool/padvyernoola nogoo]
type (noun) тип [teep]
  another type of ... ... другого типа [... droogova teepa]
typical типичный [teepeechni]
tyre шина [shiyna]

U

ugly некрасивый [nyekraseevi]
UK Соединённое Королевство [sa-yedeenyon-na-yeh karalyefstva]
Ukraine Украина [ookra-eena]
Ukrainian (adj) украинский [ookra-eenskee]
ulcer язва [yazva]
umbrella зонтик [zonteek]
uncle дядя [dyadya]

uncomfortable неудобный [nyeh-oodobni]
unconscious без сознания [byes saznanee-ya]
under (in position) под [pot]
  (less than) меньше [myensheh]
underdone (meat) недожаренный [nyedaJaryen-ni]
underground (railway) метро [myetro]
underpants трусы [troosiy]
understand: I understand я понимаю [ya paneema-yoo]
  I don't understand я не понимаю [ya nyeh paneema-yoo]
  do you understand? вы понимаете? [viy paneema-yetyeh?]
unemployed безработный [byezrabotni]
unfashionable немодный [nyemodni]
United States Соединённые Штаты [sa-yedeenyon-ni-yeh shtati]
university университет [ooneevyerseetyet]
unleaded petrol неэтилированный бензин [nyeh-eteeleeeravan-ni byenzeen]
unlimited mileage неограниченный километраж [nyeh-agraneechyen-ni keelamyetrash]
unlock открывать/открыть [atkrivat/atrkriyt]

unpack распаковывать/
распаковать [raspak**o**vivat/
raspakav**a**t]

until до [do]

unusual необыкновенный
[nyeh-abiknav**y**en-ni]

up вверх [v-vyerн]

  up there там наверху [tam
  navyerн**oo**]

  he's not up yet он ещё не
  встал [on yesh-ch**o** nyeh fstal]

  what's up? в чём дело?
  [fchom d**y**ela?]

upmarket элитарный
[eleet**a**rni]

upset stomach
расстройство желудка
[rastr**o**ystva лe**loo**tka]

upside-down вверх дном [v-
vyerн dnom]

upstairs наверху [navyerн**oo**]

up-to-date современный
[savryem**y**en-ni]

urgent срочный [s**ro**chni]

us* мы [miy]

  with us с нами [sn**a**mee]

  for us для нас [dlya nas]

USA США [seh-sheh-**a**]

use (verb) пользоваться/
воспользоваться
[p**o**lzavatsa/vasp**o**lzavatsa]

  may I use your pen? можно
  воспользоваться вашей
  ручкой? [m**o**лna vasp**o**lzavatsa
  v**a**shay r**oo**chkl?]

useful полезный [pal**y**ezni]

usual обыкновенный
[abiknav**y**en-ni]

  the usual (drink etc) то, что

обычно [to, shto ab**i**ychna]

usually обычно [ab**i**ychna]

V

**vacancy: do you have any
vacancies?** у вас есть
свободные номера? [oo vas
yest svab**o**dni-yeh namyer**a**?]

vacation отпуск [**o**tpoosk]

  on vacation в отпуске
  [v**o**tpooskyeh]

vaccination прививка
[preev**ee**fka]

vacuum cleaner пылесос
[pilyes**o**s]

valid (ticket etc)
действительный
[dyaystv**ee**tyelni]

  how long is it valid for? на
  сколько времени он
  действителен? [na sk**o**lka
  vr**y**emyenee on
  dyaystv**ee**tyelyen?]

valley долина [dal**ee**na]

valuable (adj) ценный [tsen-ni]

  **can I leave my valuables
  here?** можно оставить
  здесь ценные вещи?
  [m**o**лna ast**a**veet zdyes tsen-ni-yeh
  v**y**esh-chee?]

value ценность f [tsen-nast]

van фургон [foorg**o**n]

vanilla ваниль f [van**ee**l]

  a vanilla ice cream
  ванильное мороженое
  [van**ee**lna-yeh mar**o**лena-yeh]

vase ваза [v**a**sa]

veal телятина [tyel**ya**teena]

vegetables овощи [**o**vash-chee]

vegetarian (noun: man/woman) вегетарианец/вегетарианка [vyegeetaree-**a**nyets/vyegeetaree-**a**nka]

vending machine (торговый) автомат [(targ**o**vi) aftam**a**t]

very очень [**o**chyen]

very little for me совсем чуть-чуть для меня [safs**ye**m choot-ch**o**ot dlya myen**ya**]

I like it very much мне очень нравится [mnyeh **o**chyen nr**a**veetsa]

vest (under shirt) майка [m**i**ka]

via через [ch**ye**ryes]

video (noun: film) видео [**vee**dee-o]

video recorder видеомагнитофон [**vee**dee-omagneetaf**o**n]

view вид [veet]

village деревня [dyer**ye**vnya]

vinegar уксус [**oo**ksoos]

visa виза [**vee**za]

visit (verb) посещать/посетить [pasyesh-ch**a**t/pasyet**ee**t]

I'd like to visit ... (said by man/woman) я хотел/хотела бы посетить ... [ya hat**ye**l/hat**ye**la biy pasyet**ee**t ...]

vital: it's vital that ... абсолютно необходимо, чтобы ... [apsal**yoo**tna nyeh-apHad**ee**ma, sht**o**bi ...]

vodka водка [**vo**tka]

voice голос [**go**las]

voltage напряжение [napreej**ye**nee-yeh]

vomit тошнить/стошнить [tashn**ee**t/stashn**ee**t]

W

waist талия [t**a**lee-ya]

waistcoat жилет [Jil**ye**t]

wait ждать/подождать [Jdat/padaJd**a**t]

wait for me подождите меня [padaJd**ee**tyeh men**ya**]

don't wait for me не ждите меня [nyeh Jd**ee**tyeh myen**ya**]

can I wait until my wife/my friend gets here? я могу подождать до прихода моей жены/моего друга? [ya mag**oo** padaJd**a**t da preen**o**da ma-**yay** Jen**iy**/ma-yev**o** dr**oo**ga?]

can you do it while I wait? вы можете это сделать при мне? [viy m**o**Jetyeh **e**ta zd**ye**lat pree mnyeh?]

could you wait here for me? вы можете меня здесь подождать? [viy m**o**Jetyeh myen**ya** zdyes padaJd**a**t?]

waiter официант [afeetsi-**a**nt]

waiter! официант! [afeetsi-**a**nt!]

waiting room (doctor's etc) приёмная [pree-**yo**mna-ya] (station) зал ожидания [zal aJid**a**nee-ya]

waitress официантка
[afeetsi-**a**ntka]
  waitress! девушка!
  [d**ye**vooshka!]
**wake: can you wake me
up at 5.30?** пожалуйста,
разбудите меня в
половине шестого
[pa**J**alsta, razboode**et**yeh men**ya**
fpalav**ee**nyeh shest**o**va]
  wake-up call телефонный
  будильник [tyelyef**o**n-ni
  boode**el**neek]
Wales Уэльс [oo-**el**s]
walk: is it a long walk? это
далеко пешком? [eta dalyek**o**
pyeshk**o**m?]
  it's only a short walk это в
  нескольких шагах отсюда
  [eta vn**ye**skalkeeн shaga**н**
  ats**yoo**da]
  I'll walk я пойду пешком
  [ya pid**oo** pyeshk**o**m]
  I'm going for a walk я иду
  прогуляться [ya eed**oo**
  pragool**ya**tsa]
Walkman® плейер [pl**ay**-yer]
wall стена [sty**e**na]
wallet бумажник
[boom**a**Jneek]
**wander: I like just wandering
around** я люблю бродить
[ya lyoob**lyoo** brad**ee**t]
want: I want ... я хочу ... [ya
Hach**oo** ...]
  I don't want any ... я не
  хочу ... [ya nyeh Hach**oo** ...]
  I want to go home я хочу
  пойти домой [ya Hach**oo** pitee

damoy]
  I don't want to я не хочу [ya
  nyeh Hach**oo**]
  he wants to ... он хочет ...
  [on H**o**chyet ...]
  what do you want? что вы
  хотите? [shto viy Hat**ee**tyeh?]
ward (in hospital) палата [pal**a**ta]
warm тёплый [t**yo**pli]
  I'm so warm мне жарко
  [mnyeh **J**arka]
was*: he was он был ... [on
biyl ...]
  she was она была ... [ona
  bila ...]
  it was это было ... [eta
  b**iy**la ...]
wash (verb: hands etc) мыть/
помыть [miyt/pam**iy**t]
  (clothes) стирать/постирать
  [steer**a**t/pasteer**a**t]
  can you wash these? вы
  можете это постирать?
  [viy m**o**Jetyeh eta pasteer**a**t?]
washhand basin раковина
[rak**a**veena]
washing (clothes) бельё [byel**yo**]
washing machine
стиральная машина
[steer**a**lna-ya mash**iy**na]
washing powder
стиральный порошок
[steer**a**lni parash**o**k]
**washing-up: to do the
washing-up** мыть/помыть
посуду [miyt/pam**iy**t pas**oo**doo]
washing-up liquid жидкость
для мытья посуды **f**
[**J**iytkast dlya mit**ya** pas**oo**di]

wasp оса [asa]

watch (wristwatch) часы pl [chas**iy**]

  will you watch my things for me? присмотрите, пожалуйста, за моими вещами [preesmatr**ee**tyeh, pa**J**alsta, za ma-**ee**mee vyesh-cham**ee**]

watch strap ремешок для часов [ryem**ye**shok dlya chas**of**]

water вода [vad**a**]

  may I have some water? можно мне воды, пожалуйста? [**mo**Jna mnyeh vad**iy**, pa**J**alsta?]

waterproof (adj) непромокаемый [nyepramaka-**ye**mi]

water-skiing воднолыжный спорт [vadna-**liy**Jni sport]

way: it's this way в эту сторону [v**e**too st**o**ranoo]

  it's that way в ту сторону [ftoo st**o**ranoo]

  is it a long way to ...? далеко ли до … [dalyek**o**lee da ...?]

  no way! ни в коем случае! [nee fk**o**-yem sl**oo**cha-yeh!]

dialogue

  could you tell me the way to ...? скажите, пожалуйста, как дойти до ...? [ska**J**i**iy**tyeh, pa**J**alsta, kak dit**ee** da ...?]

  go straight on until you reach the traffic lights

идите прямо, до светофора [eed**ee**tyeh pr**ya**ma, da svyetaf**o**ra]

  turn left сверните налево [svyern**ee**tyeh nal**ye**va]

  take the first turn on the right первый поворот направа [**p**yervi pavar**o**t napr**a**va]

  see **where**

we* мы [miy]

weak слабый [sl**a**bi]

weather погода [pag**o**da]

dialogue

  what's the weather forecast? какой прогноз погоды? [kak**oy** pragn**o**s pag**o**di?]

  it's going to be fine будет хорошая погода [**boo**dyet Har**o**sha-ya pag**o**da]

  it's going to rain будет дождливо [**boo**dyet da**J**dl**ee**va]

  it'll brighten up later обещают просветление позже [ab**ye**sh-cha-yoot prasvyetl**ye**nee-yeh po**J**-**J**eh]

wedding свадьба [sv**a**dba]

wedding ring обручальное кольцо [abr**oo**chalna-yeh kalts**o**]

Wednesday среда [sryed**a**]

week неделя [nyed**ye**lya]

  a week (from) today ровно

через неделю [**ro**vna ch**ye**ryes ny**e**dy**e**lyoo]

a week (from) tomorrow
через неделю, считая с завтрашнего дня [ch**ye**ryes ny**e**dy**e**lyoo, sh-ch**ee**ta-ya z-z**a**ftrashnyeva dnya]

weekend конец недели [kan**ye**ts nyedy**e**lee]

at the weekend в субботу-воскресенье [vsoob-b**o**too-vaskrysy**e**nyeh]

weight вес [vyes]

weird странный [str**a**n-ni]

welcome: welcome to ...
добро пожаловать [dabr**o** paJ**a**lavat]

you're welcome (don't mention it) не за что [ny**e**zashta]

well: I don't feel well мне нехорошо [mnyeh nyeH**a**rash**o**]

she's not well ей нехорошо [yay nyeH**a**rash**o**]

you speak English very well вы очень хорошо говорите по-английски [viy **o**chyen H**a**rash**o** gavar**ee**tyeh pa-angl**ee**skee]

well done! молодец! [mal**a**d**ye**ts]

this one as well этот тоже [**e**tat t**o**Jeh]

well well! ну и ну! [noo ee noo!]

dialogue

how are you? как вы поживаете? [kak viy paJiva-

yetyeh?]

very well, thanks, and you? спасибо, хорошо, а вы? [spas**ee**ba, H**a**rash**o**, a viy?]

---

well-done (meat) хорошо прожаренный [H**a**rash**o** praJ**a**ryen-ni]

Welsh уэльский [oo-**e**lskee]

I'm Welsh я из Уэльса [ya eez oo-**e**lsa]

were*: we were мы были ... [miy b**iy**lee ...]

you were вы были ... [viy b**iy**lee ...]

they were они были ... [an**ee** b**iy**lee ...]

West: the West Запад [z**a**pat]

west запад [z**a**pat]

in the west на западе [na z**a**padyeh]

western западный [z**a**padni]

West Indian (adj) вест-индский [vyest-**ee**ntskee]

wet мокрый [m**o**kri]

what? что? [shto?]

what's that? что это? [shto-eta?]

what should I do? что мне делать? [shto mnyeh dy**e**lat?]

what a view! вот это вид! [v**o**teta veet!]

what bus do I take? на какой автобус мне надо сесть? [na kak**oy** aft**o**boos mnyeh n**a**da syest?]

wheel колесо [kalyes**o**]

wheelchair инвалидная

коляска [eenval**ee**dna-ya kal**ya**ska]

when? когда? [kagd**a**?]

when we get back когда мы вернёмся [kagd**a** miy vyern**yo**msya]

when's the train? когда поезд? [kagd**a** p**o**-yest?]

where? где? [gdyeh?]

I don't know where it is я не знаю, где это [ya nyeh zn**a**-yoo, gd**yeh**-eta]

dialogue

where is the cathedral? где собор? [gdyeh sab**o**r?]

it's over there вон там [von tam]

could you show me where it is on the map? вы можете показать это на карте? [viy m**o**Jetyeh pakaz**a**t eta na k**a**rtyeh?]

it's just here вот здесь [vot zdyes]

see way

which: which bus? какой автобус? [kak**o**y aft**o**boos?]

dialogue

which one? какой из них? [kak**o**y eez neeн?]

that one тот [tot]

this one? этот? [etat?]

no, that one нет, тот [nyet, tot]

while: while I'm here пока я здесь [pak**a** ya zdyes]

whisky виски **n** [v**ee**skee]

white белый [b**ye**li]

white wine белое вино [b**ye**la-yeh veen**o**]

who? кто? [kto?]

who is it? кто там? [kto tam?]

the man who ... человек, который ... [chyelav**ye**k, kat**o**ri ...]

whole: the whole week всю неделю [vsyoo nyed**ye**lyoo]

the whole lot всё [fsyo]

whose: whose is this? чьё это? [chyo eta?]

why? почему? [pacheem**oo**?]

why not? почему бы нет? [pacheem**oo**bi nyet?]

wide широкий [shir**o**kee]

wife жена [Jena]

will*: will you do it for me? вы это сделаете для меня? [viy eta sd**ye**la-yetyeh dlya myen**ya**?]

wind (noun) ветер [v**ye**tyer]

window окно [akn**o**]

near the window у окна [oo akn**a**]

in the window (of shop) в витрине [v-veetr**ee**enyeh]

window seat место у окна [m**ye**sta oo akn**a**]

windscreen ветровое стекло [vyetrav**o**-yeh styekl**o**]

windscreen wipers стеклоочистители [styekla-acheest**ee**tyelee], дворники [dv**o**rneekee]

windsurfing виндсёрфинг

[veents**yor**feenk]

windy ветреный [**vye**tryen-ni]

wine вино [**vee**no]

can we have some more wine? можно ещё вина, пожалуйста [**mo**Jna yesh-cho veen**a**, paJalsta]

wine list карта вин [**k**arta veen]

winter зима [zeem**a**]

in the winter зимой [zeem**oy**]

winter holiday зимний отпуск [**zee**mnee **o**tpoosk]

wire проволока [**pro**valaka]

(electric) провод [**pro**vat]

wish: best wishes с наилучшими пожеланиями [sna-ee**loo**chshimee paJilanee-yamee]

with с [s]

I'm staying with ... я живу у ... [ya Jiv**oo** oo ...]

without без [byes]

witness (man/woman) свидетель/свидетельница [sveed**ye**tyel/sveed**ye**tyelneetsa]

will you be a witness for me? (to man/woman) вы можете быть моим свидетелем/ моей свидетельницей? [viy mo**J**etyeh biyt ma-**ee**m sveed**ye**tyel-yem/ma-**yay** sveed**ye**tyelneetsay?]

woman женщина [**J**ensh-cheena]

wonderful замечательный [zamyech**a**tyelni]

won't*: it won't start не заводится [nyeh zav**o**deetsa]

wood (material) дерево [**dye**ryeva]

(forest) лес [lyes]

wool шерсть f [sherst]

word слово [**slo**va]

work (noun) работа [rab**o**ta]

(verb) работать [rab**o**tat]

it's not working это не работает [eta nyeh rab**o**ta-yet]

I work in ... я работаю в ... [ya rab**o**ta-yoo v ...]

world мир [meer]

worry: I'm worried я беспокоюсь [ya byespako**yoos**]

worse: it's worse это хуже [**e**ta **Hoo**Jeh]

worst самый плохой [**sa**mi pla**Hoy**]

worth: is it worth a visit? стоит ли туда ехать? [**sto**-eetlee tood**a ye**Hat?]

would: would you give this to ...? передайте это, пожалуйста ... [pyeryed**I**tyeh eta, paJalsta ...]

wrap: could you wrap it up? заверните, пожалуйста [zavyern**ee**tyeh, paJalsta]

wrapping paper обёрточная бумага [ab**yor**tachna-ya boom**a**ga]

wrist запястье [zap**ya**styeh]

write писать/написать [pees**at**/napees**at**]

could you write it down? запишите, пожалуйста [zapeesh**iy**tyeh, paJalsta]

how do you write it? как это пишется? [kak eta pee**shet**sa?]

writing paper почтовая

бумага [pachtova-ya boomaga]

wrong неправильно [nyepraveelna]

it's the wrong key это не тот ключ [eta nyeh tot klyooch]

this is the wrong train вы не на том поезде [viy nyeh na tom po-yezdyeh]

the bill's wrong счёт ошибочный [sh-chot ashiybachni]

sorry, wrong number (said by man/woman) извините, я не туда попал/попала [eezveeneetyeh, ya nyeh tooda papal/papala]

sorry, wrong room (said by man/woman) извините, я ошибся/ошиблась номером [eezveeneetyeh, ya ashiybsya/ashiyblas nomyeram]

there's something wrong with ... что-то не так с ... [shto-ta nyeh tak s ...]

what's wrong? в чём дело? [fchom dyela?]

X
—

X-ray рентгеновский снимок [ryentgyenafskee sneemak]

Y
—

yacht яхта [yaHta]

yard двор [dvor]

year год [got]

yellow жёлтый [Jolti]

yes да [da]

yesterday вчера [fchyera]

yesterday morning вчера утром [fchyera ootram]

the day before yesterday позавчера [pazafchyera]

yet ещё [yesh-cho]

dialogue

is it here yet? оно ещё не пришло? [ano yesh-cho nyeh preeshlo?]
no, not yet нет ещё [nyet yesh-cho]
you'll have to wait a little longer yet вам придётся ещё немного подождать [vam preedyotsa yesh-cho nyemnoga padaJdat]

yoghurt йогурт [yogoort]

you* (sing pol or pl) вы [viy] (sing, fam) ты [tiy]

this is for you это для вас [eta dlya vas]

with you с вами [svamee]

young молодой [maladoy]

your*/yours* (sing pol or pl) ваш m [vash], ваша f [vasha], ваше n [vasheh], ваши pl [vashee]

(sing, fam) твой m [tvoy], твоя f [tva-ya], твоё n [tva-yo], твои pl [tva-ee]

is this yours? это ваше? [eta vasheh?]

youth hostel молодёжная
  гостиница [malad**yo**Jna-ya
  gast**ee**neetsa]

Z

zero нуль **m** [nool]
  below zero ниже нуля
  [nee.Jeh nool**ya**]
zip молния [m**o**lnee-ya]
  could you put a new zip on?
  вставьте, пожалуйста,
  новую молнию [fst**a**ftyeh,
  pa.J**a**lsta, n**o**voo-yoo m**o**lnee-yoo]
zip code почтовый индекс
  [pacht**o**vi **ee**ndeks]
zoo зоопарк [zo-op**a**rk]

Russian

→

English

Colloquialisms

The following are words you may well hear. You shouldn't be tempted to use any of the stronger ones unless you are sure of your audience.

алкаш [alkash] wino, boozer
баксы [baksi] dollars
безобразие! [byezabrazee-yeh!] it's disgraceful!
блин! [bleen!] damn!
выпивка [viypeefka] bevvy, drink
деревянные [dyeryevyan-ni-yeh] roubles
дура/дурак [doora/doorak] idiot, thickhead
ёлки-палки! [yolkee-palkee!] bloody hell!
ерунда! [eroonda!] nonsense!
здорово! [zdorava!] great!
иди к чёрту! [eedee kchortoo!] go to hell!
козёл! [kazyol!] idiot!
какого чёрта ...? [kakova chorta ...?] what the hell ...?
какой ужас! [kakoy ooJas!] that's awful!
класс! [klass!] great!, brilliant!
клёвый! [klyovi!] knockout!, brill!, fantastic!
кретин [kryeteen] twit
к черту! [kchortoo!] to hell with it!
лимон [leemon] a million
молодец! [maladyets!] well done!
ничего себе! [neechyevo syebyeh!] not bad!
отвяжись! [atvyaJiys!] get lost!
парень [paryen] bloke
пошёл ты! [pashol tiy!] get lost!
псих [pseeH] nutter
ребята [ryebyata] (the) lads, (the) guys
сволочь [svolach] bastard
с приветом [spreevyetam] crackers, nuts
хреновый [Hryenovi] rotten, lousy
хрен с ним! [Hryen sneem!] to hell with it!
чёрт! [chort!] damn!, shit!
чёрт знает что [chort zna-yet shto] God only knows
чёрт с тобой! [chort staboy!] to hell with you!
чокнутый [choknooti] barmy
ужасно! [ooJasna!] it's awful!, it's ghastly!
штука [shtooka] a thousand
это обдираловка [eta abdeeralafka] it's a rip-off

A

A bus stop

авария [a**va**ree-ya] accident; breakdown

август [**av**goost] August

авиакомпания [avee-a-kamp**a**nee-ya] airline

авиапочта [avee-a-p**o**chta] airmail

  авиапочтой [**a**vee-a-p**o**chti] by airmail

Австралия [afstr**a**lee-ya] Australia

Австрия [**a**fstree-ya] Austria

автобус [aft**o**boos] bus

автовокзал [aftavakz**a**l] bus station

автоматический [aftamat**ee**chyeskee] automatic

автомобилист [aftamabeel**ee**st] car driver

автомобиль m [aftamab**ee**l] car

автоответчик [afta-atv**ye**tcheek] answering machine

автостоянка [aftasta-**ya**nka] car park, parking lot

автострада [aftastr**a**da] motorway, freeway, highway

агентство [ag**ye**nstva] agency

адвокат [advak**a**t] lawyer

администратор [admeeneestr**a**tar] manager

адрес [**a**dryes] address

адресат [adryes**a**t] addressee

адресная книга [**a**dryesna-ya kn**ee**ga] address book

Азербайджан [azyerbidj**a**n] Azerbaijan

аккумулятор [ak-koomool**ya**tar] battery (for car)

акселератор [aksyelyer**a**tar] accelerator

акцент [akts**e**nt] accent

алкоголь m [alkag**o**l] alcohol

аллергия [al-lyerg**ee**-ya] allergy

алмаз [alm**a**s] diamond

Америка [am**ye**reeka] America

американский [amyereek**a**nskee] American

амперный: 13-и амперный [amp**ye**rni] 13-amp

английская булавка [angl**ee**ska-ya bool**a**fka] safety pin

английский [angl**ee**skee] English

английский язык [angl**ee**skee yaz**iy**k] English (language)

англичане [angleech**a**nyeh] the English

англичанин [angleech**a**neen] Englishman

англичанка [angleech**a**nka] English woman

Англия [**a**nglee-ya] England

антигистамин [anteegeestam**ee**n] antihistamine

антикварная вещь [anteekv**a**rna-ya vyesh-ch] antique

антикварный [anteekv**a**rni] antiquarian; antique

антикварный магазин [anteekv**a**rni magaz**ee**n] antique shop

аппендицит [ap-pyendeets**iyt**]
  appendicitis
аппетит [ap-pyet**eet**] appetite
апрель m [apr**yel**] April
аптека [apt**ye**ka] chemist,
  pharmacy
арестовать [aryestav**at**] to
  arrest
Армения [arm**ye**nee-ya]
  Armenia
аромат [aram**at**] flavour
Архангельск [arн**a**ngyelsk]
  Archangel
аспирин [aspeer**een**] aspirin
Афганистан [afganeest**an**]
  Afghanistan
афиша [af**ee**sha] poster
аэропорт [a-erap**ort**] airport
Аэрофлот [a-erafl**ot**] Aeroflot

Б

бабушка [ba**boo**shka]
  grandmother
багаж [bag**ash**] luggage,
  baggage
багажник [bag**a**Jneek] boot (of
  car), (US) trunk
бак [bak] tank
бакалея [bakal**yeh**-ya]
  groceries
балалайка [balal**i**ka] balalaika
балкон [balk**on**] balcony
Балтийское море [balt**ee**ska-
  yeh m**o**ryeh] Baltic Sea
бальзам для волос [balz**am**
  dlya val**os**] conditioner
бампер [b**a**mpyer] bumper,

(US) fender
банк [bank] bank
банкнота [bankn**o**ta]
  banknote, (US) bill
банкомат [bankam**at**] cash
  dispenser, ATM
баня [b**a**nya] bathhouse
бар [bar] bar
бармен [b**a**rmyen] barman
бассейн [bas**yay**n] swimming
  pool
батарейка [batar**yay**ka] battery
батарея [batar**yeh**-ya] radiator
башня [b**a**shnya] tower
бегать/бежать [b**ye**gat/bye.Jat]
  to run
  бегать/бежать трусцой
  [b**ye**gat/bye.Jat tr**oo**sts**oy**] to jog
беда [byed**a**] trouble;
  misfortune
бедный [b**ye**dni] poor
бедро [byedr**o**] thigh; hip
бежать [bye.J**at**] to run
бежевый [b**ye**.Jevi] beige
без [byez] without
  без двадцати два [byez
  dvatsat**ee** dva] twenty to two
безопасность [byezap**a**snast]
  safety
  в безопасности
  [fbyezap**a**snastee] safe
безработный [byezrab**o**tni]
  unemployed
белокурый [byelak**oo**ri] blond
Белорусь [byelar**oos**] Belarus
белый [b**ye**li] white
Бельгия [b**ye**lgee-ya] Belgium
бельё [byel**yo**] washing;
  underwear

бензин [byenzeen] petrol, gasoline

берег [byeryek] coast; shore
на берегу моря [na byeryegoo morya] at the seaside

берегись ... [byeryegees ...] beware of ...

беременная [byeryemyen-na-ya] pregnant

бесплатный [byesplatni] free of charge

беспокоиться [byespako-eetsa] to worry about

бесполезный [byespalyezni] useless

беспорядок [byesparyadak] mess

беспошлинный [byesposhleen-ni] duty-free

библиотека [beeblee-atyeka] library

бизнес [beeznes] business

билет [beelyet] ticket

билет в один конец [beelyet vadeen kanyets] single ticket, one-way ticket

билетная касса [beelyetna-ya kas-sa] ticket office

билеты [beelyeti] tickets

бить/побить [beet/pabeet] to hit; to beat

благодарить/поблагодарить [blagadareet/pablagadareet] to thank

благодарный [blagadarni] grateful

бланк [blank] form

ближайший [bleeJishi] nearest

ближе [bleeJeh] nearer

близкий [bleeskee] near, close

близнецы [bleeznyetsiy] twins

близорукий [bleezarookee] shortsighted

блокнот [blaknot] notebook

блоха [blaHa] flea

блузка [blooska] blouse

блюдо [blyooda] dish

блюдце [blyoodtseh] saucer

бог [boH] God

богатый [bagati] rich

Болгария [balgaree-ya] Bulgaria

более [bolyeh-yeh] more

болезнь f [balyezn] disease; illness

болеть/заболеть [balyet/zabalyet] to be ill; to fall ill; to be sore, to ache, to hurt

болеутоляющее средство [bolyeh-ootalyayoosh-chyeh sryetstva] painkiller

боль f [bol] ache; pain

боль в желудке [bol vJelootkyeh] stomach ache

больница [balneetsa] hospital

больной [balnoy] ill, (US) sick; sore; patient

больше [bolsheh] more

большинство [balshinstvo] most (of); majority

большой [balshoy] big, large

бомж [bomJ] homeless person

борода [barada] beard

борт-проводник [bort-pravadneek] steward

боюсь: я боюсь [ya bayoos] I'm afraid

бояться [ba-**ya**tsa] to be afraid (of)

браслет [bras**lyet**] bracelet

брат [brat] brother

бриллиант [breel-lee-**ant**] diamond

британский [breet**an**skee] British

бритва [**breet**va] razor

бритвенное лезвие [**breet**vyen-na-yeh **lye**zvee-yeh] razor blade

бриться/побриться [**breet**sa/pa**breet**sa] to shave

бровь f [brof] eyebrow

бросать/бросить [bra**sat**/**bro**seet] to throw

брошь f [brosh] brooch

брошюра [bra**shoo**ra] brochure; leaflet

брюки [bry**oo**kee] trousers, (US) pants

будет [**boo**dyet] he will; she will; it will; he will be; she will be; it will be

будете [**boo**dyetyeh] you will; you will be

будешь [**boo**dyesh] you will; you will be

будильник [boo**dee**lneek] alarm clock

будить/разбудить [boo**deet**/razboo**deet**] to wake

буду [**boo**doo] I will; I will be

будут [**boo**doot] they will; they will be

будущее [**boo**doosh-chyeh-yeh] future

будьте здоровы! [**boo**dtyeh zda**ro**vi!] bless you!

буква [**book**va] letter (of alphabet)

букинист [bookee**nee**st] secondhand bookseller

букинистический магазин [bookeenee**stee**chyeskee maga**zeen**] secondhand bookshop/bookstore

булавка [boo**laf**ka] pin

булочная [**boo**lachna-ya] bakery

бульвар [bool**var**] boulevard

бумага [boo**ma**ga] paper

бумажник [boo**ma**neek] wallet

бумажные носовые платки [boo**ma**ni-yeh nasa**viy**-yeh plat**kee**] tissues, Kleenex®

буря [**boo**rya] storm

бутылка [boo**tiyl**ka] bottle

буфет [boo**fyet**] snack bar, café

бы: я хотел бы ... [ya ha**tyel** biy ...] I would like ...

бывать/побывать [bi**vat**/pabi**vat**] to be; to frequent

бывший [**biy**fshi] former

был [biyl], **была** [bi**la**] was; were

были [**biy**lee] were

было [**biy**la] was

быстрее! [bist**ryeh**-yeh!] hurry up!

быстро [**biy**stra] quickly, fast

быстрый [**biy**stri] quick, fast

бытовая химия [bita**va**-ya **нee**mee-ya] household cleaning materials

быть [biyt] to be

бюро [byoo**ro**] office

бюро находок [byoo**ro** na**нo**dak]

lost property office

бюро обслуживания [byooro apslooJivanee-ya] service bureau

бюро путешествий [byooro pootyeshestvee] travel agent's

бюстгальтер [byoostgaltyer] bra

В

в [v] in

вагон [vagon] carriage

вагон-ресторан [vagon-ryestaran] dining car

важный [vaJni] important

ваза [vaza] vase

валюта [valyoota] foreign currency

вам [vam] (to) you

вами [vamee] (by) you

ванна [van-na] bath

ванная [van-na-ya] bath; bathroom

вас [vas] you; of you

вата [vata] cotton wool, absorbent cotton

ваш [vash], **ваша** [vasha], **ваше** [vasheh] your; yours

вашего [vasheva] (of) your; (of) yours

ваше здоровье! [vasheh zdarovyeh!] cheers!

вашей [vashay] your; yours; of your; of yours; to your; to yours; by your; by yours

вашем [vashem] your; yours

вашему [vashemoo] (to) your; (to) yours

ваши [vashi] your; yours

вашим [vashim] your; yours; by your; by yours; to your; to yours

вашими [vashimee] (by) your; (by) yours

ваших [vashiн] (of) your; (of) yours

вашу [vashoo] your; yours

в воскресенья и праздничные дни [v-vaskryesyenya ee prazneechni-yeh dnee] Sundays and public holidays

вдова [vdava] widow

вдовец [vdavyets] widower

вдруг [vdrook] suddenly

вегетарианец [vyegyetaree-anyets] vegetarian

ведро [vyedro] bucket

вежливый [vyeJleevi] polite

везде [vyezdyeh] everywhere

век [vyek] century

вёл [vyol], **вела** [vyela] led; was leading

вели [vyelee] led; were leading

Великобритания [vyeleekabreetanee-ya] Britain

великолепный [vyeleekalyepni] terrific, magnificent, splendid

велосипед [vyelaseepyet] bicycle

велосипедная трасса [vyelaseepyedna-ya tras-sa] cycle path

Венгрия [vyengree-ya] Hungary

веник [**vye**neek] bunch of birch twigs; broom

вентилятор [vyenteel**ya**tar] fan

верёвка [vyer**yo**fka] string; rope

верить/поверить [**vye**reet/pav**ye**reet] to believe

вернуть [vyern**oot**] to give back, to return

вернуться [vyern**oot**sa] to get back, to come back, to return

верный [**vye**rni] true

вероятно [vyera-**ya**tna] probably

верхний этаж [**vye**rHnee et**ash**] upper floor

верховая езда [vyerHa**va**-ya yezd**a**] horse riding

вес [vyes] weight

веселиться: веселитесь! [vyesyel**ee**tyes!] have fun!

весёлый [vyes**yo**li] cheerful

весна [vyesn**a**] spring

весной [vyesn**oy**] in spring

вести [vyest**ee**] to drive; to lead

весь [vyes] all; the whole

весь день [vyes dyen] all day

ветер [**vye**tyer] wind

вечер [**vye**chyer] evening

добрый вечер [**do**bri **vye**chyer] good evening

11 часов вечера [chas**of vye**chyera] 11 pm

вешалка [**vye**shalka] peg; rack; stand; coathanger

вещи [**vye**sh-chee] things, belongings

вещь f [vyesh-ch] thing

взбешённый [vzbyesh**on**-ni] furious

вздор [vzdor] rubbish, nonsense

взлёт [vzlyot] take-off

взрослые [vz**ro**sli-yeh] adults

взрослый [vz**ro**sli] adult

взять [vzyat] to take

взять напрокат [vzyat naprak**at**] to rent

вид [veet] view; appearance; form

видео [**vee**dyeh-o] video

видеомагнитофон [**vee**dyeh-omagneetaf**on**] video recorder

видеть/увидеть [**vee**dyet/oo**vee**dyet] to see

видоискатель m [**vee**da-eesk**a**tyel] viewfinder

виза [**vee**za] visa

визит [vee**zeet**] visit

визитка [vee**zee**tka], визитная карточка [vee**zee**tna-ya **kar**tachka] business card

вилка [**vee**lka] fork

Вильнюс [**vee**lnyoos] Vilnius

винный магазин [**veen**-ni magaz**een**] wine and spirits shop

вираж [veer**ash**] bend

витамины [veetam**ee**ni] vitamins

витрина [veetr**ee**na] shop window

включать/включить [fklyooch**at**/fklyooch**eet**] to switch on

включён [fklyooch**on**] on,

switched on; included

включено в цену [fklyoochyeno ftsenoo] included in the price

включить [fklyoocheet] to switch on

вкус [fkoos] taste

вкусный [fkoosni] nice; delicious, tasty

владелец [vladyelyets] owner

Владивосток [vladeevastok] Vladivostok

вместе [vmyestyeh] together

вместо [vmyesta] instead of

внешний [vnyeshnee] outward; external; foreign

вниз [vnees] down, downwards

внизу [vneezoo] downstairs

внимание [vneemanee-yeh] attention

внутренние рейсы [vnootryen-nee-yeh ryaysi] domestic flights

внутренний [vnootryen-nee] inner; inside; internal; domestic; inland

внутри [vnootree] inside

во время [va vryemya] during

вовремя [vovryemya] on time

вода [vada] water

водитель [vadeetyel] driver

водительские права [vadeetyelskee-yeh prava] driving licence

водить/вести [vadeet/vyestee] to drive; to lead

водопад [vadapat] waterfall

возвращать/вернуть [vazvrash-chat/vyernoot] to give

back, to return

возвращаться/вернуться [vazvrash-chatsa/vyernootsa] to get back, to come back, to return

воздух [vozdooH] air

воздушный шар [vazdooshni shar] balloon

возместить [vazmyesteet] to refund

возможно [vazmojna] possible; perhaps

возражать: вы не возражаете если я ...? [viy nyeh vazraja-yetyeh yeslee ya ...?] do you mind if I ...?

возраст [vozrast] age

возьмите тележку/корзину [vazmeetyeh tyelyeshkoo/ karzeenoo] please take a trolley/basket

войдите! [vIdeetyeh!] come in!

война [vIna] war

войти [vItee] to enter, to go in

вокзал [vakzal] station (main-line railway)

Волгоград [valgagrat] Volgograd

волосы [volasi] hair

вон: вон! [von!] get out!

вон там [von tam] over there

вонь [von] stink

вообще [va-apsh-chyeh] at all; on the whole, generally

вопрос [vapros] question

вор [vor] thief

вор-карманник [var-karman-neek] pickpocket

ворота [varota] gate

воротник [varatneek] collar

восемнадцатый [vasyemnatsati] eighteenth

восемнадцать [vasyemnatsat] eighteen

восемь [vosyem] eight

восемьдесят [vosyemdyesyat] eighty

восемьсот [vasyemsot] eight hundred

воскресенье [vaskryesyenyeh] Sunday

восток [vastok] east

к востоку от [k vastokoo ot] east of

восьмой [vasmoy] eighth

вот [vot] here is; that's

вот и всё [vot ee fsyo] that's all

вот, пожалуйста [vot, paжalsta] here is, here are; here you are

вот эти [vot etee] these

вот этот [vot etat] this one

вперёд [vpyeryot] forwards; in future; in advance

впереди [fpyeryedee] in front, ahead; in front of; before; in future

врач [vrach] doctor

вредить/повредить [vryedeet/pavryedeet] to damage

время [vryemya] time

время года [vryemya goda] season

время отправления [vryemya atpravlyenee-ya] departure time

все [fsyeh] everyone; all

всё [fsyo] everything; all

всё вместе [fsyo vmyestyeh] altogether

всегда [fsyegda] always

всего [fsyevo] in all, only

всё-таки [vsyo-takee] anyway

вспомнить [fspomneet] to remember, to recall

вспышка [fspiyshka] flash

вставать/встать [fstavat/fstat] to get up

встретить [fstryeteet] to meet

встреча [fstryecha] appointment; meeting

встречать/встретить [fstryechat/fstryeteet] to meet

всякий [fsyakee] any

вторник [ftorneek] Tuesday

второй [ftaroy] second

второй этаж [ftaroy etash] first floor, (US) second floor

вход [fHot] entrance, way in

вход бесплатный [fHot byesplatni] admission free

вход воспрещён [fHot vaspryesh-chon] no admittance

вход свободный [fHot svabodni] admission free

входите [fHadeetyeh] come in

входить/войти [fHadeet/vitee] to enter, to go in

вчера [fchyera] yesterday

вчера вечером [fchyera vyechyeram] last night (before midnight)

вчера днём [fchyera dnyom] yesterday afternoon

вчера ночью [fchyera nochyoo] last night (after midnight)

вы [viy] you

выбирать/выбрать [vibeerat/ **viy**brat] to choose

выбросить [**viy**braseet] to throw away

выглядеть [**viy**glyadyet] to look; to seem

выдача багажа [**viy**dacha bagaJa] baggage claim

выдача покупок [**viy**dacha pakoopak] purchase collection point

выиграть [**viy**-eegrat] to win

выйти [**viy**tee] to go out; to get off

выключатель m [viklyoochatyel] switch

выключать/выключить [viklyoochat/**viy**klyoocheet] to switch off

выключен [**viy**klyoochyen] off, switched off

выключить [**viy**klyoocheet] to switch off

вылет [**viy**lyet] departure

вылетать/вылететь [vilyetat/ **viy**lyetyet] to take off

выпить [**viy**peet] to drink

высокий [visokee] tall; high

высота [visata] height, altitude

выставка [**viy**stafka] exhibition

выставочный зал [**viy**stavachni zal] exhibition hall

высший [**viy**s-shee] higher; highest

выхлопная труба [viHlapna-ya trooba] exhaust pipe

выход [**viy**Hat] way out, exit; gate (at airport)

выход в город [**viy**Hat vgorat] exit

выходить/выйти [viHadeet/ **viy**tee] to go out; to get off

выход на посадку [**viy**Hat na pasatkoo] gate

выходной день ... [viHadnoy dyen ...] closed on ...

выходные [viHadniy-yeh] weekend

выше [**viy**sheh] higher

вьюга [**vyoo**ga] snowstorm

Г

г. town/city

газ [gas] gas

газета [gazyeta] newspaper

газетный киоск [gazyetni kee-osk] newsagent

газон [gazon] lawn

галантерея [galantyeryeh-ya] haberdashery

галерея [galyeryay-a] gallery

галстук [galstook] tie, necktie

гараж [garash] garage

гарантия [garantee-ya] guarantee, warranty

гардероб [gardyerop] cloakroom

гастроном [gastranom] food store

гвоздь m [gvost] nail (in wall)

где? [gdyeh?] where?

где-нибудь [gdyeh-neeboot] somewhere; anywhere

где-то [gdyeh-ta] somewhere

г-жа [gaspaJa] Mrs; Ms; Miss

гигиеническая прокладка [geegee-yen**ee**chyeska-ya prak**la**tka] sanitary towel/ napkin

гид [geet] guide

главный [g**la**vni] main, principal

гладить/погладить [g**la**deet/ pag**la**deet] to iron

глаз [glas] eye

глубокий [gloob**o**kee] deep

глупый [g**loo**pi] stupid

глухой [gloo**no**y] deaf

г-н [gaspad**ee**n] Mr

гнилой [gneel**oy**] rotten

говорить/сказать [gava**ree**t/ ska**za**t] to say; to speak
 вы говорите по-... [vi gava**ree**tyeh pa-...] do you speak ...?

год [got] year

годовщина [gadafsh-ch**ee**na] anniversary

Голландия [gal-l**a**ndee-ya] Holland

голова [gala**va**] head

головная боль [gala**vna**-ya bol] headache

голодный [gal**o**dni] hungry

голос [g**o**las] voice

голый [g**o**li] naked

гомосексуалист [gomaseksoo-al**ee**st] gay, homosexual

гора [ga**ra**] mountain

гораздо [gar**a**zda] much more

гордый [g**o**rdi] proud

гореть/сгореть [gar**yet**/zgar**yet**] to burn

горло [g**o**rla] throat

горничная [g**o**rneechna-ya] maid; cleaner

город [g**o**rat] town; city

городской [garadsk**oy**] town, city, urban

горький [g**o**rkee] bitter

горячий [gar**ya**chee] hot

господин [gaspad**ee**n] Mr; Sir

госпожа [gaspaJa] Miss; Mrs; Madam; Ms

гостеприимство [gastyepree-**ee**mstva] hospitality

гостиная [gast**ee**na-ya] lounge, living room

гостиница [gast**ee**neetsa] hotel

гость [gost]/гостья [g**o**stya] guest (male/female)

государство [gasood**a**rstva] state

готовить/приготовить [gat**o**veet/preegat**o**veet] to cook; to prepare

готовый [gat**o**vi] ready

град [grat] hail

градус [gr**a**doos] degree

грамматика [gram-m**a**teeka] grammar

грампластинки [gramplast**ee**nkee] records

граница [gran**ee**tsa] border
 за границей [za gran**ee**tsay] abroad

гребная шлюпка [gryebna-ya shly**oo**pka] rowing boat

Греция [gr**ye**tsi-ya] Greece

грипп [greep] flu

гроза [gra**za**] thunderstorm

гром [grom] thunder

громкий [gromkee] loud

громче [gromchyeh] louder

грубый [groobi] rude; coarse

грудная клетка [groodna-ya klyetka] chest

грудь f [groot] breast; chest

грузинский [groozeenskee] Georgian

Грузия [groozee-ya] Georgia

грузовик [groozaveek] lorry, truck

группа [groopa] group

группа крови [groopa krovee] blood group

грустный [groostni] sad

грязное бельё [gryazna-yeh byelyo] dirty laundry, washing

грязный [gryazni] dirty

губа [gooba] lip

губная помада [goobna-ya pamada] lipstick

гулять/погулять [goolyat/pagoolyat] to go for a walk

густой [goostoy] thick

Д

д. house

да [da] yes

давай(те) ... [davi(tyeh) ...] let's ...

давать/дать [davat/dat] to give

давление в шинах [davlyenee-yeh fshiynaн] tyre pressure

давно [davno] long ago; for a long time; long since

дадим [dadeem] we will give

дадите [dadeetyeh] you will give

дадут [dadoot] they will give

даже [daJeh] even

даже если [daJeh yeslee] even if

далёкий [dalyokee] far, far away

далеко [dalyeko] far, far away

дальше [dalsheh] further

дам [dam] I will give

дама [dama] lady

Дания [danee-ya] Denmark

дарить/подарить [dareet/padareet] to give (present)

даст [dast] he will give; she will give; it will give

дать [dat] to give

дача [dacha] house/cottage in the country

дашь [dash] you will give

два [dva] two

двадцатый [dvatsati] twentieth

двадцать [dvatsat] twenty

две [dvyeh] two

две недели [dvyeh nyedyelee] fortnight, two weeks

двенадцатый [dvyenatsati] twelfth

двенадцать [dvyenatsat] twelve

дверь f [dvyer] door

двести [dvyestee] two hundred

двойной [dvinoy] double

дворец [dvaryets] palace

дворник [dvorneek] windscreen wiper; janitor;

street cleaner

двухместный номер [dvooнmyesni nomyer] double room

двухразовое питание [dvooнrazava-yeh peetanee-yeh] half board

дебютант [dyebyootant] beginner

деверь [dyevyer] brother-in-law (husband's brother)

девичья фамилия [dyeveechya fameelee-ya] maiden name

девочка [dyevachka] girl (child)

девушка [dyevooshka] girl (young woman)

девяносто [dyevyanosta] ninety

девятнадцатый [dyevyatnatsati] nineteenth

девятнадцать [dyevyatnatsat] nineteen

девятый [dyevyati] ninth

девять [dyevyat] nine

девятьсот [dyevyatsot] nine hundred

дедушка [dyedooshka] grandfather

дежурная [dyeJoorna-ya] concierge

дежурная аптека [dyeJoorna-ya aptyeka] duty pharmacist

дезинфицирующее средство [dyezeenfeetseeroo-yoosh-chyeh sryetstva] antiseptic; disinfectant

дезодорант [dyezadarant] deodorant

действительно [dyaystveetyelna] really, indeed

действительный [dyaystveetyelni] valid

декабрь m [dyekabr] December

делать/сделать [dyelat/zdyelat] to do; to make

делиться/поделиться [dyeleetsa/padyeleetsa] to share

дело [dyela] matter, business

в самом деле [fsamam dyelyeh] really

как дела? [kak dyela?] how are you?, how are things?

день m [dyen] day

деньги [dyengee] money

день рождения [dyen raJdyenee-ya] birthday

деревня [dyeryevnya] countryside; village

дерево [dyeryeva] tree; wood

из дерева [eez dyeryeva] wooden

держать [dyerJat] to hold; to keep; to support

держитесь левой стороны [dyerJeetyes lyevi staraniy] keep to the left

десятый [dyesyati] tenth

десять [dyesyat] ten

дети [dyetee] children

детская коляска [dyetska-ya kalyaska] pram, baby carriage

детская кроватка [dyetska-ya kravatka] cot

детская порция [dyetska-ya portsi-ya] children's portion

дешевле [dyeshevlyeh] cheaper

дешёвый [dyeshovi] cheap

джинсы [dJeensi] jeans

диабетик [dee-ab**ye**teek] diabetic

диета [dee-**ye**ta] diet

дизель m [**dee**zyel] diesel

дикий [**dee**kee] wild

директор [deer**ye**ktar] director

дискотека [deeska**tye**ka] disco

длина [dl**ee**na] length

длинный [dl**ee**n-ni] long

для [dlya] for

для вас/меня [dlya vas/ my**en**ya] for you/me

для некурящих [dlya nyekoor**ya**sh-cheeh] non-smoking

дневник [dnyevn**ee**k] diary

днём [dn**yom**] in the afternoon; p.m.

дно [dno] bottom

на дне [na dn**ye**h] at the bottom of

до [do] up to, as far as; before; until

доброе утро [**do**bra-yeh **oo**tra] good morning

добрый [**do**bri] good; kind

добрый вечер [**do**bri v**ye**chyer] good evening

добрый день [**do**bri dyen] good afternoon

довольно [dav**o**lna] quite; fairly

довольно хорошо [dav**o**lna Hara**sho**] pretty good

довольный [dav**o**lni] pleased

до востребования [da vastr**ye**bavanee-ya] poste restante, general delivery

договор [daga**vo**r] contract

дождик [**do**Jdeek] shower

дождливый [daJdl**ee**vi] rainy

дождь m [dosht] rain

идёт дождь [eed**yo**t dosht] it's raining

документ [dakoom**ye**nt] document

долго [**do**lga] a long time

должен: я/он должен [ya/on d**o**lJen] I/he must

должна: я/она должна [ya/ana dalJ**na**] I/she must

долина [dal**ee**na] valley

дом [dom] house; home

дома [**do**ma] at home

он дома? [on d**o**ma?] is he in?

доплата [dap**la**ta] supplement

дорога [dar**o**ga] road

дорогой [darag**oy**] expensive, dear

дороже [dar**o**Jeh] dearer

дорожные работы [dar**o**Jni-yeh rab**o**ti] roadworks

дорожный чек [dar**o**Jni chyek] traveller's cheque/check

досадно [das**a**dna] annoying

до свидания [da sveed**a**nya] goodbye

доставать/достать [dastav**a**t/ dast**a**t] to get, to obtain

достаточно [dast**a**tachna] enough

достать [dast**a**t] to get, to obtain

дочь [doch] daughter

драка [dr**a**ka] fight

древний [dr**ye**vnee] ancient

друг [drook] friend; boyfriend

другой [droog**oy**] other;

А
Б
В
Г
Д
Е
Ё
Ж
З
И
Й
К
Л
М
Н
О
П
Р
С
Т
У
Ф
Х
Ц
Ч
Ш
Щ
Ъ
Ы
Ь
Э
Ю
Я

another, a different
в другом месте [vdroogom myestyeh] elsewhere
что-то другое [shto-ta droogoy-yeh] something else
думать/подумать [doomat/padoomat] to think
я думаю, что ... [ya dooma-yoo, shto ...] I think that ...
духи [doohee] perfume
духовка [dooHofka] oven
душ [doosh] shower
дым [diym] smoke
дыра [dira] hole
дышать [dishat] to breathe
дядя [dyadya] uncle

Е

еврейский [yevryayskee] Jewish
Европа [yevropa] Europe
европейский [yevrapyayskee] European
его [yevo] him; it; of him; of it; his; its
еда [yeda] food; meal
едим [yedeem] we eat
единый билет [yedeeni beelyet] monthly season ticket
едите [yedeetyeh] you eat
едят [yedyat] they eat
её [yeh-yo] her; it; of her; of it; hers; its
ездить [yezdeet] to go (by transport); to ride; to drive; to travel
ей [yay] her; to her; by her

ем [yem] I eat
ему [yemoo] him; it; to him; to it
если [yeslee] if
ест [yest] he eats; she eats; it eats
естественный [yestyestvyen-ni] natural
есть [yest] there is; there are
здесь есть ...? [zdyes yest ...?] is there ... here?
у меня есть ...? [oo myenya yest ...] I have ...
есть/съесть [yest/syest] to eat
ехать/ездить [yeHat/yezdeet] to go (by transport); to ride; to drive; to travel
ешь [yesh] you eat; eat
ешьте [yeshtyeh] eat
ещё [yesh-cho] still; another; another one; more
ещё более ... [yesh-cho bolyeh-yeh ...] even more ...
ещё не [yesh-cho nyeh] not yet
ещё одно пиво [yesh-cho adno peeva] another beer

Ж

Ж ladies' toilets, ladies' room
жаловаться [Jalavatsa] to complain
жаль [Jal] pity; it's a pity
как жаль [kak Jal] what a pity
жара [Jara] heat
жарить [Jareet] to fry; to grill

жвачка [Jvachka] chewing gum

ждать/подождать [Jdat/padaJdat] to wait

подождите меня! [padaJdeetyeh myenya!] wait for me!

железная дорога [Jelyezna-ya daroga] railway

железо [Jelyeza] iron (metal)

жёлтый [Jolti] yellow

желудок [Jeloodak] stomach

жена [Jena] wife

женат [Jenat] married (man)

не женат [nyeh Jenat] single

жених [JeneeH] fiancé; bridegroom

женская одежда [Jenska-ya adyeJda] ladies' clothing

женский зал [Jenskee zal] ladies' hairdresser

женский отдел [Jenskee ad-dyel] ladies' department

женский туалет [Jenskee too-alyet] ladies' toilet, ladies' room

женщина [Jensh-cheena] woman

жетон [Jeton] token

живой [Jivoy] alive; living

живот [Jivot] stomach; belly

животное [Jivotna-yeh] animal

жидкость для снятия лака [Jeetkast dlya snyatee-ya laka] nail polish remover

жизнь f [Jiyzn] life

жильё [Jilyo] accommodation

жир [Jiyr] grease, fat

жирный [Jiyrni] greasy, fatty; rich

жить [Jiyt] to live

жить в палатках [Jiyt fpalatkaн] to camp

журнал [Joornal] magazine

З

за [za] behind

забавный [zabavni] funny, amusing

заблудиться [zabloodeetsa] to lose one's way

заболеть [zabalyet] to be ill; to fall ill; to be sore

забор [zabor] fence

забота [zabota] worry; bother

заботиться/позаботиться о [zaboteetsa/pazaboteetsa o] to take care of

забывать/забыть [zabivat/zabiyt] to forget

заведующий [zavyedooyoosh-chee] manager

завернуть [zavyernoot] to wrap

зависеть: это зависит [eta zaveeseet] it depends

завод [zavot] factory, plant

завтра [zaftra] tomorrow

до завтра [da zaftra] see you tomorrow

завтра вечером [zaftra vyechyeram] tomorrow night

завтра утром [zaftra ootram] tomorrow morning

завтрак [zaftrak] breakfast

загар [zagar] suntan

загорать/загореть [zagarat/ zagaryet] to get sunburnt, to tan

загораться/загореться [zagaratsa/zagaryetsa] to catch fire

загрязнённый [zagryaznyon-ni] polluted

зад [zat] bottom (of body)

задержка [zadyershka] delay

задние фары [zadnee-yeh fari] rear lights

задний [zadnee] back; reverse

задний ход [zadnee Hot] reverse gear

задняя часть [zadnya-ya chast] back, back part

зажечь [zaJech] to light

зажигалка [zaJigalka] lighter

зажигание [zaJiganee-yeh] ignition

зажигать/зажечь [zaJigat/ zaJech] to light

заказ [zakas] order; reservation

заказано [zakazana] reserved

заказное письмо [zakazno-yeh peesmo] registered mail

заказывать/заказать [zakazivat/zakazat] to order; to book

закат [zakat] sunset

закон [zakon] law

закричать [zakreechat] to shout

закрывать/закрыть [zakrivat/ zakriyt] to close

закрыто [zakriyta] closed

закрыто на ремонт [zakriyta na ryemont] closed for repairs

закрыто на учёт [zakriyta na oochot] closed for stocktaking

закрыть [zakriyt] to close

закурить [zakooreet] to smoke

закуска [zakooska] snack; hors d'oeuvre, appetizer

зал ожидания [zal aJidanee-ya] waiting room; departure lounge

замечательный [zamyechatyelni] remarkable, wonderful

замок [zamok] lock

замок [zamak] castle

замороженный [zamaroJen-ni] frozen

замужем [zamooJem] married (woman)

не замужем [nyeh zamooJem] single

замшевый [zamshevi] suede

занавеска [zanavyeska] curtain

занимать/занять [zaneemat/ zanyat] to borrow; to occupy; to take up

заниматься/заняться [zaneematsa/zanyatsa] to occupy oneself with; to study; to begin to

занято [zanyata], занятый [zanyati] engaged, occupied; engaged, busy

занять [zanyat] to borrow

запад [zapat] west

к западу от [k zapadoo at] west of

запасной выход [zapasnoy

víyнat] emergency exit

запах [zapa**н]** smell

запирать/запереть [zapeerat/
za**pyer**yet]** to lock

записная книжка-календарь
[za**pee**sna-ya kneeshka-kalyen**dar]**
diary; planner

заплатить [zaplat**eet]** to pay

заполнить [zapol**neet]** to fill in

запор [zapor]** bar; bolt; lock;
constipation

заправочная станция
[za**pra**vachna-ya **stan**tsi-ya]**
petrol/gas station; garage

запрещено [zapryesh-chye**no]**
prohibited, forbidden

запчасти [zapchas**tee]** spare
parts

запястье [zapyas**tyeh]** wrist

зарабатывать/заработать
[za**ra**bativat/zara**bo**tat]** to earn

заработок [zarabatak]** salary

заражение [zara**J**enee-yeh]**
infection; contamination

заранее [zaranyeh-yeh]** in
advance

засмеяться [zasmyeh-**yatsa]** to
laugh

засоренный [zasoryen-ni]**
blocked

застегните привязные
ремни [zastyegn**ee**tyeh
preevyaz**niy**-yeh ryem**nee]** fasten
seatbelts

застёжка-молния [zastyoshka-
molnee-ya]** zip

застенчивый [zastyencheevi]**
shy

затвор объектива [zatvor

abyekt**ee**va]** shutter (on camera)

затормозить [zatarmaz**eet]** to
brake

защищать/защитить [zash-
cheesh-ch**at**/zash-cheet**eet]** to
protect, to defend

звать/позвать [zvat/pazvat]**
to call

  как вас зовут? [kak vas
za**voot?]** what's your name?

  меня зовут ... [myenya
za**voot ...]** my name is ...

звезда [zvyezda]** star

звонить/позвонить [zvaneet/
pazvan**eet]** to ring; to phone

звонок [zvanok]** bell; phone
call

здание [zdanee-yeh]** building

здесь [zdyes]** here

здоровый [zdarovi]** healthy;
huge

здоровье [zdarovyeh]** health

  за ваше здоровье! [za vasheh
zda**ro**vyeh!]** your health!,
cheers!

здравствуйте [zdrastvooytyeh]**
hello; how do you do?

зелёный [zyelyoni]** green

земля [zyemlya]** earth; world;
ground

зеркало [zyerkala]** mirror

зима [zeema]** winter

  зимой [zeemoy]** in winter

змея [zmyeh-ya]** snake

знакомить/познакомить
[zna**ko**meet/pazna**ko**meet]** to
introduce

знакомиться/познакомиться
[zna**ko**meetsa/pazna**ko**meetsa]**

to get to know, to become acquainted with, to meet

знать [znat] to know

я не знаю [ya nyeh zna-yoo] I don't know

значить [znacheet] to mean

что это значит? [shto eta znacheet?] what does it mean?

золовка [zalofka] sister-in-law (husband's sister)

золото [zolata] gold

зонтик [zonteek] umbrella

зоопарк [za-apark] zoo

зрелый [zryeli] ripe

зуб [zoop] tooth

зубная боль [zoobna-ya bol] toothache

зубная паста [zoobna-ya pasta] toothpaste

зубная щётка [zoobna-ya sh-chotka] toothbrush

зубной врач [zoobnoy vrach] dentist

зубной протез [zoobnoy prates] dentures

зуд [zoot] itch

зять [zyat] son-in-law

И

и [ee] and

иголка [eegolka] needle

игра [eegra] game

играть/сыграть [eegrat/sigrat] to play

игрушка [eegrooshka] toy

идея [eedyeh-ya] idea

идти/ходить [eet-tee/Hadeet] to

go (on foot), to walk; to suit

известный [eezvyesni] famous

извините! [eezveeneetyeh!] excuse me!, sorry!

извините, пожалуйста [eezveeneetyeh, paJalsta] excuse me

извиняться/извиниться [eezveenyatsa/eezveeneetsa] to apologize

я очень извиняюсь [ya ochyen eezveenya-yoos] I'm really sorry

из-за [eez-za] because of

изнасиловать [eeznaseelavat] to rape

икона [eekona] icon

или [eelee] or

или ... или ... [eelee ... eelee ...] either ... or ...

им [eem] him; it; by him; by it; them; to them

имеется ... [eemyeh-yetsa ...] there is ...

иметь [eemyet] to have

имеются ... [eemyeh-yootsa ...] there are ...

ими [eemee] (by) them

имя [eemya] name, first name

иначе [eenachyeh] otherwise

инвалид [eenvaleet] disabled

иногда [eenagda] sometimes

иностранец [eenastranyets]/ **иностранка** [eenastranka] foreigner (man/woman)

иностранный [eenastran-ni] foreign

институт иностранных языков [eensteetoot eenastranniн yazik**ov**] language school

инструктор [eenstr**oo**ktar] instructor

инструмент [eenstroom**yent**] tool; instrument

интересный [eentyer**yes**ni] interesting

Интернет [eentern**et**] Internet

Интурист [eentoor**eest**] Intourist

информация [eenfarm**a**tsi-ya] information

Ирландия [eerl**a**ndee-ya] Ireland

искать [ee**sk**at] to look for

искренний [**ee**skryen-nee] sincere

искупаться [eesk**oo**patsa] to go swimming

искусственный [eesk**oo**stvyen-ni] artificial

искусство [eesk**oo**stva] art

Испания [eesp**a**nee-ya] Spain

исполнитель [eesp**a**ln**ee**tyel] executive; performer

использовать [eesp**o**lzavat] to use

испорченный [eesp**o**rchyen-ni] faulty; rotten

исторический [eestar**ee**chyeskee] historical

история [eest**o**ree-ya] history

исчезать/исчезнуть [eeschyez**at**/eeschy**ez**noot] to disappear

Италия [eet**a**lee-ya] Italy

итог [eet**ok**] total; result

их [ee**н**] their; theirs; them; of them

июль m [ee-**yool**] July

июнь m [ee-**yoon**] June

К
___

к [k] to; towards

к. block

кабинет врача [kabeen**yet** vr**a**cha] doctor's surgery

каблук [kabl**ook**] heel

каждый [k**a**Jdi] each; every

каждый день [k**a**Jdi dyen] every day

каждый раз [k**a**Jdi ras] every time

Казак [kaz**ak**] Cossack

Казахстан [kazaнst**an**] Kazakhstan

казачий [kaz**a**chee] Cossack

как [kak] like, as

как? [kak?] how?

как дела? [kak dyel**a**?] how are you?, how are things?

календарь m [kalyend**ar**] calendar

камень m [k**a**myen] stone

камера хранения [k**a**myera нran**ye**nee-ya] left luggage office, baggage checkroom

Канада [kan**a**da] Canada

канал [kan**al**] canal; channel

канат [kan**at**] rope

каникулы [kan**ee**kooli] school holidays

канун Нового года [kan**oon** n**o**vava g**o**da] New Year's Eve

канцтовары [k**a**ntstavari] stationery

А
Б
В
Г
Д
Е
Ё
Ж
З
И
Й
К
Л
М
Н
О
П
Р
С
Т
У
Ф
Х
Ц
Ч
Ш
Щ
Ъ
Ы
Ь
Э
Ю
Я

капля [kaplya] drop

капот [kapot] bonnet, (US) hood

карандаш [karandash] pencil

карий [karee] brown (eyes)

карман [karman] pocket

карта [karta] map; playing card

картина [karteena] painting

картинная галерея [karteen-na-ya galyeryeh-ya] art gallery

картон [karton] cardboard

карточка (бизнесмена) [kartachka (beeznyesmyena)] business card

Каспийское море [kaspeeska-yeh moryeh] Caspian Sea

касса [kas-sa] cash desk; booking office; box office

кассета [kas-syeta] cassette

кассетный магнитофон [kas-syetni magneetafon] cassette recorder

кастрюля [kastryoolya] saucepan

катастрофа [katastrofa] disaster

кататься на коньках [katatsa na kankaн] to skate

кататься на лыжах [katatsa na liyzaн] to ski

католик [katoleek] Catholic

кафе [kafeh] café

кафетерий [kafyeteree] cafeteria

качество [kachyestva] quality

кашель m [kashel] cough

кашлять [kashlyat] to cough

каштановый [kashtanavi]

brown, chestnut (hair)

каюта [ka-yoota] cabin

кв., квартира [kvarteera] flat, apartment

квартирная плата [kvarteerna-ya plata], квартплата [kvartplata] rent

квитанция [kveetantsi-ya] receipt; ticket

кеды [kyedi] trainers

кем [kem] who; (by) whom

кемпинг [kempeenk] campsite

Киев [kee-yev] Kiev

кило [keelo] kilo

километр [keelamyetr] kilometre

кино(театр) [keeno(-tyeh-atr)] cinema, movie theater

кинокамера [keenakamyera] camcorder

кинофильм [keenafeelm] film, movie

кислый [keesli] sour

кисть f [keest] paintbrush

Китай [keetI] China

кладбище [kladbeesh-chyeh] cemetery

класс [klas] class

классика [klaseeka] classical music or literature

классическая музыка [klaseechyeska-ya moozika] classical music

классический [klas-seechyeskee] classical

класть/положить [klast/palaJeet] to put; to lay

клей [klyay] glue

клейкая лента [klyayka-ya

lyenta] Sellotape®, Scotch tape®

клиент [klee-**yent**] client

климат [**klee**mat] climate

клиника [**klee**neeka] clinic

клуб [kloop] club

ключ [klyooch] key

книга [k**nee**ga] book

книжечка [k**nee**Jechka] book of 10 tickets

книжный магазин [k**nee**Jni maga**zeen**] bookshop, bookstore

ковёр [kav**yor**] carpet; rug

когда? [kag**da**?] when?

когда-нибудь [kag**da**-nee**boot**] at some time; ever; one day

вы когда-нибудь ...? [vi kag**da**-nee**boot** ...?] have you ever ...?

когда-то [kag**da**-ta] one day; some time

кого [ka**vo**] who; (of) whom

код [kot] code

кожа [**ko**Ja] skin; leather

кожаный [**ko**Jani] leather

койка [**koy**ka] bunk bed

колготки [kal**got**kee], колготы [kal**go**ti] tights, pantyhose

колено [ka**lye**na] knee

колесо [ka**lye**so] wheel

количество [ka**lee**chyestva] quantity

коллекция [kal-l**yek**tsi-ya] collection

колокол [**ko**lakal] bell

кольцо [kal**tso**] ring; circle

ком [kom] who; whom

команда [ka**man**da] team

командировка [kamandeer**of**ka] business trip

комар [ka**mar**] mosquito

комиссионный (магазин) [kamees-see-**on**-ni (maga**zeen**)] secondhand shop

Коммунистическая партия [kam-mooneestee**chy**eska-ya par**tee**-ya] Communist Party

комната [**kom**nata] room

компания [kam**pa**nee-ya] company

компостер [kam**pos**tyer] ticket punch

компьютер [kamp**yoo**tyer] computer

кому [ka**moo**] who; (to) whom

конверт [kan**vyert**] envelope

кондитерская [kan**dee**tyerska-ya] confectioner's

кондиционирование воздуха [kandeetsi-an**ee**ravanee-yeh **voz**dooНa] air-conditioning

конец [kan**yets**] end

конечно [kan**yesh**na] of course

конечный пункт [kan**ye**chni poonkt] terminus

консервный нож [kan**syer**vni nosh] tin-opener

консульство [**kon**soolstva] consulate

контактные линзы [kan**tak**tni-yeh **leen**zi] contact lenses

контролёр [kantral**yor**] ticket inspector

конфета [kan**fye**ta] sweet, candy

концерт [kan**tsert**] concert

концертный зал [kantsertni zal] concert hall

кончать/кончить [kanchat/koncheet] to finish

коньки [kankee] skates

кооператив [ka-apyerateef] co-operative

копейка [kapyayka] kopeck

у меня ни копейки денег [oo myenya nee kapyaykee dyenyek] I'm broke

корабль m [karabl] ship

корзина [karzeena] basket

коридор [kareedor] corridor

коричневый [kareechnyevi] brown

коробка [karopka] box

коробка передач [karopka pyeryedach] gearbox

королева [karalyeva] queen

король m [karol] king

короткий [karotkee] short

короткий путь [karotkee poot] shortcut

корп., корпус [korpoos] block

корь f [kor] measles

косметика [kasmyeteeka] make-up; cosmetics

костыли [kastilee] crutches

кость f [kost] bone

костюм [kastyoom] suit

который [katori] which

который час? [katori chas?] what time is it?

кофта [kofta] cardigan

кошелёк [kashelyok] purse, coin purse

кошка [koshka] cat

кошмар [kashmar] nightmare

к перронам [k per-ronam] to the platforms/tracks

к поездам [k pa-yezdam] to the trains

кража [kraja] theft

край [kri] edge

крайний: по крайней мере [pa krinyay myeryeh] at least

кран [kran] tap, faucet

красивый [kraseevi] nice; beautiful; handsome

красить/покрасить [kraseet/pakraseet] to paint

Красная Площадь [krasna-ya plosh-chat] Red Square

краснуха [krasnooнa] German measles

красный [krasni] red

красть/украсть [krast/ookrast] to steal

кредитная карточка [kryedeetna-ya kartachka] credit card

крем [kryem] cream; butter cream

крем для бритья [kryem dlya breetya] shaving foam

крем для обуви [kryem dlya oboovee] shoe polish

крем для снятия косметики [kryem dlya snyatee-ya kasmyeteekee] cleansing cream

Кремль m [kryeml] Kremlin

крепость f [kryepast] fortress; strength

кресло-каталка [kryesla-katalka] wheelchair

критическое положение [kreeteechyeska-yeh palajeneeyeh] emergency

кричать/закричать [kreechat/
zakreechat] to shout

кровать f [kravat] bed

кровь f [krof] blood

кроме [kromyeh] except

кроме воскресений [kromyeh
vaskryesyenee] except Sundays

круглый [kroogli] round

круиз [kroo-eez] cruise

крутой [krootoy] steep

крыло [krilo] wing

Крым [kriym] Crimea

крыша [kriysha] roof

крышка [kriyshka] lid

к себе [ksyebyeh] pull

ксерокс [ksyeraks] photocopy;
photocopier

кто? [kto?] who?

кто-нибудь [kto-neeboot], кто-
то [kto-ta] someone; anyone

кувшин [koofshiyn] jug

кузен [koozen], кузина
[koozeena] cousin (male/female)

кукла [kookla] doll

кулинария [kooleenaree-ya]
delicatessen

купальная шапочка
[koopalna-ya shapachka] bathing
cap

купальник [koopalneek]
swimming costume

купаться/искупаться
[koopatsa/eeskoopatsa] to go
swimming

купе [koopeh] compartment

купить [koopeet] to buy

купол [koopal] cupola, dome

курить/закурить [kooreet/

zakooreet] to smoke

курс (валюты) [koors (valyooti)]
exchange rate

куртка [koortka] jacket;
anorak

кусок [koosok] piece

кухня [kooHnya] kitchen;
cooking, cuisine

кухонная посуда [kooHan-na-
ya pasooda] cooking utensils

кухонное полотенце [kooHan-
na-yeh palatyentseh] tea towel

Л

ладно [ladna] all right, OK

лак для волос [lak dlya valos]
hair spray

лак для ногтей [lak dlya
naktyay] nail polish

лампа [lampa] lamp

лампочка [lampachka] light
bulb

ластик [lasteek] rubber, eraser

Латвия [latvee-ya] Latvia

лгать/солгать [lgat/salgat] to
lie, to tell a lie

левша [lyefsha] left-handed

левый [lyevi] left

лёгкие [lyoHkee-yeh] lungs

лёгкий [lyoHkee] light (not
heavy); easy

лёд [lyot] ice

леденец [lyedyenyets] lollipop

лезбиянка [lyezbee-yanka]
lesbian

лезвие бритвы [lyezvee-yeh
breetvi] razor blade

лейкопластырь [lyaykaplastir] plaster, Bandaid®

лекарство [lyekarstva] medicine, drug

ленивый [lyeneevi] lazy

лес [lyes] forest, wood

лестница [lyesneetsa] stairs; ladder

летать/лететь [lyetat/lyetyet] to fly

лето [lyeta] summer

летом [lyetam] in summer

лечь [lyech] to lie down

ли [lee] question particle

ливень m [leevyen] downpour

лист [leest] leaf

Литва [leetva] Lithuania

литр [leetr] litre

лифт [lift] lift, elevator

лихорадка [leeнaratka] fever

лицо [leetso] face

лишний [leeshnee] spare

лишний вес багажа [leeshnee vyes bagaЈa] excess baggage

лоб [lop] forehead

ловить/поймать [laveet/pɪmat] to catch

лодка [lotka] boat

лодыжка [ladiyshka] ankle

ложиться/лечь [laЈeetsa/lyech] to lie down

ложка [loshka] spoon

ложный [loЈni] false

локоть m [lokat] elbow

ломать/сломать [lamat/slamat] to break

ломтик [lomteek] slice

Лондон [londan] London

лосьон для загара [lasyon dlya zagara] suntan lotion

лосьон для снятия косметики [lasyon dlya snyatee-ya kasmyeteekee] make-up remover

лошадь f [loshat] horse

луна [loona] moon

лучше [looch-sheh] better

лучший [looch-shi] better; best

самый лучший [sami looch-shi] the best

лыжи [liyЈi] skis

лыжные ботинки [liyЈni-yeh bateenkee] ski boots

лыжный спорт [liyЈni sport] skiing

любезный [lyoobyezni] kind, obliging

любимый [lyoobeemi] favourite

любить [lyoobeet] to love

любовь f [lyoobof] love

люди [lyoodee] people

M

M gents' toilet, men's room; underground, metro, (US) subway

магазин [magazeen] shop

магазин беспошлинной торговли [magazeen byesposhleen-nɪ targovlee] duty-free shop

магнитофонная кассета [magneetafon-na-ya kasyeta] tape, cassette мазь f [mas] ointment

май [mɪ] May

маленький [malyenkee] small; little; short

мало [mala] not much; not many

мало времени [mala vryemyenee] not much time

мальчик [malcheek] boy

мама [mama] mum

марка [marka] stamp; make (of car etc)

марки [markee] stamps

март [mart] March

маршрут [marshroot] route, itinerary

маршрутное такси [marshrootna-yeh taksee] minibus

масло [masla] oil

масло для загара [masla dlya zagara] suntan oil

мастер [mastyer] foreman; expert; hair stylist

матрас [matras] mattress

матрёшка [matryoshka] Russian doll

мать f [mat] mother

машина [mashiyna] car; vehicle

мебель f [myebyel] furniture

медленно [myedlyen-na] slowly

медленный [myedlyen-ni] slow

медовый месяц [myedovi myesyats] honeymoon

медсестра [myetsyestra] nurse

между [myeJdoo] between

междугородный автобус [myeJdoogarodni aftoboos] coach, long-distance bus

международный звонок [myeJdoo-garodni zvanok] long-distance call

международный телефон [myeJdoo-garodni tyelyefon] long-distance phone

международные рейсы [myeJdoonarodni-yeh ryaysi] international flights

международный [myeJdoonarodni] international

международный звонок [myeJdoonarodni zvanok] international call

международный телефон [myeJdoonarodni tyelyefon] international telephone

мелочь f [myelach] small change

менеджер [menedjer] manager

менее [myenyeh-yeh] less

меньше [myensheh] smaller; less

меня [myenya] me; of me

у меня [oo myenya] I have

менять/поменять [myenyat/pamyenyat] to change

мёртвый [myortvi] dead

мест нет [myest nyet] full

места [myesta] seats

местное время [myesna-yeh vryemya] local time

местность f [myesnast] area

местный звонок [myesni zvanok] local call

место [myesta] place; seat

на месте [na myestyeh] on the spot

место для курения [m**ye**sta dlya koor**ye**nee-ya] smoking area

месяц [m**ye**syats] month

месячные [m**ye**syachni-yeh] period

металл [m**ye**tal] metal

метр [m**ye**tr] metre

метро [m**ye**tro] underground, metro, (US) subway

мех [m**ye**н] fur

меха [m**ye**нa] fur shop

механик [m**ye**нaneek] mechanic

меховая шапка [m**ye**нav**a**-ya sh**a**pka] fur hat

мешать [m**ye**shat] to disturb; to stir; to mix; to prevent

милиционер [meeleetsi-an**ye**r] policeman

милиция [meel**ee**tsi-ya] police

миллион [mee-lee-**o**n] million

Минск [m**ee**nsk] Minsk

минута [meen**oo**ta] minute

мир [m**ee**r] world; peace

мне [mn**ye**h] me; to me

многие [mn**o**gee-yeh] many; many people

много [mn**o**ga] a lot (of); many; much

мной [mn**o**y] (by) me

могу: я могу [ya mag**oo**] I can

мода [m**o**da] fashion

модный [m**o**dni] fashionable

моё [ma**yo**] my; mine

моего [ma-y**evo**] (of) my; (of) mine

мине; by my; by mine

моём [ma-y**o**m] my; mine

моему [ma-yem**oo**] (to) my; (to) mine

может быть [m**o**jet biyt] maybe

можно [m**o**jna] one can, one may; it is possible

можно ...? [m**o**jna ...?] can I ...?

мои [ma-**ee**] my; mine; of my; of mine

моим [ma-**ee**m] (by) my; (by) mine; (to) my; (to) mine

моими [mo-**ee**mee] (by) my; (by) mine

моих [ma-**ee**н], **мой** [m**o**y] my; mine

мокрый [m**o**kri] wet

Молдова [mald**o**va] Moldova

молния [m**o**lnee-ya] lightning; zip, zipper

молодой [malad**oy**] young

молодые люди [malad**iy**-eh ly**oo**dee] young people

моложе [mal**o**jeh] younger

море [m**o**ryeh] sea

мороженое [mar**o**jena-yeh] ice cream

мороз [mar**o**s] frost

морозилка [maraz**ee**lka] freezer

Москва [mask**va**] Moscow

мост [m**o**sst] bridge

мотор [mat**o**r] engine

моторная лодка [mat**o**rna-ya l**o**tka] motorboat

мотоцикл [matats**ee**kl] motorbike

мочь/смочь [moch/smoch] can, to be able to

мою [ma-**yoo**] my; mine

моя [ma-**ya**] my; mine

муж [moosh] husband

мужская одежда [mooshska-ya ad**ye**Jda] menswear

мужской зал [mooshsk**oy** zal] men's hairdresser

мужской туалет [mooshsk**oy** too-al**yet**] gents' toilet, men's room

мужчина m [moosh-ch**ee**na] man

музей [mooz**yay**] museum

музыка [**moo**zika] music

музыкальный [moozik**a**lni] musical

мусор [**moo**sar] rubbish, trash

мусорный ящик [**moo**sarni **ya**sh-cheek] dustbin, trashcan

муха [**moo**на] fly (insect)

мы [miy] we

мыло [**miy**la] soap

мыть/помыть [miyt/pam**iyt**] to wash

мыть/помыть посуду [miyt/pam**iyt** pas**oo**doo] to do the washing-up

мышь f [miysh] mouse

мягкие контактные линзы [**mya**нkee-yeh kant**a**ktni-yeh l**ee**nzi] soft lenses

мягкий [**mya**нkee] soft

мясной магазин [myasn**oy** magaz**een**] butcher's

мясо [**mya**sa] meat

мяч [myach] ball

Н

на [na] on; at

наберите номер [nabyer**ee**tyeh n**o**myer] dial the number

наб., набережная [nabyery**e**Jna-ya] embankment

на вынос [na **viy**nas] to take away, (US) to go

на себя [na syeb**ya**] pull

наверху [navyerн**oo**] at the top; upstairs

там наверху [tam navyerн**oo**] up there

над [nat] over; above

над головой [nad galav**oy**] overhead

надеяться [nad**yeh**-yatsa] to hope

надо [n**a**da] it is necessary; one must; need

мне надо ... [mnyeh n**a**da ...] I need ...

надоесть: мне надоело ... [mnyeh nada-**ye**la ...] I'm fed up with ...

назад [naz**at**] back; backwards; ago

три дня назад [tree dnya naz**at**] three days ago

название [nazv**a**nee-yeh] name; title

наиболее [na-eeb**o**lyeh-yeh] the most

найти [n**i**t**ee**] to find

накладная [nakladn**a**-ya] invoice

наконец [nakan**yets**] at last

налево [nalyeva] to the left

наличные: платить
наличными [plateet
naleechnimee] to pay cash

налог [nalok] tax

нам [nam] (to) us

нами [namee] (by) us

нападать/напасть [napadat/
napast] to attack

напасть [napast] to attack

написать [napeesat] to write

напиток [napeetak] drink

наполнять/наполнить
[napalnyat/napolneet] to fill

направление [napravlyenee-yeh]
direction

направо [naprava] to the
right

например [napreemyer] for
example

напрокат [naprakat] for hire,
to rent

напротив [naproteef] opposite

народ [narot] people; nation

народная музыка [narodna-ya
moozika] folk music

нарочно [narochna]
deliberately

наружное [narooJna-yeh] for
external use only

наружный [narooJni]
external; outdoor

нас [nas] us; of us

у нас [oo nas] we have

насекомое [nasyekoma-yeh]
insect

насморк [nasmark] cold

настольный теннис [nastolni
ten-nees] table tennis

настоящий [nasta-yash-chee]
genuine, real

настроение [nastra-yenee-yeh]
mood

натощак [natash-chak] on an
empty stomach

наука [na-ooka] science

научить [na-oocheet] to teach

нахальный [naнalni] cheeky,
impertinent

находить/найти [naнadeet/
nitee] to find

национальность f [natsi-
analnast] nationality

начало [nachala] beginning

начальник [nachalneek] head,
chief, boss

начинать/начать [nacheenat/
nachat] to begin, to start

наш [nash], наша [nasha] ,
наше [nasheh] our; ours

нашего [nasheva] (of) our;
(of) ours

нашей [nashay] our; ours;
of our; of ours; to our; to
ours; by our; by ours

нашем [nashem] our; ours

нашему [nashemoo] (to) our;
(to) ours

наши [nashi] our; ours

нашим [nashim] (by) our; (by)
ours; (to) our; (to) ours

нашими [nashiymee] (by) our;
(by) ours

наших [nashiн] (of) our; (of)
ours

нашу [nashoo] our; ours

не [nyeh] not

небо [nyeba] sky

неважно [nyeva**J**na] it doesn't matter

невероятный [nyevyera-**yat**ni] incredible

невеста [nyev**yes**ta] fiancée; bride

невозможно [nyevazmo**J**na] it's impossible

не высовываться из окон [nyeh vis**o**vivatsa eez **o**kan] do not lean out of the windows

него [nyev**o**] his; its

у него [oo nyev**o**] he has; it has

недалеко (от) [nyedalyek**o** (at)] not far (from)

неделя [nyed**ye**lya] week

в неделю [vnyed**ye**lyoo] per week

на этой неделе [na **e**ti nyed**ye**lyeh] this week

две недели [dvyeh nyed**ye**lee] fortnight, two weeks

недоразумение [nyedarazoom**ye**nee-yeh] misunderstanding

неё [nyeh-**yo**] her; hers; it; its

у неё [oo nyeh-**yo**] she has; it has

независимый [nyezav**ee**seemi] independent

не за что [n**ye**h za shta] you're welcome, don't mention it

ней [nyay] her; it

некоторые [n**ye**katari-yeh] some; a few

не курить [nyeh koor**ee**t] no smoking

нелепый [nyel**ye**pi] ridiculous

нём [nyom] him; it

немедленно [nyem**ye**dlyen-na] immediately

немецкий [nyem**ye**tskee] German

немецкий язык [nyem**ye**tskee yaz**iyk**] German (language)

немного [nyem**no**ga] a little bit

ненавидеть [nyenav**ee**dyet] to hate

не нырять [nyeh nir**yat**] no diving

необходимо [nyeh-apHad**ee**ma] it's necessary

не останавливается в ... [nyeh astan**a**vleeva-yetsa v ...] does not stop at ...

неправильный [nyepr**a**veelni] wrong, incorrect

не прислоняться [nyeh preeslan**ya**tsa] do not lean against the door

неприятный [nyepree-**yat**ni] unpleasant

не работает [nyeh rab**o**ta-yet] out of order

не разрешается ... [nyeh razryesha-yetsa ...] do not ...

нервный [n**ye**rvni] nervous

нёс [nyos] carried; was carrying; were carrying

несколько [n**ye**skolka] several; a few

несла [nyes**la**] carried; was carrying; were carrying

несли [nyesl**ee**] carried; were carrying

несносный [nyesn**o**sni] intolerable

нести [nyest**ee**] to carry

нет [nyet] no

нет, спасибо [nyet, spaseeba] no, thank you

нет входа [nyet fHoda] no entry

нет выхода [nyet viyHada] no exit

не трогать [nyeh trogat] do not touch

неустойчивый [nyeh-oostoycheevi] changeable; unstable

ни ... ни ... [nee ... nee ...] neither ... nor ...

нигде [neegdyeh] nowhere

нижнее бельё [neeJnyeh-yeh byelyo] underwear

низкий [neeskee] low

никогда [neekagda] never

никто [neekto] nobody

ними: с ними [sneemee] with them

нитка [neetka] thread

них [neeH] their; theirs; them

у них [oo neeH] they have

ничего [neechyevo], ничто [neeshto] nothing

но [no] but

Новая Зеландия [nova-ya zyelandee-ya] New Zealand

новогодняя ночь [navagodnya-ya noch] New Year's Eve

новости [novastee] news

новый [novi] new

новый год [novi got] New Year

с Новым годом! [snovim godam!] happy New Year!

нога [naga] leg; foot

ноготь m [nogat] fingernail; toenail

нож [nosh] knife

ножницы [noJneetsi] scissors

ноль m [nol] zero

номер [nomyer] number; hotel room

номер на двоих [nomyer na dva-eeH] double room

номер с двумя кроватями [nomyer zdvoomya kravatyamee] twin room

номерной знак [namyernoy znak] number plate

Норвегия [narvyegee-ya] Norway

нормально [narmalna] not bad, OK

нормальный [narmalni] normal

нос [nos] nose

носить/нести [naseet/nyestee] to carry

носки [naskee] socks

носовой платок [nasavoy platok] handkerchief

ночная рубашка [nachna-ya roobashka] nightdress

ночь f [noch] night

спокойной ночи [spakoyni nochee] good night

ноябрь m [na-yabr] November

нравиться [nraveetsa] to like

мне нравится ... [mnyeh nraveetsa ...] I like ...

нуль [nool] zero

нырять/нырнуть [niryat/nirnoot] to dive

O

o [a] about

оба/обе [oba/obyeh] both

обед [abyet] lunch

обёрточная бумага
[abyortachna-ya boomaga]
wrapping paper

обещать [abyesh-chat] to
promise

обижать/обидеть [abeeJat/
abeedyet] to offend

облако [oblaka] cloud

область f [oblast]
administrative region

облачный [oblachni] cloudy

обмен валюты [abmyen
valyooti] currency exchange

обогреватель m [abagryevatyel]
heater

обратный адрес [abratni
adryes] sender's address

обратный билет [abratni
beelyet] return ticket, round-
trip ticket

обручён/обручена [abroochon/
abroochyena] engaged (man/
woman: to be married)

обслуживание [apslooJivanee-
yeh] service

обслуживать/обслужить
[apslooJivat/apslooJit] to serve

обувь f [oboof] footwear

общежитие [apsh-chyeJeetee-
yeh] hostel

общество [opsh-chyestva]
society

объектив [abyekteef] lens

объяснение [abyasnyenee-yeh]
explanation

объяснять/объяснить
[abyasnyat/abyasneet] to
explain

обыкновенный [abiknavyen-
ni] usual

обычай [abiychI] custom

обычно [abiychna] usually

овощи [ovash-chee] vegetables

овощной магазин [avash-
chnoy magazeen] greengrocer's

огонь m [agon] fire

ограничение скорости
[agraneechyenee-yeh skorastee]
speed limit

одеваться/одеться [adyevatsa/
adyetsa] to get dressed

одежда [adyeJda] clothes

одеколон после бритья
[adyekalon poslyeh breetya]
aftershave

Одесса [adyesa] Odessa

одеться [adyetsa] to get
dressed

одеяло [adyeh-yala] blanket

один [adeen] alone; one

одиннадцатый [adeenatsati]
eleventh

одиннадцать [adeenatsat]
eleven

одна [adna] alone; one

одно [adno] one

одноместный номер [adna-
myesni nomyer] single room

одолжить [adalJeet] to lend

ожерелье [aJeryelyeh] necklace

ожог [aJok] burn

озеро [ozyera] lake

окно [akno] window

около [okala] near; about

октябрь m [aktyabr] October

окулист [akooleest] optician

он [on] he; it

она [ana] she; it

они [anee] they

оно [ano] it

опаздывать/опоздать (на) [apazdivat/apazdat (na)] to arrive/be late; to miss

опасность f [apasnast] danger

опасный [apasni] dangerous

опера [opyera] opera

операция [apyeratsi-ya] operation

опоздать (на) [apazdat (na)] to arrive/be late; to miss

опрокинуть [aprakeenoot] to knock over

оптика [opteeka] optician's

опухший [apooHshi] swollen

оранжевый [aranjevi] orange (colour)

организация [arganeezatsi-ya] organization

организовать [arganeezavat] to organize

оркестр [arkyestr] orchestra

оса [asa] wasp

осень f [osyen] autumn, (US) fall

осенью [osyenyoo] in the autumn, in the fall

осмотр [asmotr] check-up

особенно [asobyen-na] especially

особняк [asabnyak] detached house

особый [asobi] special

оставаться/остаться [astavatsa/astatsa] to stay; to remain

оставить [astaveet] to leave behind; to forget

остановиться [astanaveetsa] to stop

остановитесь! [astanaveetyes!] stop!

остановка [astanofka] stop

остановка автобуса [astanofka aftoboosa] bus stop

остаток [astatak] rest

остаться [astatsa] to stay; to remain

осторожно! [astaroJna!] be careful!; look out!

осторожно, двери закрываются! [astaroJna, dvyeree zakriva-yootsa!] caution, the doors are closing!

осторожно, окрашено [astaroJna, akrashena] wet paint

осторожный [astaroJni] careful

остров [ostraf] island

острый [ostri] hot, spicy; sharp

от [ot] from

ответ [atvyet] answer

ответить [atvyeteet] to answer

ответственный [atvyetstvyen-ni] responsible

отвечать/ответить [atvyechat/ atvyeteet] to answer

отвратительный [atvrateetyelni] disgusting

отдел [ad-dyel], отделение [ad-dyelyenee-yeh] department

отделение милиции [ad-dyelyenee-yeh meeleetsi-ee] police station

отдельно [ad-dyelna] separately

отдельный [ad-dyelni] separate

отдельный номер [ad-dyelni nomyer] single room

отдохнуть [ad-daнnoot] to take a rest

отдых [od-diн] holiday, vacation; rest

отдыхать/отдохнуть [ad-diнat/ad-daнnoot] to take a rest

отец [atyets] father

открывалка [atkrivalka] bottle-opener

открывать/открыть [atkrivat/atkrit] to open

открытка [atkritka] card; postcard

открыто [atkriyta] open

открытый [atkriyti] open

открыть [atkriyt] to open

отлично! [atleechna!] excellent!

отличный [atleechni] excellent

отменять/отменить [atmyenyat/atmyeneet] to cancel

отоларинголог [atalareengolak] ear, nose and throat specialist

отопление [ataplyenee-yeh] heating

отправитель [atpraveetyel] sender

отправить [atpraveet] to send

отправление [atpravlyenee-yeh] departure

отправлять/отправить [atpravlyat/atpraveet] to send

от себя [at syebya] push

отъезд [atyest] departure

офис [ofees] waiter

официант [afeetsi-ant] waiter

официантка [afeetsi-antka] waitress; barmaid

очаровательный [acharavatyelni] lovely, charming

очевидец [achyeveedyets] witness

очевидно [achyeveedna] obviously

очень [ochyen] very; very much

очень приятно! [ochyen pree-yatna!] pleased to meet you!

очередь f [ochyeryet] queue, (US) line

стоять в очереди [sta-yat vochyeryedee] to queue, to line up

очки [achkee] glasses, eyeglasses

очки от солнца [achkee at sontsa] sunglasses

ошибиться [ashibeetsa] to be mistaken

я ошибся/ошиблась [ya ashiypsa/ashiyblas] I've made a mistake (said by man/woman)

ошибка [ashiypka] mistake, error

П

падать/упасть [padat/oopast]
  to fall

падать/упасть в обморок
  [padat/oopast vobmarak] to
  faint

пакет [pakyet] packet; parcel;
  paper bag

палатка [palatka] tent

палец [palyets] finger

палец ноги [palyets nagee] toe

палуба [palooba] deck

пальто [palto] coat

памятник [pamyatneek]
  monument

папа [papa] dad

папироса [papeerosa] Russian
  non-filter cigarette

пара [para] pair; couple

парикмахер [pareekmaнyer]
  hairdresser

парикмахерская
  [pareekmaнyerska-ya] barber's,
  hairdresser's

парилка [pareelka] steam
  room

парк [park] park

паром [parom] ferry

пароход [paraнot] steamer

партер [parter] stalls

партия [partee-ya] party

парус [paroos] sail

парусная лодка [paroosna-ya
  lotka] sailing boat

парусник [paroosneek] sailing
  boat

парусный спорт [paroosni
  sport] sailing

паспорт [paspart] passport

паспортный контроль
  [paspartni kantrol] passport
  control

пассажир [pasaJeer] passenger

Пасха [pasнa] Easter

паук [pa-ook] spider

пахнуть [paнnoot] to smell

пачка [pachka] packet; pack;
  bundle

педаль f [pyedal] pedal

пейзаж [pyayzash] landscape;
  scenery

пелёнка [pyelyonka] nappy,
  diaper

пельменная [pyelmyen-na-ya]
  café selling ravioli

пеницилин [pyeneetsileen]
  penicillin

пенсионер [pyensee-anyer]

пенсионерка, [pyensee-
  anyerka] old-age pensioner
  (man/woman)

пепельница [pyepyelneetsa]
  ashtray

пер. lane

первая помощь [pyerva-ya
  pomash-ch] first aid

первый [pyervi] first

первый класс [pyervi klas]
  first class

первый этаж [pyervi etash]
  ground floor, (US) first floor

перевал [pyeryeval] pass
  (mountain)

переводить/перевести
  [pyeryevadeet/pyeryevyestee] to
  translate; to interpret

переводчик [pyeryevotcheek] translator; interpreter

переговорный пункт [pyeryegavorni poonkt] communications centre

перед [pyeryed] in front of; just before

передняя часть [pyeryednya-ya chast] front

переезд [pyeryeh-yest] level crossing, (US) grade crossing

перейти [pyeryeh-eetee] to cross

перекрёсток [pyeryekryostak] cross-roads; junction, intersection

перелом [pyeryelom] fracture

переодеться [pyeryeh-adyetsa] to get changed

переполненный [pyeryepolnyen-ni] crowded

перерыв [pyeryeriyf] break; interval

перерыв на обед с ... до ... [pyeryeriyf na abyet s ... do ...] closed for lunch from ... to ...

пересадка [pyeryesatka] change; transfer

пересесть [pyeryesyest] to change (trains etc)

пересылать/переслать [pyeryesilat/pyeryeslat] to forward

переулок [pyeryeh-oolak] lane

переход [pyeryeHot] transfer; passage; crossing; underpass, subway

переходить/перейти

[pyeryeHadeet/pyeryeh-eetee] to cross

переходник [pyeryeHadneek] adaptor

перманент [pyermanyent] perm

перчатки [pyerchatkee] gloves

песня [pyesnya] song

песок [pyesok] sand

петь [pyet] to sing

печатный материал [pyechatni matyeree-al] printed matter

печень m [pyechyen] liver

пешеход [pyeshenot] pedestrian

пешеходная зона [pyeshenodna-ya zona] pedestrian precinct

пешеходный переход [pyeshenodni pyeryenot] pedestrian crossing

пешком [pyeshkom] on foot

пещера [pyesh-chyera] cave

пивной бар [peevnoy bar], пивнушка [peevnooshka] bar, beer cellar, pub

пилка для ногтей [peelka dlya naktyay] nailfile

писать/написать [peesat/ napeesat] to write

писчебумажный магазин [peesh-chyeboomaJni magazeen] stationer's

письмо [peesmo] letter

питательный [peetatyelni] nutritious

пить/выпить [peet/viypeet] to drink

питьевая вода [peetyeva-ya vada] drinking water

пиццерия [peetser**ee**-ya] pizzeria

пишущая машинка [**pee**shoosh-cha-ya mash**iy**nka] typewriter

пищевое отравление [peesh-chevo-yeh atravl**ye**nee-yeh] food poisoning

пл. square

плавание [pl**a**vanee-yeh] swimming

плавать запрещается [pl**a**vat zapryesh-cha-yetsa] no swimming

плавать/плыть [pl**a**vat/pl**iy**t] to swim

плавки [pl**a**fkee] swimming trunks

плакат [plak**a**t] poster

плакать [pl**a**kat] to cry

пластинка [plast**ee**nka] record

пластмассовый [plasm**a**s-savi] plastic

платите в кассу [plat**ee**tyeh f **ka**s-soo] pay at the cash desk

платить/заплатить [plat**ee**t/ zaplat**ee**t] to pay

платный [pl**a**tni] paid; to be paid for

платок [plat**o**k] headscarf

платформа [platf**o**rma] platform, (US) track

платье [pl**a**tyeh] dress

плащ [plash-ch] raincoat

племянник [plyem**ya**n-neek] nephew

племянница [plyem**ya**n-neetsa] niece

плёнка [pl**yo**nka] film (for camera)

плечо [plyech**o**] shoulder

пломба [pl**o**mba] filling

плоский [pl**o**skee] flat

плохо [pl**o**нa] bad; badly
мне плохо [mnyeh pl**o**нa] I feel ill

плохой [plaн**oy**] bad

площадь f [pl**o**sh-chat] square

плыть [pl**iy**t] to swim

плэйер [pl**a**yer] personal stereo

пляж [pl**ya**sh] beach

по [po] along; according to; on
по-английски [pa-angl**ee**skee] in English

поблагодарить [pablagadar**ee**t] to thank

побриться [pabr**ee**tsa] to shave

повар [p**o**var] cook

поверить [pav**ye**reet] to believe

поворачивать/повернуть [pavar**a**cheevat/pavyern**oo**t] to turn

повредить [pavryed**ee**t] to damage

повторять/повторить [pavtar**ya**t/paftar**ee**t] to repeat

повязка [pav**ya**ska] bandage

погладить [pagl**a**deet] to iron; to stroke

погода [pag**o**da] weather

погулять [pagool**ya**t] to go for a walk

под [pot] below; under; underneath

178

под. entrance number

подавленный [padavlyen-ni] depressed

подарить [padareet] to give (present)

подарок [padarak] present, gift

подбородок [padbarodak] chin

подвал [padval] basement

подвозить/подвезти [padvazeet/padvyestee] to give a lift to

поделиться [padyeleetsa] to share

подержанный [padyerJan-ni] secondhand

подмётка [padmyotka] sole

подниматься/подняться [padneematsa/padnyatsa] to go up

поднос [padnos] tray

подняться [padnyatsa] to go up

подобный [padobni] similar

подождать [padaJdat] to wait

подойти [padItee] to approach; to arrive; to come

подписать [patpeesat] to sign

подпись f [potpees] signature

подросток [padrostak] teenager

подруга [padrooga] friend; girlfriend

подтвердить [pat-vyerdeet] to confirm

подумать [padoomat] to think

подушка [padooshka] pillow

подфарники [patfarneekee] sidelights

подходить/подойти [padhadeet/padItee] to approach; to arrive; to come

подъезд [padyest] entrance

подъёмник [padyomneek] ski-lift, chairlift

поезд [po-yest] train

поездка [pa-yestka] journey, trip

пожалуйста [paJalsta] please

пожар [paJar] fire, blaze

пожарная команда [paJarna-ya kamanda] fire brigade

пожарный выход [paJarni viyHat] fire exit

пожелание: с наилучшими пожеланиями [sna-eeloochshimee paJelanee-yamee] best wishes

поживаете: как вы поживаете? [kak viy paJivayetyeh?] how are you?

позаботиться о [pazaboteetsa o] to take care of

позавчера [pazafchyera] the day before yesterday

позвать [pazvat] to call

позвонить [pazvaneet] to ring; to phone

поздно [pozna] late; it's late

поздравляю! [pazdravlya-yoo!] congratulations!

позже [poJ-Jeh] later on

познакомить [paznakomeet] to introduce

познакомиться [paznakomeetsa] to get to know, to become acquainted with, to meet поймать [pimat] to catch

пока [paka] while

пока! [paka!] bye!

показывать/показать [pakazivat/pakazat] to show

покидать/покинуть [pakeedat/pakeenoot] to leave

по крайней мере [pa krinyay myeryeh] at least

покрасить [pakraseet] to paint

покупатель [pakoopatyel] customer; buyer

покупать/купить [pakoopat/koopeet] to buy

покупки [pakoopkee] shopping

идти за покупками [eet-tee za pakoopkamee] to go shopping

пол [pol] floor; sex

полдень m [poldyen] midday, noon

поле [polyeh] field

полезный [palyezni] useful

поликлиника [paleekleeneeka] surgery; medical centre

политика [paleeteeka] politics

политический [paleeteechyeskee] political

поллитра [pol-leetra] half a litre

полночь f [polnach] midnight

полный [polni] full

половина [palaveena] half

половина второго [palaveena ftarova] half past one

положить [palaJeet] to put, to place

полотенце [palatyentseh] towel

получать/получить [paloochat/paloocheet] to receive

полчаса [polchasa] half an hour

поменять [pamyenyat] to change

померить [pamyereet] to try on

помнить/вспомнить [pomneet/fspomneet] to remember, to recall

я помню [ya pomnyoo] I remember

помогать/помочь [pamagat/pamoch] to help

помогите! [pamageetyeh!] help!

помощь f [pomash-ch] help, aid, assistance

помыть [pamiyt] to wash

помыть посуду [pamiyt pasoodoo] to do the washing-up

помыться [pamiytsa] to wash (oneself)

понедельник [panyedyelneek] Monday

понимать/понять [paneemat/panyat] to understand

я не понимаю [ya nyeh paneema-yoo] I don't understand

понос [panos] diarrhoea

понять [panyat] to understand

поп-музыка [pop-moozika] pop music

попробовать [paprobavat] to taste; to try

порт [port] harbour, port

портфель **m** [partf**yel**] briefcase

порция [**p**ortsi-ya] portion

порядок [par**ya**dak] order

у меня всё в порядке [oo myen**ya** fsyo fpar**ya**tkyeh] fine, I'm OK, everything's OK

посадка [pas**a**tka] landing; boarding; arrival

посадочный талон [pas**a**dachni tal**o**n] boarding pass

посещать/посетить [pasyesh-ch**a**t/pasyet**ee**t] to visit

послание [paslan**ee**-yeh] message

послать [pasl**a**t] to send

после [p**o**slyeh] after

последний [pasl**ye**dnee] last

послезавтра [p**o**slyez**a**ftra] the day after tomorrow

послушать [pasl**oo**shat] to listen (to)

посмотреть (на) [pasmatr**yet** (na)] to look (at); to watch

посольство [pas**o**lstva] embassy

поставить [past**a**veet] to put

поставить машину [past**a**veet mash**i**ynoo] to park

постараться [past**a**ratsa] to try

постель **f** [past**ye**l] bed

постельное бельё [past**ye**lna-yeh byel**yo**] bed linen

постирать [pasteer**a**t] to do the washing

посторонним вход воспрещён [pastar**o**neem fhot vaspryesh-ch**o**n] private, staff only

посуда [pas**oo**da] crockery

посылать/послать [pasil**a**t/pasl**a**t] to send

посылка [pas**i**ylka] parcel

потерять [patyer**ya**t] to lose

по техническим причинам [pa tyeнн**ee**chyeskeem preech**ee**nam] for technical reasons

потолок [patal**o**k] ceiling

потом [pat**o**m] then; afterwards

потому что [patam**oo** shta] because

потребитель [patryebee**t**yel] consumer

потрясающий [patryas**a**-yoosh-chee] tremendous

похмелье [paнм**ye**lyeh] hangover

похожий [paнo**лi] like, similar to

поцеловать [patselav**a**t] to kiss

поцелуй [patsel**oo**] kiss

почему? [pachyem**oo**?] why?

починить [pacheen**ee**t] to mend, to repair

почки [p**o**chkee] kidneys

почта [p**o**chta] post office; mail

почта до востребования [p**o**chta da-vastr**ye**bavanee-ya] poste restante, general delivery

почтальон [pachtal**yo**n] postman, mailman

почти [pacht**ee**] almost

почтовая бумага [pach**to**va-ya
boo**ma**ga] writing paper

почтовый индекс [pach**to**vi
eendeks] postcode, zip code

почтовый ящик [pach**to**vi
yash-cheek] letterbox,
mailbox

пояс [**po**-yas] belt

потерять [patery**at**] to lose

пр. avenue

правильный [**pra**veelni] right,
correct

правительство [pra**vee**tyelstva]
government

православная церковь
[pravas**la**vna-ya t**se**rkaf] Russian
Orthodox Church

правый [**pra**vi] right

праздник [**pra**zneek] public
holiday

празднование [pra**zna**vanee-
yeh] celebration

практичный [prak**tee**chni]
practical

прачечная [**pra**chyechna-ya]
laundry

прачечная-
самообслуживания
[**pra**chyechna-ya-sama-
aps**loo**Jivanee-ya] launderette

пребывание [pryebi**va**nee-yeh]
stay

предварительный заказ
[pryedvar**ee**tyelni za**kas**]
reservation

предварительный заказ
билетов [pryedvar**ee**tyelni za**kas**
beel**ye**taf] seat reservation

предлагать/предложить

[pryedlag**at**/pryedla**J**e**et**] to offer,
to suggest

предложение [pryedla**J**e**nee**-
yeh] offer, proposal

предложить [pryedla**Jeet**] to
offer, to suggest

предохранитель m
[pryeda**H**ran**ee**tyel] fuse

предпочитать [pryetpacheet**at**]
to prefer

председатель m [pryedsyed**a**tyel]
chairman

представитель m
[pryetstav**ee**tyel] representative;
agent

презерватив [pryezyervat**ee**f]
condom

прекрасный [pryek**ra**sni]
beautiful; fine; excellent

прелестный [pryel**ye**sni] pretty

преподаватель m
[pryepadav**a**tyel] teacher;
lecturer

Прибалтика [preeb**a**lteeka]
Baltic States

прибыль f [**pree**bil] profit

прибытие [preeb**iy**tee-yeh]
arrival

привет [pree**vye**t] hello, hi

прививка [pree**vee**fka]
vaccination

привлекательный
[preevlyek**a**tyelni] attractive

привычка [pree**viy**chka] habit

привязной ремень
[preevyazn**oy** ryem**yen**] seatbelt

приглашать/пригласить
[preeglash**at**/preeglas**eet**] to
invite

приглашение [preeglashenee-yeh] invitation

пригород [preegarat] suburbs

пригородный поезд [preegaradni po-yest] local train, suburban train

пригородная касса [preegaradna-ya kas-sa] ticket office for suburban trains

приготовить [preegatoveet] to cook; to prepare

приезд [pree-yest] arrival

приезжать/приехать [pree-yezjat/pree-yeHat] to arrive (by transport)

приём посылок [pree-yom pasiylak] parcels counter

приехать [pree-yeHat] to arrive (by transport)

прийти [preetee] to come, to arrive (on foot)

прикурить: у вас есть прикурить? [oo vas yest preekooreet?] have you got a light?

прилёт [preelyot] arrival

пример [preemyer] example

примерно [preemyerna] approximately

принадлежать [preenadlyeJat] to belong

принимать/принять [preeneemat/preenyat] to accept, to take

принтер [preenter] printer

приносить/принести [preenaseet/preenyestee] to bring

принять [preenyat] to accept,

to take

природа [preeroda] nature

пристегните ремни [preestyegneetyeh ryemnee] fasten seat belts

приходить/прийти [preeHadeet/preetee] to come, to arrive (on foot)

причал [preechal] quay

причина [preecheena] cause; reason

приятного аппетита! [pree-yatnava apyeteeta!] enjoy your meal!

приятный [pree-yatni] pleasant, nice

пробка [propka] plug; traffic jam

проблема [prablyema] problem

пробовать/попробовать [probavat/paprobavat] to taste; to try

проверять/проверить [pravyeryat/pravyereet] to check

прогноз погоды [pragnos pagodi] weather forecast

программа [program-ma] programme

прогулка [pragoolka] walk

продавать/продать [pradavat/pradat] to sell

продаётся [prada-yotsa] for sale

продажа [pradaJa] sale; marketing

продажа билетов [pradaJa beelyetaf] tickets on sale

проданный [pradan-ni] sold

продать [pradat] to sell

продукция [pradooktsi-ya]
product

проездной билет [pra-yeznoy
beelyet] monthly season
ticket

проживание с двухразовым
питанием [praJivanee-yeh
zdvooH-razavim peetanee-yem]
half board

проживание с трёхразовым
питанием [praJivanee-yeh
stryoH-razavim peetanee-yem] full
board

производство [pra-eezvotstva]
production

произнести [pra-eeznyestee] to
pronounce

произносить/произнести
[pra-eeznaseet/pra-eeznyestee] to
pronounce

прокат [prakat] rental, hire

прокат автомобилей [prakat
aftamabeelyay] car rental

прокол [prakol] puncture

промышленность f
[pramiyshlyen-nast] industry

пропуск [propoosk] pass; hotel
card

проснуться [prasnootsa] to
wake up

проспект [praspyekt]
brochure; avenue

простите [prasteetyeh] excuse
me, sorry

простите? [prasteetyeh?]
pardon?, pardon me?

простой [prastoy] simple

простыня [prastinya] sheet

просьба [prosba] request

просьба не ... [prosba nyeh ...]
please do not ...

протестант [pratyestant]
Protestant

против [proteef] against

противозачаточное
средство [prateevazachatachna-
yeh sryetstva] contraceptive

прохладный [praHladni] cool

процент [pratsent] per cent

прочитать [pracheetat] to read

прошлый [proshli] last

в прошлом году [fproshlam
gadoo] last year

на прошлой неделе [na
proshli nyedyelyeh] last week

проявлять/проявить [pra-
yavlyat/pra-yaveet] to develop

пруд [proot] pond

прыгать/прыгнуть [priygat/
priygnoot] to jump

прыщик [priysh-cheek] spot,
pimple

прямо [pryama] straight ahead

прямой [pryamoy] direct;
straight

прямой номер [pryamoy
nomyer] direct dialling

прямой рейс [pryamoy ryays]
direct flight

птица [pteetsa] bird; poultry

публика [poobleeka] audience;
public

пуговица [poogaveetsa] button

пункт [poonkt] point; station;
place, spot; centre

пункт скорой помощи
[poonkt skori pomash-chee] first-
aid post

пустой [poostoy] empty

путеводитель **m**
[pootyevadeetyel] guidebook

путешествовать
[pootyeshestvavat] to travel

путь **m** [poot] path; way

пчела [pchyela] bee

пылесос [pilyesos] vacuum
cleaner

пьеса [pyesa] play (theatre)

пьяный [pyani] drunk

пятка [pyatka] heel (of foot)

пятнадцатый [pyatnatsati]
fifteenth

пятнадцать [pyatnatsat] fifteen

пятница [pyatneetsa] Friday

пятно [pyatno] stain

пятый [pyati] fifth

пять [pyat] five

пятьдесят [pyadyesyat] fifty

пятьсот [pyatsot] five hundred

Р
∎

p. rouble

работа [rabota] job; work

работает с ... до ... [rabota-yet s
... do ...] open from ... to ...

работать [rabotat] to work
это не работает [eta nyeh
rabota-yet] it's not working

рад [rat] glad

радио [radee-o] radio

раз [ras] time (occasion)
один раз [adeen ras] once

разбудить [razboodeet] to
wake up

разве? [razvyeh?] really?

разведён [razvyedyon],
разведена [razvyedyena]
divorced (man/woman)

развилка [razveelka] junction;
fork (in road)

разговаривать [razgavareevat]
to talk

разговаривать с водителем
запрещается [razgavareevat
svadeetyelyem zapryesh-cha-yetsa]
do not speak to the driver

разговор [razgavor]
conversation

раздевалка [razdyevalka]
changing room

размен [razmyen] change

размер [razmyer] size

разный [razni] various,
different

разочарованный
[razacharovan-ni] disappointed

разрешается [razryesha-yetsa]
it is allowed

разрешать/разрешить
[razryeshat/razryeshiyt] to let,
to allow

разрешение [razryeshenee-yeh]
permission; licence

разрешить [razryeshiyt] to let,
to allow

разумный [razoomni] sensible

район [rion] district

раковина [rakaveena] sink

ракушка [rakooshka] shell

рана [rana] injury

раненый [ranyeni] injured

рано [rana] early

раскладушка [raskladooshka]
campbed

распаковать (чемодан) [raspakavat (chyemadan)] to unpack

расписание [raspeesanee-yeh] timetable, (US) schedule

распродажа [raspradaJa] sale

рассказ [raskas] story

рассказать [raskazat] to tell

расслабиться [ras-slabeetsa] to relax

расстояние [ras-sta-yanee-yeh] distance

расстройство желудка [rastroystva Jelootka] indigestion

растение [rastyenee-yeh] plant

расчёска [raschoska] comb

ребёнок [ryebyonak] child; baby

ребро [ryebro] rib

ревматизм [ryevmateezm] rheumatism

ревнивый [ryevneevi] jealous

регистратура [ryegeestratoora] reception

регистрация [ryegeestratsi-ya] check-in; registration

регистрация багажа [ryegeestratsi-ya bagaJa] check-in

регулировщик [ryegooleerovshcheek] traffic warden

регулярный рейс [ryegoolyarni ryays] scheduled flight

редкий [ryetkee] rare

резать [ryezat] to cut

резина [ryezeena] rubber

резиночка [ryezeenachka] rubber band

рейс [ryays] flight

река [ryeka] river

реклама [ryeklama] advertisement; advertising

рекламировать [ryeklameeravat] to advertise

рекомендовать [ryekamyendavat] to recommend

религия [ryeleegee-ya] religion

ремень вентилятора [ryemyen vyenteelyatara] fan belt

ремесленные изделия [ryemyeslyen-ni-yeh eezdyelee-ya] crafts

ремонт [ryemont] repair

ремонт обуви [ryemont oboovee] shoe repairs

ремонт сумок [ryemont soomak] bag repairs

ресторан [ryestaran] restaurant

рецепт [ryetsept] prescription; recipe

решать/решить [ryeshat/ ryeshiyt] to decide

решение [ryeshyenee-yeh] decision

Рига [reega] Riga

родина [rodeena] native country; home(land)

родители [radeetyelee] parents

родиться [radeetsa] to be born

родственники [rotstvyenneekee] relatives

Рождество [raJdyestvo] Christmas

с Рождеством! [sraJdyestvom!] merry Christmas!

роза [**ro**za] rose

розетка [raz**ye**tka] socket

розовый [**ro**zavi] pink

рок-музыка [rok-m**oo**zika]
rock music

роман [ram**an**] novel

Россия [ras-**see**-ya] Russia

рот [rot] mouth

рубашка [roo**ba**shka] shirt

рубль m [roobl] rouble

руины [roo-**ee**ni] ruins

рука [rook**a**] arm; hand

руками не трогать [rook**a**mee
nyeh tr**o**gat] do not touch

руль m [rool] steering wheel

русская [**roo**ska-ya] Russian

русские [**roo**skee-yeh] the
Russians

русский [**roo**skee] Russian

русский язык [**roo**skee yaz**i**yk]
Russian (language)

Русь [roos] Russia (historical)

ручей [rooch**yay**] stream

ручка [**roo**chka] handle; pen

ручная кладь [rooch**na**-ya klat]
hand luggage, hand baggage

ручной тормоз [rooch**noy**
tormas] handbrake

рыба [**ri**yba] fish

рыбная ловля [**ri**ybna-ya l**o**vlya]
fishing

рыбная ловля запрещена
[**ri**ybna-ya l**o**vlya zapryesh-chyen**a**]
no fishing

рыбный магазин [**ri**ybni
magaz**een**] fishmonger's

рыжий [**ri**yJi] red-headed

рынок [**ri**ynak] market

рюкзак [ryoogz**ak**] rucksack

рюмка [r**yoo**mka] wine glass

ряд [ryat] row

рядом (c) [r**ya**dam (s)] next to

C

c [s] with

с нарочным [sn**a**rachnim]
special delivery

сад [sat] garden

садиться/сесть [sad**ee**tsa/syest]
to sit down; to get in

салфетка [salf**ye**tka] napkin

самовар [samav**ar**] samovar

самолёт [samal**yot**] plane

самолётом [samal**yo**tam] by
air

самообслуживание [sama-
apsl**oo**Jivanee-yeh] self-service

самый [**sa**mi] the most

санитарный день [san**ee**tarni
dyen] closed for cleaning

Санкт Петербург [sankt
pyetyerb**oo**rk] St Petersburg

сапог [sap**ok**] boot

сауна [**sa**-oona] sauna

свадьба [sv**a**dba] wedding

свежий [sv**ye**J] fresh

свёкор [sv**yo**kar] father-in-law
(husband's father)

свекровь [svyekr**of**] mother-
in-law (husband's mother)

свёрток [sv**yo**rtak] package

свет [svyet] light

светло- [sv**ye**tla-] light (colour)

светофор [svyetaf**or**] traffic
lights

свеча [svyech**a**] candle

свеча зажигания [svyecha zaJiganee-ya] sparkplug

свинья [sveenya] pig

свитер [sveeter] sweater, jumper

свободно [svabodna] free; vacant; fluent

свободный [svabodni] free; vacant; fluent

свободных мест нет [svabodniн myest nyet] no vacancies

своё [sva-yo], свои [sva-ee], свой [svoy], своя [sva-ya] my; your; his; its; her; our; their; mine; yours; hers; ours; theirs

свояченица [sva-yachyeneetsa] sister-in-law (wife's sister)

связываться/связаться (с) [svyazivatsa/svyazatsa (s)] to get in touch with

святой [svyatoy] holy; saint

священник [svyash-chyen-neek] priest

сгореть [zgaryet] to burn

сделать [zdyelat] to do; to make

сделать пересадку [zdyelat pyeryesatkoo] to change (trains etc)

себе [syebyeh], себя [syebya] myself; yourself; himself; herself; itself; ourselves; yourselves; themselves

север [syevyer] north

к северу от [k syevyeroo at] north of

Северная Ирландия

[syevyerna-ya eerlandee-ya] Northern Ireland

сегодня [syevodnya] today

сегодня вечером [syevodnya vyechyeram] this evening, tonight

сегодня днём [syevodnya dnyom] this afternoon

сегодня утром [syevodnya ootram] this morning

седьмой [syedmoy] seventh

сейчас [syaychas] now, at the moment

секретарша f [syekryetarsha] secretary

секретарь m [syekryetar] secretary

секс [seks] sex

секунда [syekoonda] second

семнадцатый [syemnatsati] seventeenth

семнадцать [syemnatsat] seventeen

семь [syem] seven

семьдесят [syemdyesyat] seventy

семьсот [syemsot] seven hundred

семья [syemya] family

сенная лихорадка [syen-na-ya leeнaratka] hayfever

сентябрь m [syentyabr] September

сердечный приступ [syerdyechni preestoop] heart attack

сердитый [syerdeeti] angry

сердце [syertseh] heart

серебро [syeryebro] silver

середина [syeryedeena] middle

серый [syeri] grey

серьги [syergee] earrings

серьёзный [syeryozni] serious

сестра [syestra] sister

сесть [syest] to sit down; to get in

Сибирь f [seebeer] Siberia

сигара [seegara] cigar

сигарета [seegaryeta] cigarette

сильный [seelni] strong

синий [seenee] blue

синяк [seenyak] bruise

скажите, пожалуйста ... [skaJeetyeh, paJalsta ...] can you tell me ...?

сказать [skazat] to say; to speak

скала [skala] cliff; rock

скандальный [skandalni] shocking

скатерть f [skatyert] tablecloth

сквозняк [skvaznyak] draught

скидка [skeetka] discount

складная детская коляска [skladna-ya dyetska-ya kalyaska] pushchair, (US) stroller

склон [sklon] slope

сковорода [skavarada] frying pan

скользкий [skolskee] slippery

сколько? [skolka?] how much?; how many?

сколько вам лет? [skolka vam lyet?] how old are you?

сколько это стоит? [skolka eta sto-eet?] how much is it?

скорая помощь [skora-ya pomash-ch] ambulance; first aid

скорее [skaryeh-yeh] rather

скорее! [skaryeh-yeh!] quickly!

скоро [skora] soon

скорость f [skorast] speed; gear

скрывать/скрыть [skrivat/ skriyt] to hide

скрыть [skriyt] to hide

скучный [skooshni] boring

слабительное [slabeetyelna-yeh] laxative

слабый [slabi] weak

сладкий [slatkee] sweet (to taste)

слайд [slit] slide (photographic)

слева [slyeva] on the left

следовать [slyedavat] to follow

следующая станция ... [slyedoo-yoosh-cha-ya stantsi-ya ...] next station ...

следующий [slyedoo-yoosh-chee] next; following

в следующем году [fslyedoo-yoosh-chyem gadoo] next year

на следующей неделе [na slyedoo-yoosh-chay nyedyelyeh] next week

следующий день [slyedoo-yoosh-chee dyen] the next day

слепой [slyepoy] blind

слишком ... [sleeshkam ...] too ...

слишком много [sleeshkam mnoga] too much

не слишком много [nyeh sleeshkam mnoga] not too much

словарь m [slavar] dictionary

слово [slova] word

сложный [sloJni] complicated

сломанный [sloman-ni] broken

сломать [slamat] to break

сломаться [slamatsa] to break down

служащий [slooJash-chee] employee

служба [slooJba] service; employment; job; work; duty

служба размещения [slooJba razmyesh-chyenee-ya] reception desk

служебный вход [slooJebni fHot] staff entrance

случай [sloochee] chance

случайно [slooch1na] by chance

случаться/случиться [sloochatsa/sloocheetsa] to happen

слушать/послушать [slooshat/paslooshat] to listen (to)

слышать/услышать [sliyshat/oosliyshat] to hear

смерть f [smyert] death

сметь [smyet] to dare

смешать [smyeshat] to mix

смеяться/засмеяться [smyeh-yatsa/zasmyeh-yatsa] to laugh

смотреть/посмотреть (на) [smatryet/pasmatryet (na)] to look (at); to watch

смочь [smoch] can, to be

able to

вы сможете ...? [viy smoJetyeh ...?] will you be able to ...?

он/она сможет [on/ana smoJet] he/she will be able to

смутно [smootna] vaguely

сначала [snachala] first; at first

снег [snyek] snow

СНГ [es-en-geh] CIS

снова [snova] again; once again

сноха [snaHa] daughter-in-law

собака [sabaka] dog

соблюдайте тишину [sablyoodItyeh teeshinoo] please be quiet

собой [saboy] (by) myself; (by) yourself; (by) himself; (by) herself; (by) itself; (by) ourselves; (by) yourselves; (by) themselves

с собой [s-saboy] to take away, (US) to go

соболь m [sobal] sable

собор [sabor] cathedral

собрание [sabranee-yeh] meeting

собственный [sopstvyen-ni] own; proper; personal

Советский Союз [savyetskee sa-yoos] Soviet Union

современный [savryemyen-ni] modern

согласен: я согласен/согласна [ya saglasyen/saglasna] I agree (said by man/woman)

согласованность

расписания [saglasovan-nast raspeesanee-ya] connection

Соединённые Штаты Америки [sayedeenyon-ni-yeh shtati amyereekee] United States

сожаление: к сожалению [k saɹalyenee-yoo] unfortunately

соки-воды [sokee-vodi] fruit juices and mineral water

солгать [salgat] to lie, to tell a lie

солёный [salyoni] salty; savoury; pickled

солнечный [solnyechni] sunny

солнечный ожог [solnyechni aɹok] sunburn

солнечный свет [solnyechni svyet] sunshine

солнечный удар [solnyechni oodar] sunstroke

солнце [sontseh] sun

сон [son] dream; sleep

сопровождать [sapravaɹdat] to accompany

сорок [sorak] forty

сосед [sasyet], соседка [sasyetka] neighbour (man/woman)

сохранять/сохранить [saнranyat/saнraneet] to keep

социализм [satsi-aleezm] socialism

Сочельник [sachyelneek] Christmas Eve

спальное место [spalna-yeh myesta] couchette

спальный вагон [spalni vagon] sleeping car

спальный мешок [spalni myeshok] sleeping bag

спальня [spalnya] bedroom

спасатель m [spasatel] lifeguard

спасательный пояс [spasatyelni po-yas] lifebelt

спасибо [spaseeba] thank you

спасибо большое [spaseeba balsho-yeh] thank you very much

спать [spat] to sleep

специальность f [spyetsi-alnast] speciality

спешить [spyeshiyt] to hurry

СПИД [speed] Aids

спина [speena] back (of body)

список [speesak] list

спичка [speechka] match

спокойной ночи [spakoynay nochee] good night

спорт [sport] sport

спортивное оборудование [sparteevna-yeh abaroodavanee-yeh] sports equipment

спортивный центр [sparteevni tsentr] sports centre

справа [sprava] on the right

справедливый [spravyedleevi] fair, just

справка [sprafka] information

справочная [spravachna-ya] enquiries; directory enquiries

справочное бюро [spravachna-yeh byooro] information office

справочный стол [spravachni stol] information desk

191

спрашивать/спросить [sprashivat/spraseet] to ask

спускаться/спуститься [spooskatsa/spoosteetsa] to go down

спущенная шина [spoosh-chyen-na-ya shiyna] flat tyre

среда [sryeda] Wednesday

среди [sryedee] among

среднего размера [sryednyeva razmyera] medium-sized

средство от насекомых [sryetstva at nasyekomiн] insect repellent

средство против загара [sryetstva proteev zagara] sunblock

срок [srok] period

срочно [srochna] urgent; urgently

срочный [srochni] urgent

СССР [es-es-es-er] USSR

ставить/поставить [staveet/pastaveet] to put

стадион [stadee-on] stadium

стакан [stakan] glass

становиться/стать [stanaveetsa/stat] to become

станция [stantsi-ya] station (underground, bus etc)

станция техобслуживания [stantsi-ya tyeнap-slooJivanee-ya] garage (for repairs), service station

стараться/постараться [staratsa/pastaratsa] to try

старше [starsheh] older

старый [stari] old

стать [stat] to become

стекло [styeklo] glass (material)

стена [styena] wall

стиральная машина [steeralna-ya mashiyna] washing machine

стиральный порошок [steeralni parashok] washing powder

стирать/постирать [steerat/pasteerat] to do the washing

сто [sto] hundred

стоимость [sto-eemast] charge, cost

стоимость международной отправки [sto-eemast myeJdoonarodnay atprafkee] overseas postage

стоить [sto-eet] to cost

стол [stol] table

столкновение [stalknavyenee-yeh] crash

столовая [stalova-ya] dining room; canteen

столовые приборы [stalovi-yeh preebori] cutlery

стоп-кран [stop-kran] emergency cord

сторона [starana] side

сто тысяч [sto tiysyach] hundred thousand

стоянка [sta-yanka] car park, parking lot

стоянка такси [sta-yanka taksee] taxi rank

стоять [sta-yat] to stand

страна [strana] country

страница [straneetsa] page

странный [stran-ni] strange

страх [straн] fear

страхование [straнаvanee-yeh] insurance

стрижка [streeshka] haircut

стройный [stroyni] shapely

студент [stoodyent], студентка [stoodyentka] student (male/female)

стул [stool] chair

стыдно: мне стыдно [mnyeh stiydna] I'm ashamed

стюард [styoo-art] steward

стюардесса [styoo-ardesa] stewardess

суббота [soob-bota] Saturday

сувенир [soovyeneer] souvenir

сумасшедший [soomashetshi] mad; madman

сумка [soomka] bag

сумочка [soomachka] handbag, (US) purse

сутки [sootkee] 24 hours, day and night

сухой [sooнoy] dry

сушить [sooshiyt] to dry

схема [sнyema] diagram; network map

сцепление [stseplyenee-yeh] clutch

счастливо оставаться! [sh-chasleeva astavatsa!] good night!; enjoy your stay!

счастливого пути! [sh-chasleevava pootee!] have a good trip!

счастливый [sh-chasleevi] happy

счастье [sh-chastyeh] happiness

к счастью [k sh-chastyoo] fortunately

счёт [sh-chot] bill, (US) check

США [seh-sheh-a] USA

сшить [s-shit] to sew

съесть [syest] to eat

сыграть [sigrat] to play

сын [siyn] son

сырой [siroy] damp; raw

сюрприз [syoorprees] surprise

Т

T trolleybus or tram stop

та [ta] that; that one

табак [tabak] tobacco

таблетка [tablyetka] pill, tablet

так [tak] so; this way; like this

так! [tak!] well!

так же красиво, как ... [tak Jeh kraseeva, kak ...] as beautiful as ...

так как [tak kak] as; since

так себе [tak syebyeh] so-so

также [tagJeh] also

такси [taksee] taxi

таксофон [taksafon] public phone

талия [talee-ya] waist

талкучка [talkoochka] flea market

Таллин [tal-leen] Tallin

талон [talon] ticket

тальк [talk] talcum powder

там [tam] there

там внизу [tam vneezoo] down there

таможенная декларация [tamoJen-na-ya dyeklaratsi-ya] Customs declaration form

таможенный контроль [tamoJeni kantrol] Customs inspection

таможня [tamoJnya] Customs

тампон [tampon] tampon

танцевать [tantsevat] dance

тапочки [tapachkee] slippers

таракан [tarakan] cockroach

тарелка [taryelka] plate

тариф [tareef] charge, tariff

Ташкент [tashkyent] Tashkent

Тбилиси [tbeeleesee] Tbilisi

твёрдый [tvyordi] hard

твоего [tva-yevo] (of) your; (of) yours

твоей [tva-**yay**] your; yours; of your; of yours; to your; to yours; by your; by yours

твоему [tva-yemoo] (to) your; (to) yours

твоё [tva-**yo**] your; yours

твоём [tva-**yom**] your; yours

твои [tva-**ee**] your; yours

твоим [tva-**eem**] (by) your; (by) yours; (to) your; (to) yours

твоими [tva-**eemee**] (by) your; (by) yours

твоих [tva-**een**] (of) your; (of) yours

твой [tvoy] your; yours

твою [tva-**yoo**] your; yours

твоя [tva-**ya**] your; yours

те [tyeh] those

театр [tyeh-**atr**] theatre

театральная касса [tyeh-atralna-ya kas-sa] box office

тебе [tyeb**yeh**] you; to you

тебя [tyeb**ya**] you; of you

у тебя [oo tyeb**ya**] you have

телевизор [tyelyeveezar] television, TV set

телеграмма [tyelyegram-ma] telegram

тележка [tyel**ye**shka] trolley

телекс [tyelyeks] telex

телефон [tyelyefon] telephone

телефон-автомат [tyelyefon-aftamat] payphone

телефонная будка [tyelyefon-na-ya bootka] phone box

телефонный код [tyelyefon-ni kot] dialling code

телефонный справочник [tyelyefon-ni spravachneek] telephone directory

тело [tyela] body

тем [tyem] (by) that; (by) that one; (to) those

теми [tyemee] (by) those

тёмный [tyomni] dark

температура [tyempyeratoora] temperature

тени для век [tyenee dlya vyek] eye shadow

теннис [tyen-nees] tennis

тень f [tyen] shadow; shade

в тени [ftyenee] in the shade

тепло [tyeplo] warm; it's warm

тёплый [tyopli] warm

термометр [tyermomyetr] thermometer

термос [termas] Thermos® flask

терпеть [tyerp**yet**] to bear, to stand

терять/потерять [tyer**yat**/ pat**yeryat**] to lose

тесный [**tyes**ni] tight; cramped

тесть m [tyest] father-in-law (wife's father)

тётя [**tyot**ya] aunt

тех [tyeн] those; of those

течь f [tyech] leak

течь [tyech] to flow; to stream; to leak

тёща [**tyosh**-cha] mother-in-law (wife's mother)

тихий [**tee**нee] quiet

тише [**tee**sheh] quieter

тише! [**tee**sheh!] quiet!

тишина [**tee**shina] silence

ткань f [tkan] material

то [to] that; that one

тобой [tab**oy**] (by) you

тогда [tagd**a**] then

того [tav**o**] (of) that; (of) that one

тоже [to**Jeh**] too; also

я тоже [ya to**Jeh**] me too

той [toy] that; that one; of that; of that one; to that; to that one

толкать/толкнуть [talk**at**/ talk**noot**] to push

толкнуть [talk**noot**] to push

толпа [talp**a**] crowd

толстый [**tol**sti] fat (adj)

только [**tol**ka] only; just

только по будним дням [**tol**ka pab**oo**dneem dnyam] weekdays only

том [tom] that; that one

тому [tam**oo**] (to) that; (to) that one

тональный крем [tan**al**ni kryem] foundation cream

тонкий [**ton**kee] thin

тонуть/утонуть [tan**oot**/ ootan**oot**] to drown

торговый центр [**targo**vi tsentr] shopping centre

тормоза [tarmaz**a**] brakes

тормозить/затормозить [tarmaz**eet**/zatarmaz**eet**] to brake

тот [tot] that; that one

тот же самый [tot Jeh **sam**i] the same

тощий [**tosh**-chee] skinny

трава [trav**a**] grass; herb; weed

традиционный [tradeetsi-**on**-ni] traditional

традиция [trad**eet**si-ya] tradition

транзитная посадка [tranz**eet**na-ya pas**at**ka] intermediate stop

тратить [**trat**eet] to spend

требовать [**tryeb**avat] to demand

тревога [tryev**o**ga] alarm

третий [**trye**tee] third

три [tree] three

тридцатый [**treet**sati] thirtieth

тридцать [**treet**sat] thirty

тринадцатый [treen**at**sati] thirteenth

тринадцать [treen**at**sat] thirteen

триста [**tree**sta] three hundred

трогать/тронуть [**tro**gat/**tro**noot] to touch

тройка [**troy**ka] troika

тронуть [**tro**noot] to touch

тропинка [tra**pee**nka] path

тротуар [tratoo-**ar**] pavement, sidewalk

трубка [**troo**pka] pipe (to smoke)

трубопровод [troobapra**vot**] pipe; pipeline

трудный [**trood**ni] difficult

трусики [**troo**seekee] pants, panties

трусы [**troo**siy] underpants

ту [too] that; that one

туалет [too-a**lyet**] toilet, rest room

туалетная бумага [too-a**lyet**na-ya boomaga] toilet paper

туалеты [too-a**lyet**i] toilets, rest rooms

туман [too**man**] fog

туннель **m** [toon-**nel**] tunnel

тургруппа [toorgroop-pa] tour group

турист [too**reest**] tourist

туристическая поездка [tooreestee**chyes**ka-ya pa**yez**tka] package tour

Турция [**toor**tsi-ya] Turkey

туфли [**toof**lee] shoes

тушь для ресниц **f** [toosh dlya ryes**neets**] mascara

ты [tiy] you

тысяча [**tiy**syacha] thousand

тюрьма [tyoor**ma**] prison

тяжёлый [tya**Jo**li] heavy

тянуть [tya**noot**] to pull

У

у [oo] at; by; near; with

у них [oo neen] they have

у вас [oo vas] you have

у тебя [oo tye**bya**] you have

у неё [oo nyeh-**yo**] she has; it has

у нас [oo nas] we have

у него [oo nye**vo**] he has; it has

у меня [oo mye**nya**] I have

у вас есть ...? [oo vas yest ...?] have you got ...?

у меня нет ... [oo mye**nya** nyet ...] I don't have ...

убивать/убить [oobee**vat**/oo**beet**] to kill

убирать/убрать [oobee**rat**/oo**brat**] to take away; to clean

убить [oo**beet**] to kill

убрать [oo**brat**] to take away; to clean

уверенный [oo**vye**ryen-ni] sure

увидеть [oo**vee**dyet] to see

увлажняющий крем [oovlaJ**nya**-yoosh-chee kryem] moisturizer

увлекательный [oovlye**ka**tyelni] exciting

угол [**oo**gal] corner

удар [oo**dar**] blow; stroke

ударять/ударить [ooda**ryat**/oo**da**reet] to hit

удача [oo**da**cha] luck; success

удивительный [oodee**vee**tyelni] surprising

удлинитель [oodlee**nee**tyel] extension lead

удобный [oodobni] comfortable

удостоверение [oodastavyeryenee-yeh] certificate

уезжать/уехать [ooyezJat/ ooyeHat] to leave

ужалить [ooJaleet] to sting

ужас [ooJas], ужасно [ooJasna] it's awful, it's ghastly

ужасный [ooJasni] awful, terrible, ghastly

уже [ooJeh] already

ужин [ooJin] dinner; supper

ужинать [ooJinat] to have dinner

узкий [ooskee] narrow

узнавать/узнать [ooznavat/ ooznat] to recognize

уйти [ooytee] to go away

указатель поворота **m** [ookazatyel pavarota] indicator

укладывать/уложить вещи [ookladivat/oolaJeet vyesh-chee] to pack

укол [ookol] injection

Украина [ookra-eena] Ukraine

украсть [ookrast] to steal

укус [ookoos] bite

ул., улица [ooleetsa] street
на улице [na ooleetsyeh] outside; in the street

уличное движение [ooleechna-yeh dveeJenee-yeh] traffic

уложить вещи [oolaJeet vyesh-chee] to pack

уложить волосы феном [oolaJeet volasi fyenam] to blow-dry

улучшить [oolootshit] to

improve

улыбаться/улыбнуться [oolibatsa/oolibnootsa] to smile

улыбка [ooliypka] smile

улыбнуться [ooliybnootsa] to smile

умелый [oomyeli] skilful

умирать/умереть [oomeerat/ oomyeryet] to die

умный [oomni] clever, intelligent

умывальник [oomivalneek] washbasin

универмаг [ooneevyermak] department store

универсам [ooneevyersam] supermarket

университет [ooneevyerseetyet] university

упасть [oopast] to fall

упасть в обморок [oopast vobmarak] to faint

управляющий [oopravlya-yoosh-chee] manager

уровень масла [ooravyen masla] oil level

уродливый [oorodleevi] ugly

урок [oorok] lesson

уронить [ooraneet] to drop

услышать [oosliyshat] to hear

успех [oospyeH] success
желаю успеха! [Jelayoo oospyeHa!] good luck!

успокойтесь ! [oospakoytyes!] calm down!

усталый [oostali] tired

устройство [oostroystva] device

усы [oosiy] moustache

утонуть [ootanoot] to drown
утро [ootra] morning
  утра [ootra] in the morning;
  a.m.
  в пять часов утра [fpyat
  chasof ootra] at 5 a.m.
утюг [ootyook] iron (for clothes)
ухо [ooHa] ear
уходить/уйти [ooHadeet/ooytee]
  to go away
  уходите! [ooHadeetyeh!] go
  away!
учёт [oochot] stocktaking
учитель m [oocheetyel],
  учительница
  [oocheetyelneetsa] teacher
учиться [oocheetsa] to learn;
  to study
Уэльс [oo-els] Wales
уэльский [oo-elskee] Welsh

Ф

факс [faks] fax
факсимильный аппарат
  [fakseemeelni aparat] fax
  machine
фамилия [fameelee-ya]
  surname
фары [fari] headlights
февраль m [fyevral]
  February
фейерверк [fyay-yervyerk]
  fireworks
фен [fyen] hairdryer
ферма [fyerma] farm
Финляндия [feenlyandee-ya]
  Finland

фиолетовый [fee-alyetavi]
  purple
фирма [feerma] firm,
  company
флаг [flak] flag
фонарик [fanareek] torch
фонтан [fantan] fountain
фотоаппарат [fata-aparat]
  camera
фотограф [fatograf]
  photographer
фотографировать
  [fatagrafeeravat] to take photos
фотография [fatagrafee-ya]
  photograph
Франция [frantsi-ya] France
французский [frantsooskee]
  French
французский язык
  [frantsooskee yaziyk] French
  (language)
фрукты [frookti] fruit
фунт [foont] pound
фуражка [foorashka] cap
фургон [foorgon] van
футбол [foodbol] football
футболка [foodbolka] T-shirt
футбольное поле [foodbolna-
  yeh polyeh] football pitch

Х

халат [Halat] dressing gown
химчистка [Heemcheestka]
  dry-cleaner
хлеб [Hlyep] bread
хлопок [Hlopak] cotton
ходить [Hadeet] to go (on foot),

to walk; to suit

хозяин [Hazya-een] owner; host

хозяйственный магазин [Hazyaystvyen-ni magazeen] hardware store

хоккей [Hakyay] hockey

холм [Holm] hill

холодильник [Haladeelneek] fridge

холодный [Halodni] cold

холостяк [Halastyak] bachelor

хороший [Haroshi] good

хорошо [Harasho] well

хорошо! [Harasho!] good!

мне хорошо [mnyeh Harasho] I'm well

хотеть [Hatyet] to want

я хотел/хотела [ya Hatyel/ Hatyela] I wanted (said by man/ woman)

я хотел/хотела бы ... [ya Hatyel/Hatyela bi ...] I would like ... (said by man/woman)

хотим [Hateem] we want

хотите [Hateeteyeh] you want

хотя [Hatya] although

хотят [Hatyat] they want

хочет [Hochyet] he wants; she wants; it wants

хочется: мне хочется ... [mnyeh Hochyetsa ...] I feel like ...

хочешь [Hochyesh] you want

хочу [Hachoo] I want

храбрый [Hrabri] brave

храните в сухом/ прохладном/тёмном месте [Hraneeteyeh fsooHom/praHladnam/ tyomnam myestyeh] keep in a cool/dark/dry place

хранить [Hraneet] to keep; to preserve

хрустящий картофель [Hroostyash-chee kartofyel] crisps, (US) chips

художник [HoodoJneek] artist, painter

худой [Hoodoy] thin

худший [Hootshi] worst

хуже [HooJeh] worse

Ц

царь m [tsar] tsar

цвет [tsvyet] colour

цветная плёнка [tsvyetna-ya plyonka] colour film

цветок [tsvyetok] flower

цветочный магазин [tsvyetochni magazeen] florist's, flower shop

цветы [tsvyetiy] flowers

целовать/поцеловать [tselavat/patselavat] to kiss

целый [tseli] whole

цена [tsena] price

центр [tsentr] centre

центр города [tsentr gorada] city centre

центральное отопление [tsentralna-yeh ataplyenee-yeh] central heating

цепочка [tsepochka] chain

церковь f [tserkav] church

Ч
▬

чаевые [cha-ye**vi**yeh] tip

чайник [**chi**neek] kettle; teapot

чартерный рейс [**char**terni ryays] charter flight

час [chas] hour; one o'clock

в … часа [f … cha**sa**] at … o'clock

в … часов [f … cha**sof**] at … o'clock

часто [**chas**ta] often

частый [**chas**ti] often

часть f [chast] part

часы [cha**si**] watch; clock; hours

часы приёма [cha**si** pree-**yo**ma] visiting hours

часы работы [cha**si ra**boti] opening hours, opening times

чашка [**chash**ka] cup

чаще [**chash**-chyeh] more often

чего [**chye**vo] what; of what

чек [chyek] cheque, (US) check

чековая книжка [**chye**kava-ya **knee**shka] cheque/check book

человек [chyela**vyek**] person

челюсть f [**chye**lyoost] jaw

чем [chyem] than; what; by what

чём [chyom] what

чемодан [chyema**dan**] suitcase

чему [chye**moo**] what; to what

через [**chye**ryes] through; across; in

через три дня [**chye**ryes tree dnya] in three days

чёрно-белый [**cho**rna-b**ye**li] black and white

Чёрное море [**cho**rna-yeh **mo**ryeh] Black Sea

чёрный [**cho**rni] black

честный [**chye**sni] honest

четверг [chye**tvyerk**] Thursday

четвёртый [chet**vyo**rti] fourth

четверть f [**chye**tvyert] quarter

четверть часа [**chye**tvyert cha**sa**] quarter of an hour

четверть второго [**chye**tvyert fta**ro**va] quarter past one

без четверти два [byes **chye**tvyertee dva] quarter to two

четыре [chet**i**ryeh] four

четыреста [chyet**i**ryesta] four hundred

четырнадцатый [chet**i**rnatsati] fourteenth

четырнадцать [chet**i**rnatsat] fourteen

Чешская республика [**chye**shska-ya ryesp**oo**bleeka] Czech Republic

чинить/починить [cheen**eet**/pachee**neet**] to mend

число [chees**lo**] date; number

чистить [**chee**steet] to clean

чистый [**chee**sti] clean; pure

читать/прочитать [chee**tat**/prachee**tat**] to read

что [shto] what; that

что-нибудь [shto-**nee**boot] anything

что-то [**shto**-ta] something

чувство [**choo**stva] feeling

чувствовать [**choo**stvavat] to feel

чувствовать себя [**choo**stvavat syeb**ya**] to feel

чулки [**choo**lkee] stockings

чуть [choot] hardly, scarcely; a little

чьё: чьё это? [cho **e**ta?] whose is this?

Ш

шампунь m [sham**poo**n] shampoo

шапка [**sha**pka] hat (with flaps)

шариковая ручка [sha**ree**kava-ya **roo**chka] ballpoint pen

шарф [sharf] scarf (neck)

шашлычная [shash**lee**chna-ya] café selling kebabs

швейцар [shvyayts**ar**] porter; doorman

Швейцария [shvyayts**a**ree-ya] Switzerland

Швеция [shv**ye**tsi-ya] Sweden

шевелиться/шевельнуться [shevyel**ee**tsa/shevyeln**oo**tsa] to move; to stir

шезлонг [shez**lo**nk] deckchair

шёл [shol] went; was going

шёлковый [**sho**lkavi] silk

шерсть f [sherst] wool

шестнадцатый [shes**na**tsati] sixteenth

шестнадцать [shes**na**tsat] sixteen

шестой [shest**oy**] sixth

шесть [shest] six

шестьдесят [shesdyes**yat**] sixty

шестьсот [shes-**sot**] six hundred

шея [sh**eh**-ya] neck

шина [**shi**yna] tyre

широкий [shi**ro**kee] wide

шить/сшить [shit/s-shit] to sew

шкаф [shkaf] cupboard; wardrobe, closet

школа [**shko**la] school

шла [shla] went; was going

шли [shlee] went; were going

шло [shlo] went; was going

шляпа [sh**lya**pa] hat

шнурки [shnoor**kee**] shoelaces

шоколад [shakal**at**] chocolate

шорты [**sho**rti] shorts

шоссе [shas-**seh**] highway

Шотландия [shatl**a**ndee-ya] Scotland

шотландский [shatl**a**ndskee] Scottish

штепсельная вилка [sht**e**psyelna-ya v**ee**lka] plug (electric)

штопор [**shto**par] corkscrew

штраф [shtraf] fine

шум [shoom] noise

шумный [**shoo**mni] noisy

шурин [**shoo**reen] brother-in-law (wife's brother)

шутка [**shoo**tka] joke

Щ

щётка [sh-**cho**tka] brush

Э

экипаж [ekeepash] crew
эластичный [elasteechni] elastic
электрический [elyektreechyeskee] electric
электричество [elyektreechyestva] electricity
электричка [elyektreechka] suburban train
электронная почта [elyektron-na-ya pochta] electronic mail
Эстония [estonee-ya] Estonia
эт. floor
эта [eta] it (is); that; this; this one
этаж [etash] floor; storey
  первый этаж [pyervi etash] ground floor, (US) first floor
эти [etee] these; those
этим [eteem] (by) this; (by) this one; (to) these
этими [eteemee] (by) these
этих [eteeн] these; of these
это [eta] it (is); that; this (one)
этого [etava] (of) this; (of) this one
этой [eti] this; this one; of this; of this one; to this; to this one; by this; by this one
этом [etam] this; this one
этому [etamoo] (to) this; (to) this one
этот [etat] it (is); that; this; this one
эту [etoo] this; this one

Ю

юбка [yoopka] skirt
ювелирные изделия [yoovyeleerni-yeh eezdyelee-ya] jewellery
ювелирный магазин [yoovyeleerni magazeen] jeweller's shop
юг [yook] south
  к югу от [k yoogoo at] south of
Южная Африка [yooжna-ya afreeka] South Africa
южный [yooжni] southern
юмор [yoomar] humour

Я

я [ya] I
явиться на регистрацию [yaveetsa na ryegeestratsi-yoo] to check in
яд [yat] poison
язык [yaziyk] tongue; language
Ялта [yalta] Yalta
январь m [yanvar] January
ярлык [yarliyk] label
ярмарка [yarmarka] fair; market
ярус [yaroos] circle; tier
ясный [yasni] clear; obvious

Menu
Reader:
Food

Essential terms

bread хлеб [Hlyep]
butter масло [masla]
cup чашка [chashka]
dessert десерт [dyesyert]
fish рыба [riyba]
fork вилка [veelka]
glass стакан [stakan]
knife нож [nosh]
main course основное блюдо [asnavno-yeh blyooda]
meat мясо [myasa]
menu меню [myenyoo]
pepper перец [pyerets]
plate тарелка [taryelka]
salad салат [salat]
salt соль f [sol]
set menu комплексный обед [komplyeksni abyet]
soup суп [soop]
spoon ложка [loshka]
starter закуска [zakooska]
table стол [stol]

another ..., please ещё одно ..., пожалуйста [yesh-cho ... peeva, paJalsta]
excuse me! простите! [prasteetyeh!]
could I have the bill, please? счёт, пожалуйста [sh-chot, paJalsta]
I'd like ... (said by man/woman) я бы хотел/хотела ... [ya biy Hatyel/ Hatyela ...]

абрикос [abreek**os**] apricot

азу [az**oo**] small pieces of meat in a savoury sauce

ананас [anan**as**] pineapple

антрекот [antryek**ot**] entrecote steak

апельсин [apyels**een**] orange

апельсиновое варенье [apyels**ee**nava-yeh var**ye**nyeh] marmalade

арахис [ara**н**ees] peanuts

арбуз [arb**oos**] water melon

ассорти мясное [asart**ee** myasn**o**-yeh] assorted meats

ассорти рыбное [asart**ee** r**iy**bna-yeh] assorted fish

баклажан [bakla**ж**an] aubergine

банан [ban**an**] banana

баранина [bar**a**neena] mutton, lamb

баранина на вертеле [bar**a**neena na v**ye**rtyelyeh] mutton grilled on a skewer

баранки [bar**a**nkee] ring-shaped rolls

бараньи котлеты [bar**a**nee katl**ye**ti] lamb chops

батон [bat**on**] baguette

бекон [byek**on**] bacon

белый хлеб [b**ye**li **н**lyep] white bread

беф строганов [byef-str**o**ganaf] beef Stroganoff

битки [beetk**ee**] rissoles; hamburgers

битки из баранины [beetk**ee** eez bar**a**nini] lamb meatballs

бифштекс [beefsht**e**ks] steak

бифштекс натуральный [beefsht**e**ks nat**oo**ralni] fried or grilled steak

блинчики [bl**ee**ncheekee] pancakes

блинчики с вареньем [bl**ee**ncheekee svar**ye**nyem] pancakes with jam

блины [bleen**iy**] buckwheat pancakes, blini

блины с икрой [bleen**iy** sikr**oy**] blini with caviar

блины со сметаной [bleen**iy** sa smyet**a**ni] blini with sour cream

блюда из птицы [bl**yoo**da ees pt**ee**tsi] poultry dishes

блюдо [bl**yoo**da] dish, course

бородинский хлеб [barad**ee**nskee **н**lyep] dark rye bread

борщ [borsh-ch] beef, beetroot and cabbage soup

брынза [br**iy**nza] sheep's cheese, feta

брюссельская капуста [bryoos-s**ye**lska-ya kap**oo**sta] Brussels sprouts

бублик [b**oo**bleek] type of bagel

буженина с гарниром [b**oo**ж**e**neena zgarn**ee**ram] cold boiled pork with vegetables

булки [b**oo**lkee] rolls

булочка [b**oo**lachka] roll

бульон [b**oo**lyon] clear meat soup, bouillon

бульон с пирожками [boolyon

speerashka**mee**] clear meat
soup served with small meat
pies

бульон с фрикадельками
[bool**yon** sfreekade**l**kamee] clear
soup with meatballs

бутерброд [booterb**rot**]
sandwich

бутерброд с мясом [booterb**rot**
s**mya**sam] meat sandwich

бутерброд с сыром [booterb**rot**
s-**siy**ram] cheese sandwich

буханка [boo**Han**ka] loaf

ванильный [va**neel**ni] vanilla

вареники [var**ye**neekee] curd
or fruit dumplings

варёный [var**yo**ni] boiled

варенье [var**ye**nyeh] jam,
preserve

ватрушка [vat**roo**shka]
cheesecake

вермишель [vyermee**shel**]
vermicelli

вегетарианский [vyegyetaree-
anskee] vegetarian

ветчина [vyetchee**na**] ham

взбитые сливки [vzb**ee**ti-yeh
sleefkee] whipped cream

винегрет [veenyeg**ryet**]
Russian vegetable salad:
beetroot, potatoes, onions,
peas, carrots and pickled
cucumbers in mayonnaise
or oil

виноград [veena**grat**] grapes

вишня [**vee**shnya] sour
cherries

галушка [ga**loo**shka]
Ukrainian dumpling

гамбургер [gam**boor**gyer]
hamburger

гарнир [gar**neer**] vegetables

говядина [gav**ya**deena] beef

говядина отварная с хреном
[gav**ya**deena atvarna-ya s**Hry**enam]
boiled beef with horseradish

говядина тушёная
[gav**ya**deena too**sho**na-ya]
stewed beef

голубцы [ga**loop**ts**iy**] cabbage
leaves stuffed with meat
and rice

горох [ga**roH**] peas

горошек [ga**ro**shek] peas

горчица [gar**chee**tsa] mustard

горячие закуски [gar**ya**chee-
yeh za**koo**skee] hot starters,
hot appetizers

горячий [gar**ya**chee] hot

грейпфрут [**grayp**froot]
grapefruit

гренки [gryen**kee**] croutons

гренок [gry**enak**] toast

грецкие орехи [gr**ye**tskee-yeh
ar**ye**Hee] walnut

гречка [gr**yech**ka] buckwheat

гречневая каша [gr**yech**nyeva-
ya **ka**sha] buckwheat porridge

грибы [gree**biy**] mushrooms

грибы в сметане [gree**biy**
fsmyet**a**nyeh] mushrooms in
sour cream

грибы маринованные
[gree**biy** mareen**o**vani-yeh]
marinated mushrooms

груша [gr**oo**sha] pear

гуляш из говядины [goolyash eez gavyadeeni] beef goulash

гусь [goos] goose

десерт [dyesyert] dessert

джем [djem] jam

дичь [deech] game

домашний [damashnee] home-made

домашняя птица [damashnya-ya pteetsa] poultry

дыня [diynya] melon

еда [yeda] food; meal

ежевика [yeJeveeka] blackberries

жареная рыба [Jaryena-ya riyba] fried fish

жареный [Jaryeni] grilled; fried; roast

жареный картофель [Jaryeni kartofyel] fried potatoes

жареный на вертеле [Jaryeni na vyertyel-yeh] grilled on a skewer

желе [Jelyeh] jelly

жир [Jiyr] lard

жульен [Joolyen] mushrooms or meat cooked with onions and sour cream

завтрак [zaftrak] breakfast

закуска [zakooska] snack; starter, appetizer

закуски [zakooskee] starters, appetizers

заливная рыба [zaleevna-ya riyba] fish in aspic

заливной [zaleevnoy] in aspic

замороженные продукты [zamaroJen-ni-yeh pradookti] frozen food

запеканка [zapyekanka] baked pudding; shepherd's pie

запечённый [zapyechonni] baked

зелёный горошек [zyelyoni garoshek] green peas

зелёный лук [zyelyoni look] spring onions

зелёный салат [zyelyoni salat] green salad

земляника [zyemlyaneeka] wild strawberries

зразы [zrazi] meat cutlets stuffed with rice, buckwheat or mashed potatoes

изделия из теста [eezdyelee-ya ees tyesta] pastry dishes

изюм [eezyoom] sultanas; raisins

икра [eekra] caviar

икра баклажанная [eekra baklaJanna-ya] mashed fried aubergines with onions and tomatoes

икра зернистая [eekra zyerneesta-ya] fresh caviar

икра кетовая [eekra kyetova-ya] red caviar

индейка [eendyayka] turkey

инжир [eenJiyr] figs

кабачки [kabachkee] courgettes

камбала [kambala] plaice

капуста [kapoosta] cabbage

карп [karp] carp

карп с грибами [karp zgreebamee] carp with mushrooms

картофель [kartofyel] potatoes

картофельное пюре [kartofyelna-yeh pyooreh] mashed potatoes

картофель с ветчиной и шпиком [kartofyel zvyetcheenoy ee shpeekam] potatoes with ham and bacon fat

картофель фри [kartofyel free] chips, French fries

каша [kasha] porridge

каштан [kashtan] chestnut

кебаб [kebap] kebab

кекс [kyeks] fruit cake

кета [kyeta] Siberian salmon

кетчуп [kyetchoop] ketchup

кильки [keelkee] sprats

кисель [keesyel] thin fruit jelly

кисель из клубники [keesyel ees kloobneekee] strawberry jelly

кисель из чёрной смородины [keesyel ees chorni smarodeeni] blackcurrant jelly

кислая капуста [keesla-ya kapoosta] sauerkraut

кислые щи [keesli-ya sh-chee] sauerkraut soup

клубника [kloobneeka] strawberries

клюква [klyookva] cranberries

колбаса [kalbasa] salami sausage

комплексный обед [komplyeksni abyet] set menu

компот [kampot] stewed fruit in a light syrup; compote

компот из груш [kampot eez groosh] stewed pears

компот из сухофруктов [kampot ees sooнa-frooktaf] stewed dried fruit

консервы [kansyervi] tinned foods

конфета [kanfyeta] sweet, candy

копчёная колбаса [kapchona-ya kalbasa] smoked sausage

копчёная сёмга [kapchona-ya syomga] smoked salmon

копчёные свиные рёбрышки [kapchoni-yeh sveeniy-yeh ryobrishkee] smoked pork ribs

копчёный [kapchoni] smoked

коржики [korJikee] shortbread

корица [kareetsa] cinnamon

котлета [katlyeta] cutlet; burger; rissole

котлеты по-киевски [katlyeti pa-kee-yefskee] chicken Kiev

котлеты с грибами [katlyeti zgreebamee] steak with mushrooms

кофейный [kafyayni] coffee-flavoured; coffee

краб [krap] crab

крабовые палочки [krabavi-yeh palachkee] crab sticks

красная икра [krasna-ya eekra] red caviar

красная смородина [krasna-ya

smarodeena] redcurrants
креветки [kryevyetkee] prawns
крем [kryem] butter cream
кровь: с кровью [s krovyoo] rare
кролик [kroleek] rabbit
кукуруза [kookoorooza] sweet corn
кулебяка [koolyebyaka] pie with meat, fish or vegetables
курица [kooreetsa] chicken

лапша [lapsha] noodles
лесные орехи [lyesniy-yeh aryeнee] hazelnuts
лимон [leemon] lemon
ломтик [lomteek] slice
лососина [lasaseena] smoked salmon
лосось [lasos] salmon
лук [look] onions

майонез [mi-anes] mayonnaise
макаронные изделия [makaron-ni-yeh eezdyelee-ya] pasta
макароны [makaroni] macaroni
малина [maleena] raspberries
мандарин [mandareen] mandarin; tangerine
манная каша [man-na-ya kasha] semolina
маргарин [margareen] margarine
маслины [masleeni] olives
масло [masla] butter; oil
мёд [myot] honey
медовый [myedovi] honey

меню [myenyoo] menu
мидии [meedee-ee] mussels
миндаль [meendal] almonds
моллюски [mal-lyooskee] shellfish
молоко [malako] milk
молочный [malochni] milk; dairy
молочный кисель [malochni keesyel] milk jelly
морковь [markof] carrots
мороженое [maroжena-yeh] ice cream
мороженое малиновое [maroжena-yeh maleenava-yeh] raspberry ice cream
мороженое 'пломбир' [maroжena-yeh plambeer] originally ice cream with candied fruit, but nowadays often just plain vanilla ice cream
мороженое клубничное [maroжena-yeh kloobneechna-yeh] strawberry ice cream
мороженое молочное [maroжena-yeh malochna-yeh] dairy ice cream
мороженое молочное с ванилином [maroжena-yeh malochna-yeh svaneeleenam] vanilla dairy ice cream
мороженое шоколадное [maroжena-yeh shakaladna-yeh] chocolate ice cream
морская капуста [marska-ya kapoosta] sea kale
морские продукты [marskee-yeh pradookti] seafood

мука [**moo**ka] flour
мясной [myas**noy**] meat
мясной бульон [myas**noy** bool**yon**] clear meat soup
мясо [**mya**sa] meat

на вертеле [na **vyer**tyelyeh] on a skewer
на вынос [na **viy**nas] to take away, to go
национальные русские блюда [natsi-an**a**lni-yeh **roo**skee-yeh **blyoo**da] Russian national dishes
начинка [na**chee**nka] filling

обед [ab**yet**] lunch
овощи [**o**vash-chee] vegetables
овощной [avash-ch**noy**] vegetable
овощной суп [avash-ch**noy** soop] vegetable soup
огурец [agoo**ryets**] cucumber
огурцы со сметаной [agoort**siy** sa smyet**ani**] cucumber with sour cream
окорок [**o**karak] gammon
окрошка [ak**ro**shka] cold soup made with kvas (see p. 268), vegetables and meat
оладьи [a**la**dee] thick pancakes
оливки [a**leef**kee] olives
омар [a**mar**] lobster
омлет [am**lyet**] omelette
омлет натуральный [am**lyet** natoo**ra**lni] plain omelette
омлет с ветчиной [am**lyet** svyetchee**noy**] ham omelette

орехи [ar**ye**Hee] nuts
осётр запечённый в сметане [as**yo**tr zapyech**oni** fsmyet**a**nyeh] sturgeon baked in sour cream
осетрина заливная [asyetr**ee**na zal**ee**vna-ya] sturgeon in aspic
осетрина под белым соусом [asyetr**ee**na pat **byel**im **so**-oosam] sturgeon in white sauce
осетрина с гарниром [asyetr**ee**na zgarn**ee**ram] sturgeon with vegetables
осетрина с пикантным соусом [asyetr**ee**na spee**ka**ntnim **so**-oosam] sturgeon in piquant sauce
основное блюдо [asnavn**o**-yeh **blyoo**da] main course
отбивная котлета [atbeevn**a**-ya kat**lye**ta] chop
отварная рыба [atvarn**a**-ya **riy**ba] poached fish
отварной [atvarn**oy**] boiled; poached
отварной цыплёнок [atvarn**oy** tsipl**yo**nak] boiled chicken

палтус [**pal**toos] halibut
панированный [panee**ro**vanni] in breadcrumbs
панированный цыплёнок [panee**ro**vanni tsipl**yo**nak] chicken in breadcrumbs
паштет [pash**tyet**] pâté; pie
пельмени [pyelm**ye**nee] type of ravioli
первое блюдо [**pyer**va-yeh

blyooda] first course

перец [pyeryets] pepper

персик [pyerseek] peach

петрушка [pyetrooshka] parsley

печёнка [pyechonka] liver

печёный [pyechoni] baked

печенье [pyechyenyeh] biscuit, cookie; pastry

печень трески в масле [pyechyen tryeskee vmasl-yeh] cod liver in oil

пирог [peerok] pie; tart; cake

пирог с повидлом [peerok spaveedlam] jam tart

пирог с мясом [peerok smyasam] meat pie

пирог с яблоками [peerok syablakamee] apple pie

пирожки [peerashkee] pies

пирожки с капустой [peerashkee skapoosti] cabbage pies

пирожки с мясом [peerashkee smyasam] meat pies

пирожки с творогом [peerashkee stvoragam] cottage cheese pies

пирожное [peeroJna-yeh] pastries; cake, pastry

пицца [peetsa] pizza

плавленый сыр [plavlyeni siyr] processed cheese

плов [plof] pilaf

повидло [paveedla] jam

под белым соусом [pat byelim so-oosam] in white sauce

поджаренный [padJaryen-ni]

grilled; fried

поджаренный хлеб [padJaryen-ni Hlyep] toast

под майонезом [pad mi-anezam] in mayonnaise

подсолнечное масло [patsolnyechna-yeh masla] sunflower oil

пожарские котлеты [paJarskee-yeh katlyeti] minced chicken patties

помидор [pameedor] tomato

пончики [poncheekee] doughnuts

порция [portsi-ya] portion

почки [pochkee] kidneys

приправа к салату [preeprava k salatoo] salad dressing

простокваша [prastakvasha] natural set yoghurt

пряник [pryaneek] gingerbread

пряность [pryanast] spice

птица [pteetsa] poultry

рагу из баранины [ragoo eez baraneeni] lamb ragout

рагу из говядины [ragoo eez gavyadeeni] beef ragout

рак [rak] crayfish

рассол [ras-sol] pickle

рассольник [ras-solneek] meat or fish soup with pickled cucumbers

ржаной хлеб [rJanoy Hlyep] rye bread

рис [rees] rice

ромштекс с луком [romshteks slookam] rump steak with

А
Б
В
Г
Д
Е
Ё
Ж
З
И
Й
К
Л
М
Н
О
П
Р
С
Т
У
Ф
Х
Ц
Ч
Ш
Щ
Ъ
Ы
Ь
Э
Ю
Я

onions

ростбиф с гарниром [**r**ostbeef zgarn**ee**ram] roast beef with vegetables

рубленое мясо [**roo**blyena-yeh **my**asa] minced meat

рубленые котлеты [**roo**blyeni-yeh katl**yet**i] rissoles

рулет [r**oo**lyet] meat and potato roll; swiss roll

рулет из рубленой телятины [r**oo**lyet eez r**oo**blyeni tyel**ya**teeni] minced veal roll

русская кухня [**roo**ska-ya k**oo**ннya] Russian cuisine

рыба [**riy**ba] fish

рыбные блюда [**riy**bni-yeh bl**yoo**da] fish dishes

рыбный [**riy**bni] fish

ряженка [**rya**лenka] fermented baked milk, similar to thick yoghurt

салат [sal**at**] lettuce; salad

салат зелёный [sal**at** zyel**yo**ni] green salad

салат из картофеля [sal**at** ees kart**o**fyelya] potato salad

салат из лука [sal**at** eez l**oo**ka] spring onion salad

салат из огурцов [sal**at** eez agoorts**of**] cucumber salad

салат из помидоров [sal**at** ees pameed**o**raf] tomato salad

салат из помидоров с брынзой [sal**at** ees pameed**o**raf zbr**iy**nzı] tomato salad with sheep's cheese

салат из редиски [sal**at** eez

ryed**ee**skee] radish salad

салат из яблок [sal**at** eez **ya**blak] apple salad

салат мясной [sal**at** myasn**oy**] meat salad

салат с крабами [sal**at** skr**a**bamee] crab salad

салат столичный [sal**at** stal**ee**chni] potato salad with meat, carrots, peas and mayonnaise

сало [s**a**la] salted pork fat, sliced and eaten with rye bread (Ukrainian)

самообслуживание [sama-apsl**oo**jivanee-yeh] self-service

сандвич [s**a**ndveech] sandwich

сардельки [sard**el**kee] thick frankfurters

сардины [sard**ee**ni] sardines

сардины в масле [sard**ee**ni vm**a**slyeh] sardines in oil

сахар [s**a**нar] sugar

свежий [sv**ye**лi] fresh

свёкла [sv**yo**kla] beetroot

свинина [sveen**ee**na] pork

свинина жареная с гарниром [sveen**ee**na лaryena-ya zgarn**ee**ram] fried pork with vegetables

свинина с квашеной капустой [sveen**ee**na skv**a**sheni kap**oo**sti] pork with sauerkraut

свиной [sveen**oy**] pork

свиные отбивные [sveen**iy**-yeh atbeevn**iy**-yeh] pork chops

с гарниром [zgarn**ee**ram] with vegetables

селёдка малосольная [syelyotka malasolna-ya] slightly salted herring

сельдь [syeld] herring

сёмга [syomga] salmon

скумбрия горячего копчения [skoombree-ya garyachyeva kapchyenee-ya] smoked mackerel

скумбрия запечённая [skoombree-ya zapyechona-ya] baked mackerel

сладкий [slatkee] sweet

сладкое [slatka-yeh] dessert, sweet course

слива [sleeva] plum

сливки [sleefkee] cream

сливочное масло [sleevachna-yeh masla] butter

с майонезом [smi-anezam] with mayonnaise

сметана [smyetana] sour cream

солёное печенье [salyona-yeh pyechyenyeh] savoury biscuits

солёные огурцы [salyoni-yeh agoortsiy] pickled cucumbers

солёные помидоры [salyoni-yeh pameedori] pickled tomatoes

солёный [salyoni] salty; savoury; salted; pickled

соль [sol] salt

солянка [salyanka] spicy soup made from fish or meat and vegetables; stewed meat and cabbage with spices

сосиски [saseeskee] frankfurters

соус [so-oos] sauce

спаржа [sparja] asparagus

с рисом [s reesam] with rice

стерлядь [styerlyat] small sturgeon

студень [stoodyen] meat jelly; galantine; aspic

судак [soodak] pike-perch

судак в белом вине [soodak vbyelam veen-yeh] pike-perch in white wine

судак жареный в тесте [soodak Jareni ftyestyeh] pike-perch fried in batter

суп [soop] soup

суп из свежих грибов [soop ees svyeJih greebof] fresh mushroom soup

суп картофельный [soop kartofyelni] potato soup

суп-лапша с курицей [soop lapsha skooreetsay] chicken noodle soup

суп мясной [soop myasnoy] meat soup

суп с грибами [soop zgreebamee] mushroom soup

суп томатный [soop tamatni] tomato soup

с хреном [sHryenam] with horseradish sauce

сыр [siyr] cheese

сырник [siyrneek] small cheesecake; cottage cheese pancake or fritter

сырой [siroy] raw

творог [tvarok] cottage cheese

телятина [tyelyateena] veal

телячьи отбивные [tyelyachee atbeevniy-yeh] veal chops

тесто [tyesta] pastry; dough

тефтели с рисом [tyeftyelee sreesam] meatballs with rice

тмин [tmeen] thyme

томатный соус [tamatni so-oos] tomato sauce

торт [tort] cake, gateau

травы [travi] herbs

треска [tryeska] cod

тунец [toonyets] tuna fish

тушёный [tooshoni] stewed

укроп [ookrop] dill

уксус [ooksoos] vinegar

устрицы [oostreetsi] oysters

утка [ootka] duck

уха [ooha] fish soup

фаршированная рыба [farshirovan-na-ya riyba] stuffed fish

фаршированные помидоры [farshirovan-ni-yeh pameedori] stuffed tomatoes

фаршированный [farshirovan-ni] stuffed

фасоль [fasol] French beans; haricot beans

филе [filyeh] fillet

фирменные блюда [feermyen-ni-yeh blooda] speciality dishes

фисташки [feestashkee] pistachio nuts

форель [faryel] trout

фрикадельки [freekadyelkee] meatballs

фрикадельки из телятины в соусе [freekadyelkee ees tyelyateeni vso-oosyeh] veal meatballs in gravy

фруктовое мороженое [frooktova-yeh maroJena-yeh] fruit ice cream

фрукты [frookti] fruit

харчо [Harcho] Georgian thick, spicy mutton soup

хлеб [Hlyep] bread

холодной [Halodni] cold

холодные закуски [Halodni-yeh zakooskee] cold starters, cold appetizers

хорошо прожаренный [Harasho praJaryen-ni] well-done

хрен [Hryen] horseradish

хрустящий картофель [Hroostyash-chee kartofyel] crisps, (US) chips

цветная капуста [tsvyetna-ya kapoosta] cauliflower

цыплёнок [tsiplyonak] chicken

цыплёнок в тесте [tsiplyonak ftyestyeh] chicken in pastry

цыплёнок по-охотничьи [tsiplyonak pa-aHotneechee] chicken chasseur

цыплёнок 'табака' [tsiplyonak tabaka] Georgian chicken with garlic, grilled or fried

цыплёнок фрикасе [tsiplyonak freekaseh] chicken fricassee

чахохбили [chaнонбeelee]
Georgian-style chicken
casserole

черешня [cheryeshnya] sweet
cherries

чёрная смородина [chorna-ya
smarodeena] blackcurrants

черника [chyerneeka]
bilberries

чёрный перец [chorni pyeryets]
black pepper

чёрный хлеб [chorni Hlyep]
black bread, rye bread

чеснок [chyesnok] garlic

чечевица [chyechyeveetsa]
lentils

шашлык [shashliyk] kebab

шашлык из баранины
[shashliyk eez baraneeni] lamb
kebab

шашлык из свинины с
рисом [shashliyk ees sveeneeni
sreesam] pork kebab with
rice

шницель [shneetsel] schnitzel

шницель с яичницей
глазуньей [shneetsel sya-
eeshneetsay glazoonyay]
schnitzel with fried egg

шоколад [shakalat] chocolate

шпинат [shpeenat] spinach

шпроты [shproti] sprats

щи [sh-chee] cabbage soup

щука [sh-chooka] pike

эскалоп [eskalop] escalope

эскимо [eskeemo] choc-ice

яблоко [yablaka] apple

яблочный пирог [yablachni
peerok] apple pie

язык [yaziyk] tongue

яичница [ya-eeshneetsa] fried
egg; omelette

яичница болтунья [ya-
eeshneetsa baltoonya] scrambled
eggs

яичница глазунья [ya-
eeshneetsa glazoonya] fried eggs

яйцо [yitso] egg

яйцо вкрутую [yitso fkrootoo-
yoo] hard-boiled egg

яйцо всмятку [yitso fsmyatkoo]
soft-boiled egg

яйцо под майонезом
[yitso pad mi-anezam] egg
mayonnaise

Menu
Reader:
Drink

Essential terms

beer пиво [**pee**va]
bottle бутылка [boo**tiy**lka]
brandy коньяк [kan**yak**]
coffee кофе **m** [**ko**fyeh]
cup чашка [**chash**ka]
fruit juice фруктовый сок [frook**to**vi sok]
gin джин [djin]
gin and tonic джин с тоником [djin s**to**neekam]
glass стакан [sta**kan**]
  (wine glass) бокал [ba**kal**]
milk молоко [mala**ko**]
mineral water минеральная вода [meenye**ral**na-ya va**da**]
red wine красное вино [**kra**sna-yeh vee**no**]
soda (water) газированная вода [gazee**ro**van-na-ya va**da**]
soft drink безалкогольный напиток [byezalka**gol**ni na**pee**tak]
sugar сахар [**sa**Har]
tea чай **m** [chI]
tonic (water) тоник [**to**neek]
vodka водка [**vot**ka]
water вода [va**da**]
whisky виски [**vee**skee]
white wine белое вино [**bye**la-yeh vee**no**]
wine вино [vee**no**]
wine list карта вин [**kar**ta veen]

another beer, please ещё одно пиво, пожалуйста [yesh-**cho** ad**no** **pee**va, pa**Jal**sta]
a cup of tea, please чашку чая, пожалуйста [**chash**koo cha-ya, pa**Jal**sta]
a glass of ... стакан ... [sta**kan**]

абрикосовый сок [abrekosavi ˙sok] apricot juice

Акашени [akashenee] Georgian red wine

апельсиновый сок [apyelseenavi sok] orange juice

аперитив [apyereeteef] aperitif

Арарат® [ararat] brandy from Armenia

армянксий коньяк [armyanskee kanyak] Armenian brandy

бальзам [balzam] alcoholic herbal drink flavoured with honey and fruit

безалкогольный напиток [byezalkagolni napeetak] soft drink

безо льда [byezalda] without ice

без сахара [byes saнara] without sugar

белое вино [byela-yeh veeno] white wine

Белый Аист® [byeli a-eest] brand of cognac

Боржоми® [barJomee] brand of mineral water

брют [bryoott] dry, brut

вермут [vyermoot] vermouth

вино [veeno] wine

виноградный сок [veenagradni sok] grape juice

виски [veeskee] whisky

вишнёвый сок [veeshnyovi sok] cherry juice

вода [vada] water

водка [votka] vodka

водка Зубровка® [votka zoobrofka] bison grass vodka

водка Лимонная® [votka leemon-na-ya] lemon vodka

водка Московская® [votka maskofska-ya] brand of vodka

водка Охотничья® [votka aнotneechya] hunter's vodka flavoured with juniper berries, ginger and cloves

водка Перцовка [votka pyertsovka] pepper vodka

водка Старка® [votka starka] apple and pear-leaf vodka

водка Столичная® [votka staleechna-ya votka] brand of vodka

газированная вода [gazeerovan-na-ya vada] fizzy water

газированный [gazeerovan-ni] fizzy

горилка [gareelka] Ukrainian vodka

Гурджани [goordJanee] Georgian dry white wine

грузинское вино [groozeenska-yeh veeno] Georgian wine

джин [djin] gin

джин с тоником [djin stoneekom] gin and tonic

заварка [zavarka] strong leaf tea brew to which boiling water is added игристое вино [eegreesta-yeh veeno] sparkling wine

какао [kaka-o] cocoa

карта вин [karta veen] wine list

квас [kvas] kvas – non-alcoholic drink made from fermented bread and water

кефир [kyefeer] sour yoghurt drink

Киндзмараули [kindzmara-oolee] Georgian red wine

кисель [keesyel] thickened fruit juice drink

клюквенный морс [klyookvyen-ni mors] cranberry drink

Кока-Кола® [koka-kola] Coca-Cola®

коктейль [kaktayl] cocktail

компот [kampot] fruit syrup drink with pieces of fresh or dried fruit

коньяк [kanyak] brandy

кофе [kofyeh] coffee

кофе по-турецки [kofyeh pa-tooryetskee] Turkish coffee

кофе с молоком [kofyeh smalakom] coffee with milk

красное вино [krasna-yeh veeno] red wine

креплёное вино [kryeplyona-yeh veeno] fortified wine

кумыс [koomiys] fermented drink made from mare's milk

лёд [lyot] ice; ice cubes

ликёр [leekyor] liqueur

лимон [leemon] lemon

лимонад [leemanat] lemonade

Массандра [mas-sandra] Crimean fortified wine

минеральная вода [meenyeralna-ya vada] mineral water

молоко [malako] milk

Московское® [maskofska-yeh] brand of bottled light ale

Мукузани [mookoozanee] Georgian red wine

напитки [napeetkee] drinks

напиток [napeetak] drink

Нарзан® [narzan] brand of mineral water

настойка [nastoyka] liqueur made from berries or other fruit

пиво [peeva] beer

пиво Балтика® [peeva balteeka] brand of bottled beer

пиво Жигулёвское® [peeva Jigoolyofska-yeh] brand of bottled beer

пиво Очаковское® [peeva achakofska-yeh] brand of bottled beer

пиво Тверское [peeva tversko-yeh] dark beer

полусладкий [palooslatkee] medium-sweet

полусладкое вино [palooslatka-yeh veeno] medium-sweet

wine
полусухое вино [poloosooно-yeh veeno] medium-dry wine
полусухой [poloosooноy] medium-dry
Пепси® [pepsee] Pepsi®
портвейн [portvyayn] port-style drink

растворимый кофе [rastvareemi kofyeh] instant coffee
ром [rom] rum

Саперави [sapyeravi] Georgian red wine
сахар [saнar] sugar
светлое пиво [svyetla-yeh peeva] lager
сладкий [slatkee] sweet
сладкое вино [slatka-yeh veeno] dessert wine
сливки [sleefkee] cream
с молоком [smalakom] with milk
сок [sok] juice
со льдом [saldom] with ice
с сахаром [s-saнaram] with sugar
столовое вино [stalova-yeh veeno] table wine
сухой [sooноy] dry

томатный сок [tamatni sok] tomato juice
травяной чай [travyanoy chi] herbal tea

Фанта® Fanta®

Цинандали [tsinandalee] Georgian dry white wine

чай [chi] tea
чай с лимоном [chi sleemonam] lemon tea
чёрный кофе [chorni kofyeh] black coffee

шампанское [shampanska-yeh] champagne

яблочный сок [yablachni sok] apple juice

А
Б
В
Г
Д
Е
Ё
Ж
З
И
Й
К
Л
М
Н
О
П
Р
С
Т
У
Ф
Х
Ц
Ч
Ш
Щ
Ъ
Ы
Ь
Э
Ю
Я

How the

Language

Works

Pronunciation

Throughout this book Russian words have been transliterated into romanized form (see the Cyrillic Alphabet on pages 226-227) so that they can be read as though they were English bearing in mind the notes on pronunciation given below:

a	as in **a**t	iy	i as in b**i**t followed
ay	as in m**ay**		by y as in **y**es
e	as in m**e**t	J	like the s in mea**s**ure
g	hard g as in **g**et	o	as in n**o**t
H	a guttural ch as in the	s	as in mi**ss**
	Scottish word lo**ch**	y	as in **y**es
i	as in b**i**t	ye	as in **ye**s
I	i sound as in **I** or **eye**		

Letters given in bold type indicate the part of the word to be stressed.

Abbreviations

acc	accusative case	m	masculine
adj	adjective	n	neuter
dat	dative case	nom	nominative case
f	feminine	pl	plural
fam	familiar	pol	polite
gen	genitive case	prep	prepositional case
instr	instrumental case	sing	singular

Notes

When two forms of the verb are given in the dictionary sections, the first form is the imperfective aspect and the second is the perfective aspect (see page 249 for further information).

The Cyrillic Alphabet

Set out below is the Cyrillic alphabet, the names of the letters and the system of transliteration used in this book:

А, а	ah	a as in at
Б, б	beh	b
В, в	veh	v
Г, г	geh	g as in get or v
Д, д	deh	d
Е, е	yeh	ye as in yes
Ё, ё	yo	yo as in yonder
Ж, ж	Jeh	J: pronounced like the s in measure
З, з	zeh	z
И, и	ee	ee
Й, й	ee kratka-yeh	sometimes y as in boy, but usually silent
К, к	ka	k
Л, л	el	l
М, м	em	m
Н, н	en	n
О, о	o	when stressed, o as in not; when unstressed, a as in at
П, п	peh	p
Р, р	er	r
С, с	es	s
Т, т	teh	t
У, у	oo	oo as in boot
Ф, ф	ef	f
Х, х	Ha	H: a guttural ch as in Scottish loch
Ц, ц	tseh	ts as in hats
Ч, ч	cheh	ch as in church
Ш, ш	sha	sh as in ship
Щ, щ	sh-cha	sh-ch
Ъ, ъ	tvyordi znak	hard sign: no sound, but indicates hardening of preceding consonant
Ы, ы	iy	i as in bit followed by y as in yes
Ь, ь	myaHkee znak	soft sign: no sound but softens the preceding letter

Э, э	eh	e as in **e**nd
Ю, ю	yoo	yoo
Я, я	ya	ya as in **ya**m

б, в, г, д and з may be pronounced p, f, k, t and s respectively, usually when they occur at the end of a word or when preceding certain consonants. For example:

выход	**вход**
viyHat	f**Hot**
exit	entrance

Combinations and Diphthongs

АЙ, ай	ɪ: i sound as in **I** or **eye; ee** if unstressed
ЕЙ, ей	yay
ИЙ, ий	ee
ОЙ, ой	oy as in b**oy**; ɪ: i sound as in **I** or **eye** if unstressed
ЫЙ, ый	i as in b**i**t

Russian Handwriting

Handwritten Russian does not always resemble the printed characters. The letters below are examples of actual Russian handwriting:

А, а	*А а а*	К, к	*К Ж к к*	Х, х	*Х Х х х*
Б, б	*Б Б б*	Л, л	*Л л*	Ц, ц	*Ц ц*
В, в	*В В в*	М, м	*М м*	Ч, ч	*Ч ч*
Г, г	*Г Г г*	Н, н	*Н н*	Ш, ш	*Ш ш*
Д, д	*Д Д g*	О, о	*О о*	Щ, щ	*Щ щ*
Е, е	*Е е*	П, п	*П п*	Ъ, ъ	*ъ*
Ё, ё	*Ё ё/е*	Р, р	*Р Р р р*	Ы, ы	*Н ы*
Ж, ж	*Ж ж*	С, с	*С с*	Ь, ь	*ь*
З, з	*З з*	Т, т	*Т т т*	Э, э	*Э э*
И, и	*И и*	У, у	*У у*	Ю, ю	*Ю Ю ю*
Й, й	*Й й*	Ф, ф	*Ф ф ф*	Я, я	*Я я*

Articles

There are no articles (a, an, the) in Russian:

окно	полотенце
akno	palatyentseh
window/a window/the window	towel/a towel/the towel

Context clarifies the equivalent English article:

вы не возражаете, если я открою окно ...?
viy nyeh vazraJa-yetyeh, **ye**slee ya atkro-yoo akn**o**?
do you mind if I open the window?

дайте мне, пожалуйста, полотенце
d**i**tyeh mnyeh paJalsta, palat**ye**nseh
can I have a towel?

Nouns and Cases

Nouns

Russian nouns have one of three genders — masculine, feminine or neuter. The gender is determined by the noun ending. Most nouns ending in a consonant are masculine:

вагон	отец	дом
vag**on**	at**ye**ts	dom
carriage	father	house

Nouns ending in -й are also masculine:

музей	трамвай
mooz**yay**	tramv**i**
museum	tram

Most nouns ending in -a or -я are feminine:

машина	сестра
mash**i**yna	syestr**a**
car	sister

учительница
oocheetyelneetsa
teacher (woman)

тётя
tyotya
aunt

спальня
spalnya
bedroom

гостья
gostya
guest (woman)

Most nouns ending in a soft sign -ь are feminine, but some are masculine (indicated by **f** or **m** in the English-Russian section of this book):

мелочь f
myelach
small change

дверь f
dvyer
door

кровать f
kravat
bed

рубль m
roobl
rouble

день m
dyen
day

картофель m
kartofyel
potato

Most nouns ending in -o or -e are neuter:

блюдо
blyooda
dish

пиво
peeva
beer

вино
veeno
wine

море
moryeh
sea

отделение
od-dyelyenee-yeh
department

Nouns ending in -мя are neuter:

время
vryemya
time

имя
eemya
first name

Some nouns ending in -a or -я that refer to males are masculine:

229

мужчина	дядя
moosh-**chee**na	**dya**-dya
man	uncle

Cases

Russian has six cases: nominative, accusative, genitive, dative, instrumental and prepositional. Noun endings change depending on the case. The case endings used depend on the following factors:

whether the noun is masculine inanimate (objects), masculine animate (people or animals), feminine or neuter

whether the noun is singular or plural

whether the noun stem ends in г, к, х, ч, щ, ж or ш, in which case и is used instead of ы in the ending.

Nominative Case

The nominative is the case of the subject of a sentence. In the following examples, 'shop' and 'he' are in the nominative:

магазин открыт	он сегодня приехал
magaz**een** atkr**iyt**	on syev**od**nya pree-**ye**Hal
the shop is open	he arrived today

Accusative Case

The object of most verbs takes the accusative. In the following examples the objects (the sights, stamps and pen) are in the accusative:

мы хотим осмотреть достопримечательности
miy Hat**ee**m asmatr**yet** dastapreemyecha**t**yelnastee
we want to see the sights

вы продаёте марки?
viy prada-**yo**tyeh m**ar**kee?
do you sell stamps?

вы не одолжите ручку?

viy nyeh adal*j*ityeh **roo**chkoo?

may I borrow your pen?

Some prepositions indicating motion or direction towards something are followed by the accusative:

в	**на**
v	na
to; into	to; onto

через	**в Москву**
ch**ye**ryes	vmaskv**oo**
through	to Moscow

мы едем на вокзал	**я пройду через парк**
miy **ye**dyem na vakz**al**	ya prid**oo** ch**ye**ryes park
we're going to the station	I'll walk through the park

Genitive Case

The genitive is used to indicate possession:

машина Кати

mash**i**yna **ka**tee

Katya's car

There is no word for 'of' in Russian. The genitive is used to translate 'of':

бутылка водки	**плитка шоколада**
boot**i**ylka **vo**tkee	pl**ee**tka shakal**a**da
a bottle of vodka	a bar of chocolate

The genitive is also used after some prepositions, for example:

до	**у**	**около**
do	oo	**o**kala
until; to	by; at	near, by; beside; about

до Москвы	у Саши	около гостиницы
da maskv**iy**	oo s**a**shi	**o**kala gast**ee**neetsi
to Moscow	at Sasha's house	beside the hotel

Dative Case

The dative is used for indirect objects with verbs like 'to give' and 'to send'. It often corresponds to 'to' (as in 'to me') in English:

дайте мне ..., пожалуйста	я дал ему это
d**i**tyeh mnyeh ..., pa**J**alsta	ya dal yem**oo** **e**ta
please give me ...	I gave it to him

See the forms of personal pronouns on pages 246–247.

The dative is also used after some prepositions, for example:

к	по
k	pa
to, towards	on; along

к вокзалу	по улице
k vakz**a**loo	pa **oo**leetseh
to the station	along the street

Instrumental Case

The instrumental is used to show by whom or by what means an action is carried out. It is used to translate 'by' when referring to means of transport:

мы приехали поездом	авиапочтой
miy pree-**ye**Halee p**o**-yezdam	avee-a-p**o**cht**i**
we came by train	by airmail

The instrumental is also used with some prepositions:

под	перед	с
pot	p**ye**ryet	s
under	before; in front of	with

под столом
pat stal**o**m
under the table

перед обедом
p**ye**ryed ab**ye**dam
before lunch

я пью чай с лимоном
ya pyoo chi sleem**o**nam
I take tea with lemon

Prepositional Case

The prepositional is used with most prepositions which indicate the position or location of something:

на
na
at; on

в
v
at; in

на самолёте
na samal**yo**tyeh
on the plane

в городе
vg**o**ratyeh
in the town

на улице
na **oo**leetseh
on the street

на вокзале
na vakz**a**lyeh
at the station

It is also used with the preposition **о** [a] about:

они говорили о фильме
an**ee** gavar**ee**lee a f**ee**lmyeh
they were talking about the film

Numbers and Cases

Numbers in Russian also determine the case of the noun. 1 and all numbers ending in 1 (eg 21, 31 and so on) are followed by a noun in the nominative singular; 2, 3, and 4 and all numbers ending in 2, 3, and 4 (except for 11, 12, 13 and 14) take the genitive singular; all other numbers (including 11, 12, 13 and 14) take the genitive plural:

одна бутылка
adn**a** boot**iy**lka
one bottle

две бутылки
dvyeh boot**iy**lkee
two bottles

три женщины	двадцать одна женщина
tree Jensh-cheeni	dvatsat adna Jensh-cheena
three women	21 women

один час	семь часов
adeen chas	syem chasof
one hour	seven hours

двадцать четыре часа
dvatsat chyetiyryeh chasa
24 hours

See Numbers on pages 261-263.

Noun Cases

In the following tables, when the noun stem ends in г, ж, к, х, ч, ш or щ, и is used instead of ы in the noun endings, for example:

язык/языки	марка/марки
yaziyk/yaziykee	marka/markee
language/languages	stamp/stamps

masculine singular inanimate

	carriage	museum	rouble
nom	вагон	музей	рубль
	vagon	moozyay	roobl
acc	вагон	музей	рубль
	vagon	moozyay	roobl
gen	вагона	музея	рубля
	vagona	moozyeh-ya	rooblya
dat	вагону	музею	рублю
	vagonoo	moozyeh-yoo	rooblyoo
instr	вагоном	музеем	рублем
	vagonam	moozyeh-yem	rooblyom
prep	вагоне	музее	рубле
	vagonyeh	moozyeh-yeh	rooblyeh

masculine singular animate

	artist	driver
nom	**художник**	**водитель**
	Hood**o**Jneek	vad**ee**tyel
acc	**художника**	**водителя**
	Hood**o**Jneeka	vad**ee**tyelya
gen	**художника**	**водителя**
	Hood**o**Jneeka	vad**ee**tyelya
dat	**художнику**	**водителю**
	Hood**o**Jneekoo	vad**ee**tyelyoo
instr	**художником**	**водителем**
	Hood**o**Jneekam	vad**ee**tyelyem
prep	**художнике**	**водителе**
	Hood**o**Jneekyeh	vad**ee**tyelyeh

feminine singular

	car	aunt	door
nom	**машина**	**тётя**	**дверь**
	mash**iy**na	**tyo**tya	dvyer
acc	**машину**	**тётю**	**дверь**
	mash**iy**noo	**tyo**tyoo	dvyer
gen	**машины**	**тёти**	**двери**
	mash**iy**ni	**tyo**tee	dv**ye**ree
dat	**машине**	**тёте**	**двери**
	mash**iy**nyeh	**tyo**tyeh	dv**ye**ree
instr	**машиной**	**тётей**	**дверью**
	mash**iy**ni	**tyo**tyay	dv**ye**ryoo
prep	**машине**	**тёте**	**двери**
	mash**iy**nyeh	**tyo**tyeh	dv**ye**ree

neuter singular

	dish	sea	first name	department
nom	блюдо	море	имя	отделение
	bl**yoo**da	m**o**ryeh	**ee**mya	ad-dyel**ye**nee-yeh
acc	блюдо	море	имя	отделение
	bl**yoo**da	m**o**ryeh	**ee**mya	ad-dyel**ye**nee-yeh
gen	блюда	моря	имени	отделения
	bl**yoo**da	m**o**rya	**ee**myenee	ad-dyel**ye**nee-ya
dat	блюду	морю	имени	отделению
	bl**yoo**doo	m**o**ryoo	**ee**myenee	ad-dyel**ye**nee-yoo
instr	блюдом	морем	именем	отделением
	bl**yoo**dam	m**o**ryem	**ee**myenyem	ad-dyel**ye**nee-yem
prep	блюде	море	имени	отделении
	bl**yoo**dyeh	m**o**ryeh	**ee**myenee	ad-dyel**ye**nee-ee

masculine plural inanimate

	carriage	museum	rouble
nom	вагоны	музеи	рубли
	vag**o**ni	mooz**yeh**-ee	roobl**ee**
acc	вагоны	музеи	рубли
	vag**o**ni	mooz**yeh**-ee	roobl**ee**
gen	вагонов	музеев	рублей
	vag**o**naf	mooz**yeh**-yef	roobl**yay**
dat	вагонам	музеям	рублям
	vag**o**nam	mooz**yeh**-yam	roobl**yam**
instr	вагонами	музеями	рублями
	vag**o**namee	mooz**yeh**-yamee	roobl**ya**mee
prep	вагонах	музеях	рублях
	vag**o**naн	mooz**yeh**-yaн	roobl**ya**н

masculine plural animate

	artist	driver
nom	**художники** Hood**o**Jneekee	**водители** vad**ee**tyelee
acc	**художников** Hood**o**Jneekaf	**водителей** vad**ee**tyelyay
gen	**художников** Hood**o**Jneekaf	**водителей** vad**ee**tyelyay
dat	**художникам** Hood**o**Jneekam	**водителям** vad**ee**tyelyam
instr	**художниками** Hood**o**Jneekamee	**водителями** vad**ee**tyelyamee
prep	**художниках** Hood**o**JneekaH	**водителях** vad**ee**tyelyaH

feminine plural

	car	aunt	door
nom	**машины** mash**iy**ni	**тёти** **tyo**tee	**двери** dv**ye**ree
acc	**машины** mash**iy**ni	**тётей** **tyo**tyay	**двери** dv**ye**ree
gen	**машин** mash**iy**n	**тётей** **tyo**tyay	**дверей** dvyer**yay**
dat	**машинам** mash**iy**nam	**тётям** **tyo**tyam	**дверям** dvyer**yam**
instr	**машинами** mash**iy**namee	**тётями** **tyo**tyamee	**дверями** dvyer**ya**mee
prep	**машинах** mash**iy**naH	**тётях** **tyo**tyaH	**дверях** dvyer**ya**H

neuter plural

	dish	sea	first name	department
nom	блюда	моря	имена	отделения
	blyooda	marya	eemyena	ad-dyelyenee-ya
acc	блюда	моря	имена	отделения
	blyooda	marya	eemyena	ad-dyelyenee-ya
gen	блюд	морей	имён	отделений
	blyoot	maryay	eemyon	ad-dyelyenee
dat	блюдам	морям	именам	отделениям
	blyoodam	maryam	eemyenam	ad-dyelyenee-yam
instr	блюдами	морями	именами	отделениями
	blyoodamee	maryamee	eemyenamee	ad-dyelyenee-yamee
prep	блюдах	морях	именах	отделениях
	blyoodaн	maryaн	eemyenaн	ad-dyelyenee-yaн

Irregular Plurals

Several common nouns have irregular plurals:

дом/дома	[dom/dama]	house/houses
поезд/поезда	[poyest/payezda]	train/trains
город/города	[gorat/garada]	town/towns
номер/номера	[nomyer/namyera]	room/rooms; number/numbers
сестра/сёстры	[syestra/syostri]	sister/sisters
брат/братья	[brat/bratya]	brother/brothers
мать/матери	[mat/matyeree]	mother/mothers
сын/сыновья	[siyn/sinavya]	son/sons
дочь/дочери	[doch/dochyeree]	daughter/daughters
друг/друзья	[drook/droozya]	friend/friends

Some common Russian nouns do not change in the plural or according to case and are known as indeclinable nouns:

кафе	[kafeh]	cafe
кино	[keeno]	cinema
кофе	[kofyeh]	coffee
метро	[myetro]	underground, (US) subway
пальто	[palto]	overcoat
такси	[taksee]	taxi
фойе	[fl-yeh]	foyer

Prepositions

The following are some common prepositions and the cases they take (see also pages 230-232):

без [byes] (+ gen) without
в [v] (+ acc) to
в [v] (+ prep) in
для [dlya] (+ gen) for
до [do] (+ gen) before; until
за [za] (+ acc) behind; beyond; after; over
за [za] (+ instr) behind; beyond; at
между [myeJdoo] (+ instr) between; among
на [na] (+ acc) to
на [na] (+ prep) on
над [nat] (+ instr) above
напротив [naproteef] (+ gen) opposite
о [a] (+ prep) about
около [okala] (+ gen) about; near
от [ot] (+ gen) from
перед [pyeryed] (+ instr) in front of; before
по [po] (+ dat) on; along
под [pot] (+ instr) under
после [poslyeh] (+ gen) after
при [pree] (+ prep) by; at
с [s] (+ instr) with
через [chyeryes] (+ acc) through, via

Adjectives

Adjectives agree in case, gender and number with the nouns to which they refer.

Most Russian adjectives end in **-ый** and change as follows:

	singular			**plural**
	masculine	feminine	neuter	

красивый [kraseevi] beautiful

	masculine	feminine	neuter	plural
nom	красивый	красивая	красивое	красивые
	kraseevi	kraseeva-ya	kraseeva-yeh	kraseevi-yeh
acc	красивый	красивую	красивое	красивые
	kraseevi	kraseevoo-yoo	kraseeva-yeh	kraseevi-yeh
gen	красивого	красивой	красивого	красивых
	kraseevava	kraseevı	kraseevava	kraseeviн
dat	красивому	красивой	красивому	красивым
	kraseevamoo	kraseevı	kraseevamoo	kraseevim
instr	красивым	красивой	красивым	красивыми
	kraseevim	kraseevı	kraseevim	kraseevimee
prep	красивом	красивой	красивом	красивых
	kraseevam	kraseevı	kraseevam	kraseeviн

Some adjectives ending in -ий (often preceded by г, ж, к, х, ч, ш, щ) change as follows:

	singular			**plural**
	masculine	feminine	neuter	

зимний [zeemnee] winter, winter's

	masculine	feminine	neuter	plural
nom	зимний	зимняя	зимнее	зимние
	zeemnee	zeemnya-ya	zeemnyeh-yeh	zeemnee-yeh
acc	зимний	зимнюю	зимнее	зимние
	zeemnee	zeemnyoo-yoo	zeemnyeh-yeh	zeemnee-yeh
gen	зимнего	зимней	зимнего	зимних
	zeemnyeva	zeemnyay	zeemnyeva	zeemneeн
dat	зимнему	зимней	зимнему	зимним
	zeemnyemoo	zeemnyay	zeemnyemoo	zeemneem
instr	зимним	зимней	зимним	зимними
	zeemneem	zeemnyay	zeemneem	zeemneemee
prep	зимнем	зимней	зимнем	зимних
	zeemnyem	zeemnyay	zeemnyem	zeemneeн

	singular			**plural**
	masculine	feminine	neuter	
хороший Haroshi good				
nom	**хороший**	**хорошая**	**хорошее**	**хорошие**
	Haroshi	Harosha-ya	Harosheh-yeh	Haroshi-yeh
acc	**хороший**	**хорошую**	**хорошее**	**хорошие**
	Haroshi	Haroshoo-yoo	Harosheh-yeh	Haroshi-yeh
gen	**хорошего**	**хорошей**	**хорошего**	**хороших**
	Harosheva	Haroshay	Harosheva	HaroshiH
dat	**хорошему**	**хорошей**	**хорошему**	**хорошим**
	Haroshemoo	Haroshay	Haroshemoo	Haroshim
instr	**хорошим**	**хорошей**	**хорошим**	**хорошими**
	Haroshim	Haroshay	Haroshim	Haroshimee
prep	**хорошем**	**хорошей**	**хорошем**	**хороших**
	Haroshem	Haroshay	Haroshem	HaroshiH

Some adjectives ending in **-ой** (when the stress is on the ending) change as follows:

	singular			**plural**
	masculine	feminine	neuter	
большой [balshoy] big				
nom	**большой**	**большая**	**большое**	**большие**
	balshoy	balsha-ya	balsho-yeh	balshiy-yeh
acc	**большой**	**большую**	**большое**	**большие**
	balshoy	balshoo-yoo	balsho-yeh	balshiy-yeh
gen	**большого**	**большой**	**большого**	**больших**
	balshova	balshoy	balshova	balshiyH
dat	**большому**	**большой**	**большому**	**большим**
	balshomoo	balshoy	balsho-moo	balshiym
instr	**большим**	**большой**	**большим**	**большими**
	balshiym	balshoy	balshiym	balshiymee
prep	**большом**	**большой**	**большом**	**больших**
	balshom	balshoy	balshom	balshiyH

красивая картина
kraseeva-ya karteena
a beautiful picture

мне нравится русское пиво
mnyeh nraveetsa rooska-yeh peeva
I like Russian beer

это хорошая гостиница
eta Harosha-ya gasteeneetsa
it's a good hotel

Comparatives

The comparative of adjectives is generally formed by adding the words for 'more' or 'less' in front of the adjective and noun:

более
bolyeh-yeh
more

более интересный
bolyeh-yeh eentyeryesni
more interesting

менее
myenyeh-yeh
less

менее дорогой
myenyeh-yeh daragoy
less expensive

Some common adjectives have irregular comparatives:

большой [balshoy] big
больше [bolsheh] bigger
маленький [malyenkee] small
меньше [myensheh] smaller
старый [stari] old
старше [starsheh] older
дорогой [daragoy] dear
дороже [daroJeh] dearer
дешёвый [dyeshovi] cheap
дешевле [dyeshevlyeh] cheaper

'Than' is **чем** [chyem]:

это дешевле, чем я думал
eta dyeshevlyeh, chyem ya doomal
it's cheaper than I thought

Superlatives

To form the superlative, add the adverb **наиболее** [na-eebolyeh-yeh] or the particle **самый** [sami] in front of the adjective and noun:

наиболее удобный	**самый популярный**
na-eeb**o**lyeh-yeh oo**do**bni	**sa**mi papool**ya**rni
the most convenient	the most popular

Adverbs

To form the adverb, remove the final -**ый** or -**ий** from the adjective and add -**о**:

хороший	**хорошо**	**медленный**	**медленно**
Har**o**shi	Hara**sho**	m**ye**dlyen-ni	m**ye**dlyen-na
good	well	slow	slowly

Demonstratives

The demonstratives are:

этот	**эти**	**тот**	**те**
this (one)	these	that (one)	those

In Russian, the demonstrative agrees with the gender and case of the noun to which it refers. **этот** and **эти** change as follows:

	masculine	feminine	neuter	plural
nom	**этот**	**эта**	**это**	**эти**
	etat	**e**ta	**e**ta	**e**tee
acc	**этот**	**эту**	**это**	**эти**
	etat	**e**too	**e**ta	**e**tee
gen	**этого**	**этой**	**этого**	**этих**
	etava	**e**tı	**e**tava	**e**teeн
dat	**этому**	**этой**	**этому**	**этим**
	etamoo	**e**tı	**e**tamoo	**e**teem
instr	**этим**	**этой**	**этим**	**этими**
	eteem	**e**tı	**e**teem	**e**teemee
prep	**этом**	**этой**	**этом**	**этих**
	etam	**e**tı	**e**tam	**e**teeн

я этого не заказывал

ya **e**tava nyeh zak**a**zival

I didn't order this

эти открытки, пожалуйста

etee atkr**iy**tkee, pa**J**alsta

these cards please

тот and **те** change as follows:

	masculine	feminine	neuter	plural
nom	**тот**	**та**	**то**	**те**
	tot	ta	to	tyeh
acc	**тот**	**ту**	**то**	**те**
	tot	too	to	tyeh
gen	**того**	**той**	**того**	**тех**
	tav**o**	toy	tav**o**	tyeн
dat	**тому**	**той**	**тому**	**тем**
	tam**oo**	toy	tam**oo**	tyem
instr	**тем**	**той**	**тем**	**теми**
	tyem	toy	tyem	**tye**mee
prep	**том**	**той**	**том**	**тех**
	tom	toy	tom	tyeн

я зайду в тот магазин

ya zid**oo** ftot magaz**een**

I'll pop into that shop

можна взглянуть на ту книгу?

mo**J**na vzglyan**oot** na too kn**ee**goo?

can I see that book?

Possessives

Possessive adjectives and pronouns are as follows:

мой	[moy]	my; mine	наш	[nash]	our; ours
твой	[tvoy]	your (fam); yours	ваш	[vash]	your (sing pol or
его	[yevo]	his/its			pl); yours
её	[yeh-**yo**]	her; hers	их	[eeн]	their; theirs

See pages 247-248 for more on the use of **твой** and **ваш**.

	masculine	feminine	neuter	plural
	my; mine			
nom	мой	моя	моё	мои
	moy	ma-**ya**	ma-**yo**	ma-**ee**
acc	мой	мою	моё	мои
	moy	ma-**yoo**	ma-**yo**	ma-**ee**
gen	моего	моей	моего	моих
	ma-yev**o**	ma-**yay**	ma-yev**o**	ma-**ee**н
dat	моему	моей	моему	моим
	ma-yem**oo**	ma-**yay**	ma-yem**oo**	ma-**ee**m
instr	моим	моей	моим	моими
	ma-**ee**m	ma-**yay**	ma-**ee**m	ma-**ee**mee
prep	моём	моей	моём	моих
	ma-**yo**m	ma-**yay**	ma-**yo**m	ma-**ee**н

твой [tvoy] (your; yours) declines in the same way as мой.

	masculine	feminine	neuter	plural
	our; ours			
nom	наш	наша	наше	наши
	nash	na**sha**	na**sheh**	na**shi**
acc	наш	нашу	наше	наши
	nash	na**shoo**	na**sheh**	na**shi**
gen	нашего	нашей	нашего	наших
	na**sheva**	na**shay**	na**sheva**	na**shi**н
dat	нашему	нашей	нашему	нашим
	na**shemoo**	na**shay**	na**shemoo**	na**shim**
instr	нашим	нашей	нашим	нашими
	na**shim**	na**shay**	na**shim**	na**shimee**
prep	нашем	нашей	нашем	наших
	na**shem**	na**shay**	na**shem**	na**shi**н

ваш [vash] (your; yours) declines in the same way as наш.

> **отнесите это в мой номер**
> atnyese**ee**tyeh **e**ta vmoy n**o**myer
> take this to my room

вы не видели нашего гида?
viy nyeh **vee**dyelee n**a**sheva g**ee**da?
have you seen our guide?

возвращаю вашу ручку
vazvrash-ch**a**-yoo v**a**shoo r**oo**chkoo
I'm returning your pen

The following possessives are invariable:

его [yev**o**]	his/its
её [yeh-**yo**]	her; hers
их [еен]	their; theirs

это её сумка	**я его друг**	**это их автобус**
eta yeh-**yo** s**oo**mka	ya yev**o** drook	**e**ta ееn aft**o**boos
it's her bag	I'm his friend	it's their bus

The possessive adjective **свой** [svoy] is used when the object possessed relates directly to the subject of the sentence. It declines like **мой**.

я потерял свой ключ
ya patyery**al** svoy kly**oo**ch
I've lost my key

мы живём в своём собственном доме
miy Jivy**om** fsva-**yo**m s**o**pstvyen-nam d**o**myeh
we live in our own house

The possessives can be omitted when the object possessed relates directly to the subject of the sentence:

я скучаю по родителям
ya skoocha-yoo pa rad**ee**tyelyam
I miss my parents

Pronouns

Personal Pronouns

я	[ya]	I	**мы**	[miy]	we
ты	[tiy]	you (fam)	**вы**	[viy]	you (sing pol or pl)
он	[on]	he			
она	[ana]	she	**они**	[anee]	they
оно	[ano]	it			

Personal pronouns change according to case as follows:

nom	я	ты	он/оно	она
	ya	tiy	on/ano	ana
acc	меня	тебя	его	её
	myen**ya**	tyeb**ya**	yev**o**	yeh-**yo**
gen	меня	тебя	его	её
	myen**ya**	tyeb**ya**	yev**o**	yeh-**yo**
dat	мне	тебе	ему	ей
	mnyeh	tyeb**yeh**	yem**oo**	yay
instr	мной	тобой	им	ей
	mnoy	tab**oy**	eem	yay
prep	мне	тебе	нём	ней
	mnyeh	tyeb**yeh**	nyom	nyay

nom	мы	вы	они	
	miy	viy	an**ee**	
acc	нас	вас	их	
	nas	vas	eeн	
gen	нас	вас	их	
	nas	vas	eeн	
dat	нам	вам	им	
	nam	vam	eem	
instr	нами	вами	ими	
	n**a**mee	v**a**mee	**ee**mee	
prep	нас	вас	них	
	nas	vas	neeн	

The third person singular and plural pronouns take the prefix **н**- after prepositions i.e.:

> для них
> dlya neeн
> for them

'You'

There are two words for 'you' in Russian: the polite/plural form **вы** [viy] and the familiar/singular form **ты** [tiy]. **Вы** is used when you are addressing someone you do not know at all, do not know well enough to consider a friend, as a sign of respect to an elder, or if you are addressing more than one person. Ты is used when addressing a child or a friend. The corresponding possessives are: ваш for the singular polite or plural and твой for the familiar form (see pages 244-245).

Reflexive Pronouns

The reflexive pronoun себя can mean 'myself', 'yourself', 'himself', 'herself', 'itself', 'ourselves', 'yourselves' or 'themselves', depending on the context in which it is used. It changes according to case as follows:

acc	себя	instr	собой
	syeb**ya**		sab**oy**
gen	себя	prep	себе
	syeb**ya**		syeb**yeh**
dat	себе		
	syeb**yeh**		

Interrogative Pronouns

кто (who) and что (what) decline as follows:

nom	**кто**	dat	**кому**
	kto		kam**oo**
acc	**кого**	instr	**кем**
	kav**o**		kyem
gen	**кого**	prep	**ком**
	kav**o**		kom

nom	**что**	dat	**чему**
	shto		chyem**oo**
acc	**что**	instr	**чем**
	shto		chyem
gen	**чего**	prep	**чём**
	chyev**o**		chom

Verbs

Verb Aspects

The basic form of the verb given in the dictionaries in this book is the infinitive (e.g. to do, to go, to read etc). Most Russian verbs have two forms known as the imperfective and perfective aspects. In the English-Russian and Russian-English sections of this book, where useful, the two aspects of common verbs are given in this order: imperfective/perfective. For example the verb 'to do' is:

делать [d**ye**lat]/сделать [zd**ye**lat]

The imperfective aspect is generally used to form what in English would be the present and imperfect (continuous) tenses and the future (with the future tense of **быть** to be). The perfective aspect is generally used to form what in English would be expressed by the perfect tense.

Russian regular verbs usually have one of two endings and are known as first conjugation and second conjugation verbs:

first conjugation
-ать   делать to do

second conjugation
-ить   говорить to speak, to say

To form the various tenses, the ending of the verb is removed and appropriate endings are added to the basic stem.

Present Tense

The present tense corresponds to 'I leave' and 'I am leaving' in English. Using the imperfective aspect of the verb, the conjugation patterns for the present tense are as follows:

first conjugation	second conjugation
делать	говорить
dyelat	gavareet
to do	to speak, to say
я читаю	я говорю
ya dyela-yoo	ya gavaryoo
ты делаешь	ты говоришь
tiy dyela-yesh	tiy gavareesh
он/она делает	он/она говорит
on/ana dyela-yet	on/ana gavareet
мы делаем	мы говорим
miy dyela-yem	miy gavareem
вы делаете	вы говорите
viy dyela-yetyeh	viy gavareetyeh
они делают	они говорят
anee dyela-yoot	anee gavaryat

Most verbs ending in -ать or -ять conjugate in the same way as делать. The following are some common exceptions:

слышать	спать
sliyshat	spat
to hear	to sleep
я слышу	я сплю
ya sliyshoo	ya splyoo
ты слышишь	ты спишь
tiy sliyshish	tiy speesh
он/она слышит	он/она спит
on/ana sliyshit	on/ana speet
мы слышим	мы спим
miy sliyshim	miy speem
вы слышите	вы спите
viy sliyshityeh	viy speetyeh
они слышат	они спят
anee sliyshat	anee spyat

ждать	брать
Jdat	brat
to wait	to take

я жду	я беру
ya Jdoo	ya byer**oo**
ты ждёшь	ты берёшь
tiy Jdyosh	tiy byer**yosh**
он/она ждёт	он/она берёт
on/on**a** Jdyot	on/on**a** byer**yot**
мы ждём	мы берём
miy Jdyom	miy byer**yom**
вы ждёте	вы берёте
viy Jd**yo**tyeh	viy byer**yo**tyeh
они ждут	берут
an**ee** Jdoot	an**ee** byer**oot**

Most verbs ending in -**ить** and -**еть** are conjugated in a similar way to **говорить**. However, the first person singular may change slightly in that there may also be consonant changes or the addition of an **л** between the verb stem and ending:

видеть	любить
vee**d**yet	lyoob**eet**
to see	to like

я вижу	я люблю
ya vee**J**oo	ya lyoobl**yoo**
ты видишь	ты любишь
tiy vee**d**eesh	tiy l**yoo**beesh
он/она видит	он/она любит
on/an**a** vee**d**eet	on/an**a** l**yoo**beet
мы видим	мы любим
miy vee**d**eem	miy l**yoo**beem
вы видите	вы любите
viy vee**d**eetyeh	viy l**yoo**beetyeh
они видят	они любят
an**ee** vee**d**yat	an**ee** l**yoo**byat

платить	просить

plat**eet**	pras**eet**
to pay for	to ask
я плачу	я прошу
ya plach**oo**	prash**oo**
ты платишь	ты просишь
tiy pl**a**teesh	tiy pr**o**seesh
он/она платит	он/она просит
on/an**a** pl**a**teet	on/an**a** pr**o**seet
мы платим	мы просим
miy pl**a**teem	miy pr**o**seem
вы платите	вы просите
viy pl**a**teetyeh	viy pr**o**seetyeh
они платят	они просят
an**ee** pl**a**tyat	an**ee** pr**o**syat

сидеть [seed**yet**] (to sit) and all forms of the verb ходить [Had**eet**] (to walk) are conjugated like видеть.

The following verbs are irregular in the present tense:

есть	хотеть
yest	Hat**yet**
to eat	to want
я ем	я хочу
ya yem	ya Hach**oo**
ты ешь	ты хочешь
tiy yesh	tiy H**o**chyesh
он/она ест	он/она хочет
on/an**a** yest	on/an**a** H**o**chyet
мы едим	мы хотим
miy yed**ee**m	miy Hat**ee**m
вы едите	вы хотите
viy yed**ee**tyeh	viy Hat**ee**tyeh
они едят	они хотят
an**ee** yed**yat**	an**ee** Hat**yat**
пить	жить

peet	Jiyt
to drink	to live, to stay
я пью	**я живу**
ya pyoo	ya Jiv**oo**
ты пьёшь	**ты живёшь**
tiy pyosh	tiy Jiv**yo**sh
он/она пьёт	**он/она живёт**
on/an**a** pyot	on/an**a** Jiv**yo**t
мы пьём	**мы живём**
miy pyom	miy Jiv**yo**m
вы пьёте	**вы живёте**
viy p**yo**tyeh	viy Jiv**yo**tyeh
они пьют	**они живут**
an**ee** pyoot	an**ee** Jiv**oo**t

The Past Tense: Imperfective and Perfective Forms

There are two types of past tense formed by the imperfective and the perfective of the verb.

The imperfective form describes an action which is seen as continuing:

> **они покупали сувениры**
> an**ee** pakoop**a**lee soovyen**ee**ri
> they were buying souvenirs

The perfective form describes an action which is seen as completed:

> **они купили сувениры**
> an**ee** koop**ee**lee soovyen**ee**ri
> they bought souvenirs

Some perfective verbs can be formed by adding various prefixes to the imperfective form:

imperfective	perfective
делать	**сделать** to do
dyelat	zdyelat
платить	**заплатить** to pay for
plateet	zaplateet

Other perfective forms may be a different verb altogether:

imperfective	perfective
брать	**взять** to take
brat	vzyat
говорить	**сказать** to speak, to say
gavareet	skazat

Perfective verbs can sometimes be identified because they look like a simpler form of the imperfective, for example:

imperfective	perfective
открывать	**открыть** to open
atkrivat	atkriyt
давать	**дать** to give
davat	dat

To form the past tense of both the imperfective and perfective forms, remove the ending from the infinitive and add the appropriate ending for masculine, feminine, neuter or plural subjects:

masculine	feminine	neuter	plural
-л	-ла	-ло	-ли
-l	-la	-lo	-lee

вчера шёл дождь
fchyera shol dosht
it was raining yesterday

я только что поела (said by woman)
ya tolka shto pa-**yeh**la
I've only just eaten

время пролетело очень быстро
vr**ye**mya pralyet**ye**la **o**chyen b**i**ystra
time flew by

мы побывали в Кремле
miy pabiv**a**lee fkryeml**ye**h
we visited the Kremlin

masculine	feminine	neuter	plural
идти [eet-tee] to go			
шёл	**шла**	**шло**	**шли**
shol	shla	shlo	shlee
нести [nyestee] to carry			
нёс	**несла**	**несло**	**несли**
nyos	nyesl**a**	nyesl**o**	nyesl**ee**
вести [vyestee] to lead			
вёл	**вела**	**вело**	**вели**
vyol	vyel**a**	vyel**o**	vyel**ee**

Future Tense

There are two ways of forming the future tense in Russian. The imperfective future is formed with the infinitive of the main verb (imperfective aspect) and the future tense of the verb 'to be' **быть** (see next page.)

он будет встречать нас в аэропорту
on b**oo**dyet fstryech**a**t nas va-erapart**oo**
he'll be meeting us at the airport

The future can also be expressed using the 'present' tense of perfective verbs. The conjugation patterns are the same as those for the present tense on page 250.

завтра мы поедем в Суздаль
z**a**ftra miy pa-**ye**dyem fs**oo**zdal
tomorrow we'll go to Suzdal

'To Be'

In Russian, there is no equivalent of the verb 'to be' in the present tense; it is not translated:

я уверен/уверена	он здесь?
ya oov**ye**ryen/oov**ye**ryena	on zdyes?
I'm sure (said by man/woman)	is he here?

The past tense of the verb 'to be' is as follows:

masculine	feminine	neuter	plural
был	была	было	были
biyl	bil**a**	b**iy**la	b**iy**lee

The future tense of the verb 'to be' is as follows:

я буду	мы будет
ya b**oo**doo	miy b**oo**dyem
ты будешь	вы будете
tiy b**oo**dyesh	viy b**oo**dyetyeh
он/она будет	они будут
on/an**a** b**oo**dyet	an**ee** b**oo**doot

'To Have'

'To have' is translated in Russian using the preposition у followed by the genitive of the noun or pronoun; the object possessed is in the nominative:

у меня была простуда	у вас есть другие?
oo myen**ya** bil**a** prast**oo**da	oo vas yest droog**ee**-yeh?
I had a cold	do you have any others?

у нас будет достаточно времени для покупок
oo nas b**oo**dyet dast**a**chna vr**ye**myenee dlya pak**oo**pak
we'll have enough time for shopping

Negatives

To form a negative sentence, insert не (not, no) in front of the verb:

In phrases, using 'have not', 'had not' or 'will not', **нет**, **не было** and **не будет** are used respectively as follows:

> **у меня нет талонов**
> oo men**ya** nyet tal**o**naf
> I don't have any bus tickets

> **у меня не хватило денег на подарки**
> oo myen**ya** nyeh Hvat**ee**la d**ye**nyek na pad**a**rkee
> I hadn't enough money to buy presents

> **у меня не будет времени на это**
> oo myen**ya** nyeh b**oo**dyet vr**ye**myenee na **e**ta
> I won't have time for that

Double negatives are common:

ничего	**я ничего не хочу**
neechyev**o**	ya neechyev**o** nyeh Hach**oo**
nothing	I don't want anything

никогда	**я никогда там не был/была**
neekagd**a**	ya neekagd**a** tam nyeh biyl/bil**a**
never	I've never been there (said by man/woman)

Imperative

The imperative form of the verb is used to express a command such as 'come here!', 'sit down' etc. The imperative is formed by taking the second person (**ты** form) of the verb (either the imperfective or perfective depending on the context), removing the last three letters and adding the endings as follows:

	stem ending in consonant	stem ending in vowel
fam	**-и**, or **-ь**	**-й**
pol/pl	**-ите**, or **ьте**	**-йте**

иди сюда!	**идите сюда!**
eed**ee** sy**oo**da!	eed**ee**tyeh sy**oo**da!
come here!	come here!

открой дверь
atkr**oy** dvyer
open the door

откройте дверь
atkr**oy**tyeh dvyer
open the door

перестань кричать
pyeryest**a**n kreech**a**t
stop shouting

перестаньте кричать
pyeryest**a**ntyeh kreech**a**t
stop shouting

Reflexive Verbs

Reflexive verbs such as 'to wash oneself', 'to get dressed' etc are formed by adding -**ся** to verbs ending in a consonant or -**сь** to verbs ending in a vowel:

одевать
adyev**a**t
to dress

одеваться
adyev**a**tsa
to get dressed

The same endings are used for 'myself', 'yourself', 'himself', 'themselves' etc.

Some verbs only exist in the reflexive form:

бояться [ba-**ya**tsa] to be afraid of
надеяться [nad**yeh**-yatsa] to hope
нравиться [nrav**ee**tsa] to like
смеяться [smy**eh-ya**tsa] to laugh

Questions

A statement can be turned into a question by using a questioning intonation:

мы возвращаемся в гостиницу
miy vazvrash-ch**a**-yemsya vgast**ee**neetsoo
we are returning to the hotel

мы возвращаемся в гостиницу?
miy vazvrash-ch**a**-yemsya vgast**ee**neetsoo?
are we returning to the hotel?

Dates

Use the neuter form of the ordinal numbers on page 263 to express the date. These decline like adjectives (see pages 240-241).

второе ноября
ftar**o**-yeh na-yabr**ya**
the second of November

тридцать первое января
tr**ee**tsat p**ye**rva-yeh yanvar**ya**
the thirty-first of January

Days

Sunday воскресенье [vaskryes**ye**nyeh]
Monday понедельник [panyed**ye**lneek]
Tuesday вторник [ft**o**rneek]
Wednesday среда [sryed**a**]
Thursday четверг [chyetv**ye**rk]
Friday пятница [p**ya**tneetsa]
Saturday суббота [soob**o**ta]

Months

January январь [yanv**a**r]
February февраль [fyevr**a**l]
March март [mart]
April апрель [apr**ye**l]
May май [mI]
June июнь [ee-**yoo**n]
July июль [ee-**yoo**l]
August август [**a**vgoost]
September сентябрь [syent**ya**br]
October октябрь [akt**ya**br]
November ноябрь [na-**ya**br]
December декабрь [dyek**a**br]

Time

what time is it? который час? [**kat**ori chas?]

(it's) one o'clock час [chas]

(it's) two o'clock два часа [dva chas**a**]

(it's) three o'clock три часа [tree chas**a**]

(it's) four o'clock четыре часа [chyet**iy**ryeh chas**a**]

(it's) five o'clock* пять часов [pyat chas**of**]

* For numbers of five and above, use часов. See Numbers and Cases page 233.

five past one** пять минут второго [pyat meen**oot** ftar**o**va]

ten past two** десять минут третьего [**dye**syat meen**oot** tr**ye**tyeva]

quarter past one** четверть второго [**chye**tvyert ftar**o**va]

quarter past two** четверть третьего [**chye**tvyert tr**ye**tyeva]

half past one** половина второго [palav**ee**na ftar**o**va]

half past two** половина третьего [palav**ee**na tr**ye**tyeva]

** For time past the hour, refer to the next hour. половина второго 'half past one' literally means 'half of the second'.

twenty to ten без двадцати десять [byez dvatsat**ee dye**sat]

quarter to two без четверти два [byez **chye**tvyertee dva]

quarter to ten без четверти десять [byez **chye**tvyertee d**ye**sat]

at one o'clock в час [fchas]

at two/three/four o'clock в два/три/четыре часа [v dva/tree/ chyet**iy**ryeh chas**a**]

at five o'clock в пять часов [fpyat chas**of**]

at half past four в половине пятого [fpalav**ee**nyeh p**ya**tava]

14.00 hours четырнадцать ноль-ноль [chyet**iy**rnatsat nol-nol]

17.30 семнадцать тридцать [syemn**a**tsat tr**ee**tsat]

noon полдень [**po**ldyen]

midnight полночь [**po**lnach]

am утра [**oo**tra]

pm (in the afternoon) дня [dnya]

  (in the evening) вечера [**vye**chyera]

hour час [chas]
minute минута [meen**oo**ta]
second секунда [syek**oo**nda]
quarter of an hour четверть часа [ch**ye**tvyert chas**a**]
half an hour полчаса [polchas**a**]
three quarters of an hour сорок пять минут [**so**rak pyat meen**oot**]

Numbers

See Numbers and Cases page 233.

0	ноль	[nol]
1	один **m**, одна **f**, одно **n**	[ad**ee**n, adn**a**, adn**o**]
2	два **m/n**, две **f**	[dva, dvyeh]
3	три	[tree]
4	четыре	[chyet**iy**ryeh]
5	пять	[pyat]
6	шесть	[shest]
7	семь	[syem]
8	восемь	[**vo**syem]
9	девять	[d**ye**vyat]
10	десять	[d**ye**syat]
11	одиннадцать	[ad**ee**natsat]
12	двенадцать	[dvyen**a**tsat]
13	тринадцать	[treen**a**tsat]
14	четырнадцать	[chyet**iy**rnatsat]
15	пятнадцать	[pyatn**a**tsat]
16	шестнадцать	[shesn**a**tsat]
17	семнадцать	[syemn**a**tsat]
18	восемнадцать	[vasyemn**a**tsat]
19	девятнадцать	[dyevyatn**a**tsat]
20	двадцать	[dv**a**tsat]
21	двадцать один/одна/одно	[dv**a**tsat ad**ee**n/adn**a**/adn**o**]
22	двадцать два/две	[dv**a**tsat dva/dvyeh]
30	тридцать	[tr**ee**tsat]

40	сорок [**so**rak]
50	пятьдесят [pyadyes**yat**]
60	шестьдесят [shesdyes**yat**]
70	семьдесят [**sye**mdyesyat]
80	восемьдесят [**vo**syemdyesyat]
90	девяносто [dyevyan**o**sta]
100	сто [sto]
101	сто один/одна/одно [sto ad**ee**n/adn**a**/adn**o**]
102	сто два/две [sto dva/dvyeh]
200	двести [dv**ye**stee]
300	триста [**tree**sta]
400	четыреста [chyet**iy**ryesta]
500	пятьсот [pyats**o**t]
600	шестьсот [shes-s**o**t]
700	семьсот [syems**o**t]
800	восемьсот [vasyems**o**t]
900	девятьсот [dyevyats**o**t]
1,000	тысяча [**tiy**syacha]
2,000	две тысячи [dvyeh **tiy**syachi]
3,000	три тысячи [tree **tiy**syachi]
4,000	четыре тысячи [chyet**iy**ryeh **tiy**syachi]
5,000	пять тысяч [pyat **tiy**syach]
10,000	десять тысяч [d**ye**syat **tiy**syach]
20,000	двадцать тысяч [dv**a**tsat **tiy**syach]
100,000	сто тысяч [sto **tiy**syach]
1,000,000	миллион [meelee-**o**n]

Ordinals

1st	первый	[p**y**ervi]
2nd	второй	[ftar**oy**]
3rd	третий	[try**e**tee]
4th	четвёртый	[chyetv**yo**rti]
5th	пятый	[p**ya**ti]
6th	шестой	[shest**oy**]
7th	седьмой	[syedm**oy**]
8th	восьмой	[vasm**oy**]
9th	девятый	[dyev**ya**ti]
10th	десятый	[dyes**ya**ti]
11th	одиннадцатый	[ad**ee**natsati]
12th	двенадцатый	[dvy**e**natsati]
13th	тринадцатый	[tre**e**natsati]
14th	четырнадцатый	[chyet**iy**rnatsati]
15th	пятнадцатый	[pyatn**a**tsati]
16th	шестнадцатый	[shesn**a**tsati]
17th	семнадцатый	[syemn**a**tsati]
18th	восемнадцатый	[vasyemn**a**tsati]
19th	девятнадцатый	[dyevyatn**a**tsati]
20th	двадцатый	[dvats**a**ti]
21st	двадцать первый	[dv**a**tsat p**y**ervi]
22nd	двадцать второй	[dv**a**tsat ftar**oy**]
23rd	двадцать третий	[dv**a**tsat try**e**tee]
24th	двадцать четвёртый	[dv**a**tsat chyetv**yo**rti]
25th	двадцать пятый	[dv**a**tsat p**ya**ti]
26th	двадцать шестой	[dv**a**tsat shest**oy**]
27th	двадцать седьмой	[dv**a**tsat syedm**oy**]
28th	двадцать восьмой	[dv**a**tsat vasm**oy**]
29th	двадцать девятый	[dv**a**tsat dyev**ya**ti]
30th	тридцатый	[treets**a**ti]
31st	тридцать первый	[tre**e**tsat p**y**ervi]

Conversion Tables

1 centimetre = 0.39 inches   1 inch = 2.54 cm

1 metre = 39.37 inches = 1.09 yards   1 foot = 30.48 cm

1 kilometre = 0.62 miles = 5/8 mile   1 yard = 0.91 m

     1 mile = 1.61 km

km	1	2	3	4	5	10	20	30	40	50	100
miles	0.6	1.2	1.9	2.5	3.1	6.2	12.4	18.6	24.8	31.0	62.1

miles	1	2	3	4	5	10	20	30	40	50	100
km	1.6	3.2	4.8	6.4	8.0	16.1	32.2	48.3	64.4	80.5	161

1 gram = 0.035 ounces   1 kilo = 1000 g = 2.2 pounds

g	100	250	500
oz	3.5	8.75	17.5

1 oz = 28.35 g

1 lb = 0.45 kg

kg	0.5	1	2	3	4	5	6	7	8	9	10
lb	1.1	2.2	4.4	6.6	8.8	11.0	13.2	15.4	17.6	19.8	22.0

kg	20	30	40	50	60	70	80	90	100
lb	44	66	88	110	132	154	176	198	220

lb	0.5	1	2	3	4	5	6	7	8	9	10	20
kg	0.2	0.5	0.9	1.4	1.8	2.3	2.7	3.2	3.6	4.1	4.5	9.0

1 litre = 1.75 UK pints / 2.13 US pints

1 UK pint = 0.57 l   1 UK gallon = 4.55 l
1 US pint = 0.47 l   1 US gallon = 3.79 l

centigrade / Celsius $°C = (°F - 32) \times 5/9$

°C	-5	0	5	10	15	18	20	25	30	36.8	38
°F	23	32	41	50	59	64	68	77	86	98.4	100.4

Fahrenheit $°F = (°C \times 9/5) + 32$

°F	23	32	40	50	60	65	70	80	85	98.4	101
°C	-5	0	4	10	16	18	21	27	29	36.8	38.3